David Bowie and the Art of Music Video

New Approaches to Sound, Music, and Media

Series Editors: Carol Vernallis, Holly Rogers and Lisa Perrott

Forthcoming Titles:
Musical New Media by Nicola Dibben
David Bowie and the Transformation of Music Video (1984–2016 and Beyond) by Lisa Perrott
Popular Music, Race, and Media since 9/11 by Nabeel Zuberi
Haunted Soundtracks: Audiovisual Cultures of Memory, Landscape and Sound edited by K.J. Donnelly and Aimee Mollaghan
Bellini on Stage and Screen edited by Emilio Sala, Graziella Seminara and Emanuele Senici
Traveling Music Videos edited by Tomáš Jirsa and Mathias Bonde Korsgaard
Kahlil Joseph's Transmedia Works: The Audiovisual Atlantic by Joe Jackson

Published Titles:
Transmedia Directors by Carol Vernallis, Holly Rogers, and Lisa Perrott
Dangerous Mediations by Áine Mangaoang
Resonant Matter by Lutz Koepnick
Cybermedia: Science, Sound, and Vision edited by Carol Vernallis, Holly Rogers, Jonathan Leal, Selmin Kara
The Rhythm Image: Music Videos in Time by Steven Shaviro
YouTube and Music: Cyberculture and Everyday Life edited by Holly Rogers, Joana Freitas, and João Francisco Porfírio
More Than Illustrated Music: Aesthetics of Hybrid Media Between Pop, Art and Video edited by Elfi Vomberg and Kathrin Dreckmann
Remediating Sound: Repeatable Culture, YouTube and Music edited by Holly Rogers, Joana Freitas, and João Francisco Porfírio
David Bowie and the Art of Music Video by Lisa Perrott

David Bowie and the Art of Music Video

Lisa Perrott

BLOOMSBURY ACADEMIC
NEW YORK · LONDON · OXFORD · NEW DELHI · SYDNEY

BLOOMSBURY ACADEMIC
Bloomsbury Publishing Inc
1385 Broadway, New York, NY 10018, USA
50 Bedford Square, London, WC1B 3DP, UK
29 Earlsfort Terrace, Dublin 2, Ireland

BLOOMSBURY, BLOOMSBURY ACADEMIC and the Diana logo are trademarks of
Bloomsbury Publishing Plc

First published in the United States of America 2024

Copyright © Lisa Perrott, 2024

For legal purposes the Acknowledgments on p. xii constitute an
extension of this copyright page.

Cover design:
Cover image © Lisa Perrott, 2023

All rights reserved. No part of this publication may be reproduced or transmitted in any form or by any means, electronic or mechanical, including photocopying, recording, or any information storage or retrieval system, without prior permission in writing from the publishers.

Bloomsbury Publishing Inc does not have any control over, or responsibility for, any third-party websites referred to or in this book. All internet addresses given in this book were correct at the time of going to press. The author and publisher regret any inconvenience caused if addresses have changed or sites have ceased to exist, but can accept no responsibility for any such changes.

A catalog record for this book is available from the Library of Congress.

ISBN:	HB:	978-1-5013-3514-3
	PB:	978-1-5013-3592-1
	ePDF:	978-1-5013-3516-7
	eBook:	978-1-5013-3515-0

Series: New Approaches to Sound, Music, and Media

Typeset by RefineCatch Limited, Bungay, Suffolk

To find out more about our authors and books visit
www.bloomsbury.com and sign up for our newsletters.

For the Kooks, and all the Young Dudes.

Contents

List of Illustrations   viii
Acknowledgements   xii
Preface   xiv

1. The Art of Music Video   1
2. Traversing Stage and Screen   29
3. Opening the Third Eye   65
4. Painting the Truth   105
5. Future Nostalgia   157
6. Eclosion   201

Epilogue   233
Bibliography   239
Index   251

Illustrations

2.1 Bowie's final facial expression says it all. 'Love You till Tuesday' (Malcom J. Thomson, 1969) — 30

2.2 Bowie drops seductively to floor level. 'Love You till Tuesday' (Malcom J. Thomson, 1969) — 43

2.3 Bowie emulates a hybrid 'Elvis-Jagger' figure. 'Let Me Sleep Beside You' (Malcom J. Thomson, 1969) — 46

2.4 Bowie mimes arrogance. 'The Mask' (Malcom J. Thomson, 1969) — 48

2.5 Bowie's eyes accidentally make contact with the lens. 'Space Oddity' (Malcom J. Thomson, 1969) — 53

2.6 Bowie mimes floating in space. 'Space Oddity' (Malcom J. Thomson, 1969) — 54

2.7 Bowie drops his artifice in favour of an impassioned performance. 'Five Years' (Michael Appleton & Rowan Ayers, 1972) — 62

3.1 Bowie mimes the gestural traits of Hollywood starlets. 'John, I'm Only Dancing' (Mick Rock, 1972) — 75

3.2 Bowie expresses proto-punk attitude in this out-take shot. 'John, I'm Only Dancing' (Mick Rock, 1972; Re-edited by Nacho, 2017) — 79

3.3 Bowie frames his eyes with his hands. 'The Jean Genie' (Mick Rock, 1972) — 82

3.4 Bowie performs the 'Ziggy-finger-mask'. 'The Jean Genie' (Mick Rock, 1972) — 83

3.5 The visual interpretation of sonic elements is manifested by the layering of film footage. 'Space Oddity' (Mick Rock, 1972) — 87

3.6 Bowie's body language betrays his exhaustion. 'Space Oddity' (Mick Rock, 1972) — 88

3.7 Bowie's direct address to camera portrays authenticity. 'Space Oddity' (Mick Rock, 1972) — 89

3.8 Rock's close-framing lingers on Bowie's mismatched eyes. 'Life on Mars?' (Mick Rock, 1973) — 96

3.9 Bowie mimes 'Mickey Mouse has grown up a cow'. 'Life on Mars?' (Mick Rock, 1973) — 97

3.10	Bowie gestures 'spit in the eyes of fools'. 'Life on Mars?' (Mick Rock, 1973)	98
3.11	Bowie performs a gesture of sexual satisfaction. 'Life on Mars?' (Mick Rock, 1973)	99
3.12	Bowie makes a direct connection with his audience. 'Life on Mars?' (Mick Rock, 1973)	99
3.13	The outtakes reveal 'flickers of authenticity'. 'Life On Mars?' (Mick Rock, 1973; remastered by Nacho, 2021)	102
4.1	Bowie channels Buster Keaton. 'Be My Wife' (Stanley Dorfman, 1977)	115
4.2	Bowie anthropomorphizes the guitar as an object of desire. 'Be My Wife' (Stanley Dorfman, 1977)	115
4.3	Bowie enacts the antithesis of the commitment expected of a rock musician. 'Be My Wife' (Stanley Dorfman, 1977)	117
4.4	Dorfman composes body parts and props like an abstract painting. 'Be My Wife' (Stanley Dorfman, 1977)	119
4.5	Bowie's backlit pose is much like an alien emerging from haze. 'Heroes' (Stanley Dorfman and Nicholas Ferguson, 1977)	125
4.6	The alien in *Close Encounters of the Third Kind* (Steven Spielberg, 1977)	126
4.7	'The Divine Mercy', painted after St Faustina's death. (Adolf Hyła, Kraków 1944)	128
4.8	A painterly cross-dissolve. 'Heroes' (Stanley Dorfman and Nicholas Ferguson, 1977)	130
4.9	Divine light emanating from Bowie's 'thigh-gap'. 'Heroes' (Stanley Dorfman and Nicholas Ferguson, 1977)	131
4.10	Bowie performing as three back-up singers. 'Boys Keep Swinging' (David Mallet, 1979)	136
4.11	Bowie performs a back-handed lipstick smear. 'Boys Keep Swinging' (David Mallet, 1979)	138
4.12	'Jump They Say' (Mark Romanek, 1993)	139
4.13	Lady Gaga re-enacts Bowie's lipstick smear. 'Applause' (Inez and Vinoodh, 2013)	140
4.14	Lorde re-enacts Bowie's lipstick smear. 'Yellow Flicker Beat' (Live at the AMAs, 2014)	141
4.15	Bowie performing with Klaus Nomi and Joey Arias. 'Boys Keep Swinging' (*Saturday Night Live*, 1979).	142
4.16	Bowie with his self-portrait. 'Look Back in Anger' (David Mallet, 1979)	144

4.17	Bowie stares intensely into the camera lens. 'Space Oddity' (David Mallet, 1979)	148
4.18	Breaking the 'fourth wall' of the television studio. 'Space Oddity' (David Mallet, 1979)	149
4.19	A cross-dissolve creates dramatic effect. 'Space Oddity' (David Mallet, 1979)	151
4.20	Noir lighting references 1920s expressionistic film sets. 'Space Oddity' (David Mallet, 1979)	152
4.21	Expressionistic aesthetics in *The Cabinet of Dr Caligary* (Robert Wiene, 1920)	152
4.22	References to German Expressionist film. 'Space Oddity' (David Mallet, 1979)	153
5.1	'Ashes to Ashes Clown Suit Story' (Adam Buxton, 2021).	158
5.2	Storyboard image for 'Ashes to Ashes' (David Bowie, 1980) (Courtesy of the David Bowie Archive, © Victoria and Albert Museum)	166
5.3	Bowie performing as Pierrot. 'Ashes to Ashes' (David Mallet, 1980)	168
5.4	Bowie performing as Pierrot. 'Ashes to Ashes' (David Mallet, 1980)	169
5.5	Dissolve editing creates bizarre relationships. 'Ashes to Ashes' (David Mallet, 1980)	173
5.6	Pierrot becomes a freeze-frame, giving life to Major Tom. 'Ashes to Ashes' (David Mallet, 1980)	174
5.7	Pierrot walks beside an elderly woman. 'Ashes to Ashes' (David Mallet, 1980)	175
5.8	Image from *Un Chien Andalou* (Luis Buñuel and Salvador Dalí, 1929)	176
5.9	The New Romantics flank Pierrot. 'Ashes to Ashes' (David Mallet, 1980)	177
5.10	Image from *Un Chien Andalou* (Luis Buñuel and Salvador Dalí, 1929)	177
5.11	Image from Visage's video 'Fade To Grey' (Godley & Creme, 1980)	187
5.12	Bowie's emotional performance in 'Wild is the Wind' (David Mallet, 1981)	193
5.13	An expressionist play of light. 'Wild is the Wind' (David Mallet, 1981)	194
5.14	Bowie is central in the frame. 'The Drowned Girl' (David Mallet, 1981)	196
5.15	A haptic fusion of sensory organs and instruments. 'The Drowned Girl' (David Mallet, 1981)	197
6.1	The mountains lit by a nuclear explosion. 'Let's Dance' (David Mallet, 1983)	208
6.2	Joelene and Terry look at red shoes. 'Let's Dance' (David Mallet, 1983)	212

6.3	Joelene liberates herself from colonialism. 'Let's Dance' (David Mallet, 1983)	213
6.4	White gloves signify colonialism. 'Let's Dance' (David Mallet, 1983)	214
6.5	Geeling wearing a *chador*. 'China Girl' (David Mallet, 1983)	222
6.6	Layered imagery in 'China Girl' (David Mallet, 1983)	223
6.7	Layered imagery in 'China Girl' (David Mallet, 1983)	224
6.8	Geeling performing the lipstick smear. 'China Girl' (David Mallet, 1983)	229

Acknowledgements

This book has been a labour of love. Along the way, I have learnt much from David Bowie about respecting the collaborative process, and I have also learnt that some collaborations are unique for generating a 'lightning-bolt' – a spark that gives life to a song, music video, an idea or a piece of writing. While I have often thought of Bowie as the 'patron saint' of lightning-bolts, I am privileged to be sharing my life with a person who – not unlike Bowie – sparks my brain in ways that give life to new thoughts. I would not have been able to write this book without my loving partner Sean Erin Lynch, who has been a sounding board, idea generator, proof-reader and image editor. As a musician, actor and sound and lighting designer, Sean has been a vital source of expertise, which has enriched my analysis of the sonic, visual, and performance elements of the videos. My number one advocate throughout this project, Sean has taken care of my wellbeing with his infectious humour, his cooking and his strategies for making me take breaks. He has been remarkably patient with my absent-presence, knowing that I can be found hanging out in the spare room with Bowie. My family has been an immense source of strength for me, bolstering my resilience through the challenges of the past five years. I thank my daughters (Maia and Katya) for your unwavering patience, my mokopuna (George, Brooklyn and Franco) for giving me perspective and a fresh lease of life. To my dad (Ken) for the painting materials and my mum (Sonya) for the camera gear, which enabled me to paint and photograph the cover image.

There are many other people I wish to thank for contributing their time, thoughts and inspiration, even though some may not be aware that they have done so. I thank David Mallet, Nacho and Geeling Ching, who have each provided me with fascinating insights about their part in the creation of Bowie's music videos. I am indebted to Alison Blair for her research assistance. Alison's extensive knowledge of popular music, media and subcultures has been invaluable, as has her impeccable proof-reading and editing skills. I owe much thanks to friend and collaborator Holly Rogers, whose expertise in the field of audio-visual media is unmatched, and who has given me inspiration, useful feedback and steadfast support throughout this project. I acknowledge my three intellectually voracious PhD students; while Kahurangi Waititi helped catalyse my thoughts around time-travel and the mobility of storyworlds across mediums, Liwei Fang and Anthea Visage provided perceptive interpretations of the videos. I thank Oliver Stewart, John Verryt, Michael de Young and Jennifer Campion. Last but not least, I wish to express my gratitude to Jacinda Ardern, for saving numerous lives during the pandemic and for being such a wonderful role model for all women. During times of doubt and exhaustion, I only needed to look to Jacinda for inspiration, strength and clarity. This book is sprinkled with Jacinda's stardust.

Preface

The night David Bowie moved into the spare room, I realized it was time to get this book out of my head and onto the page. After several years of gestation, Bowie had started appearing in my dreams. That night, his ghost had taken up residence in my writing room. As an apparition does, he would come and go at strange times of the day and night, not even bothering to knock or announce his presence. He would be lurking in every corner, expecting to have long conversations with my partner and I over a four-course meal. He had even provided us with a menu and shopping list, and we were stressing about gathering the correct ingredients and cooking the specified dishes to his satisfaction. Being Bowie fans for over forty years, we welcomed him into our house with enthusiasm and indulged in lengthy conversations about musical arrangements, art and video. After a while though, he was like a family member who had outstayed their welcome. I heard myself saying 'We love you David, but we can't seem to do anything without you being present. Can you give us some space?' Waking from this dream, I realized this book had been hanging around in my head and my home far too long. It was time to get it out into the world.

This dream reminded me of an earlier 'visitation' from Bowie in 2015, which triggered the genesis of this book. I was standing in front of a series of screens at the *David Bowie Is* exhibition in Melbourne,[1] just before delivering a presentation about Bowie's music videos at the symposium *The Stardom and Celebrity of David Bowie*. While I relished the total immersion of process materials, music and images of Bowie dancing across the screens, I was struck by the lack of contextual information accompanying the videos, particularly as most other items in the exhibition included fascinating descriptions of Bowie's creative process. In the midst of the sensory overload, I had an epiphany – what is needed

---

[1] ACMI, 'David Bowie Is – Opening Night', YouTube video, 00:01:35, 28 July 2015, https://youtu.be/Q4p1HgWyupw.

is a book that contributes in-depth analysis of Bowie's music videos. How about a book that functions like a curated exhibition? I could be the curator, taking people on a joyride through elaborately furnished storyworlds, across time and space – even into outer-space. From that moment, the book began gestating in the 'spare room' of my head for the next seven years.

This story reveals a few things about myself. Apart from tending toward obsessive over-thinking and vivid dreams, I am a long-term Bowie fan who accidentally became an 'aca fan' – an academic whose research includes examining the artistic and cultural contributions of Bowie, along with other subjects of my fandom.[2] While scholars have debated the legitimacy and value of researching from the subjective position of fandom, I draw on the research of Toija Cinque and Sean Redmond to argue that such a position can contribute a unique perspective and rich insights.[3] My fandom might fuel an obsessive curiosity and a drive to learn more about Bowie's approach to music video, but it does not eclipse critical evaluation and analytical rigor. In-depth analysis supports my argument that Bowie was a vanguard in establishing the art of music video. While I do not consider all of Bowie's videos to be virtuoso works of art, there is much to be learnt from exploring their creative and collaborative process, along with the artistry of music video directors, who are often overlooked. One of the most significant contributions of this book, is the spotlight it shines onto artists and directors such as Mick Rock, Stanley Dorfman and David Mallet, showing how they played an important part – alongside Bowie – in establishing music video as a collaborative artform. Not only are these directors important for this reason, they must be credited for teaching Bowie about the collaborative process and how to use the form.

Although I was initially inspired to fill a gap in the literature on Bowie's music videos, my motivation to write this book goes further than a gap-filling mission. I am driven by a deep appreciation for Bowie's songs and music videos, a fascination to learn more about his artistic process, a desire to pass on knowledge to the younger generations, and a nagging urge to address a blind spot that obscures the field of vision within academia, the art world, and the creative industries. Music video has been treated as superfluous, trivial and as a dying form. While it has

---

[2] The term 'aca-fan' refers to an academic who is undertaking scholarly research focused on the object of their fandom. For more on this, see Henry Jenkins, 'Confessions of an aca-fan', *Henry Jenkins*, 22 October 2011, https://tinyurl.com/a5pew2tm.

[3] Toija Cinque and Sean Redmond, *The Fandom of David Bowie* (Cham: Palgrave Macmillan, 2020), 131–50.

been considered worthy of studying in terms of its commercial value or use as a marketing tool, this narrow concept of value overlooks its role as an artform with significant value for representing social, cultural, and political issues. Few scholars have explored the artform's potential to play an educational, therapeutic or transformative role in the day-to-day lives of citizens, and there is little in the way of in-depth analyses of music videos that remediate historical artforms or of artists who have played a key role in this process over a sustained period.

Seeing Bowie's artisanal approach to music video develop across five decades has propelled me to engage in a deep exploration of his contributions to the art of music video. This book is intended as a companion to the videos; a resource that provides social and cultural context and offers conceptual and analytical tools, all of which helps to build a more nuanced understanding of Bowie's creative process, and of music video as an artform. While I hope the book will build upon readers' existing knowledge, it is neither a dry academic study guide nor a dense theoretical treatise. Intending to inspire a diverse audience, I have approached this project much like a storybook, designed to take readers on a time-travelling adventure. Crafted for maximum accessibility, it offers a resource for artisans, practitioners and for anyone engaged in scholarship. As such, readers can expect to come across some disciplinary-specific terms and academic references. Just as it is important to acknowledge my sources, I hope the references will serve as portals for those who wish to delve deeper.

While I have included contextual information about Bowie's upbringing, influences and collaborations, this book is not a biography or a tabloid account of his personal life and relationships. There are already numerous publications offering extensive accounts of Bowie's biography.[4] This book does not provide a comprehensive compendium of Bowie's catalogue of songs, nor does it discuss all of his music videos. Scholarship on Bowie's music has already been covered exceptionally well by authors such as Chris O'Leary,[5] Nicholas Pegg,[6] Leah Kardos,[7] David Buckley[8] and Benoît Clerc.[9] While these authors undertake some

---

[4] Wendy Leigh, *Bowie: The Biography* (New York: Gallery Books, 2014); Paul Trynka, *Starman David Bowie: The Definitive Biography* (London: Sphere, 2011).
[5] Chris O'Leary, *Rebel Rebel: All the Songs of David Bowie: From '64 to '76* (Alresford: Zero Books, 2015); Chris O'Leary, 'David Bowie, Song by Song', *Pushing Ahead of the Dame*, https://bowiesongs.wordpress.com/about/
[6] Nicholas Pegg, *The Complete David Bowie* (London: Titan Books, 2016).
[7] Leah Kardos, *Blackstar Theory: The Last Works of David Bowie* (New York: Bloomsbury, 2022).
[8] David Buckley, *Strange Fascination* (London: Virgin, 2005).
[9] Benoît Clerc, *David Bowie All the Songs: The Story Behind Every Track* (New York: Black Dog & Leventhal Publishers, 2022).

examination of Bowie's videos, their focus is primarily on the songs. Since I am neither a trained musician nor a musicologist, I must acknowledge the extent to which I have relied on the work of these authors to comprehend the sonic layers of the videos. My hope is that this book will serve as a companion to their publications, which are unsurpassable in terms of providing insight into Bowie's music.

Before Bowie's death in 2016, there were already numerous scholarly publications exploring his contribution to music, art[10] and culture.[11] The scholarship in this field has continued to flourish, resulting in a plethora of insightful explorations of Bowie's engagement with the screen,[12] transmedia and inter-art,[13] philosophy,[14] performance,[15] identity,[16] stardom and celebrity.[17] There have also been exemplary studies of his music videos, by Eoin Devereux, Aileen Dillane and Martin J. Power (2018),[18] Julie Lobalzo Wright (2017),[19] Tiffany Naiman (2019)[20] and Katherine Reed (2023).[21] The book you are reading would not exist without the strong foundation laid by the authors who have contributed to what is now termed 'Bowie studies'. Building upon this valuable body of literature, this book contributes the first in-depth examination of the artistry woven through Bowie's music videos from 1969 to 1983. This timeline is

---

[10] Victoria Broackes and Geoffrey Marsh (eds), *David Bowie Is* (New York: V&A Publishing, 2013).
[11] Ian Chapman, *David Bowie: FAQ* (Connecticut: Backbeat Books, 2020).
[12] Toija Cinque, Angela Ndalianis and Sean Redmond, 'David Bowie On-Screen', *Cinema Journal* 57, no. 3 (2018): 126–30.
[13] Ana Cristina Mendes and Lisa Perrott (eds), *David Bowie and Transmedia Stardom* (Abingdon: Routledge, 2020); Alison Blair, '"Oh man, I need TV when I got T. Rex": Bowie and Bolan's Otherworldly Carnivalesque Intermediality', *Celebrity Studies* 10, no.1 (2019): 75–88.
[14] Eoin Devereux, Aileen Dillane and Martin Power (eds), *David Bowie: Critical Perspectives* (London: Routledge, 2015).
[15] Ian Dixon and Brendan Black (eds), *I'm Not a Film Star* (New York: Bloomsbury, 2022); Shelton Waldrep, *Future Nostalgia: Performing David Bowie* (New York: Bloomsbury, 2015); Stan Hawkins, 'David Bowie: 1947–2016', *Contemporary Music Review* 37, no. 3 (2018): 189–92.
[16] Lisa Perrott, 'Bowie the Cultural Alchemist: Performing Gender, Synthesizing Gesture and Liberating Identity', *Continuum* 31, no. 4 (2017): 528–41.
[17] Toija Cinque, Christopher Moore and Sean Redmond (eds), *Enchanting David Bowie: Space Time Body Memory* (New York: Bloomsbury, 2015).
[18] Eoin Devereux, Aileen Dillane and Martin J. Power, 'Saying Hello to the Lunatic Men: A Critical Reading of "Love is Lost"', *Contemporary Music Review* 37, no.3 (2018): 257–71; Devereux, Dillane and Power, *David Bowie: Critical Perspectives*, 35–55.
[19] Julie Lobalzo Wright, 'The Boy Kept Swinging: David Bowie, Music Video, and the Star Image', in Gina Arnold, Daniel Cookney, Kirsty Fairclough and Michael Goddard (eds), *Music/Video: Histories, Aesthetics, Media* (New York: Bloomsbury, 2017), 67–78.
[20] Tiffany Naiman, '"More Solemn Than a Fading Star": David Bowie's Modernist Aesthetics of Ending', in Lori Burns and Stan Hawkins (eds), *The Bloomsbury Handbook of Popular Music Video Analysis* (New York: Bloomsbury, 2019), 297–313.
[21] Katherine Reed, *David Bowie and the Moving Image: A Standing Cinema* (New York: Bloomsbury, 2023), 43–70.

appropriate, since this was the period in which Bowie played a significant role in establishing music video as a collaborative, intermedial artform. The videos I have analysed were selected on the basis of their potential for revealing insights about this process. A selection of Bowie's subsequent music videos is examined in my book *David Bowie and the Transformation of Music Video: 1984–2016 and Beyond* in my forthcoming book, which serves as a type of sequel to this book. Although each book contributes something new and distinct to the literature, it may be helpful to consider the books as siblings in an unfolding mini-series.

Format and structure

Taking inspiration from Bowie's 'magpie' approach to foraging, I have stitched together a diverse array of perspectives from multiple authors. While this cannot possibly mirror the complex tapestry woven through Bowie's videos, my intent is to leave many threads dangling, so that readers may pick up and follow them.

One of the challenges with any exploration of diverse media is to employ a consistent method for distinguishing between mediums. The following section outlines the formatting protocols I use throughout the book to differentiate each medium. Firstly, I use subheadings to clearly signpost my analysis of a song, before moving to an analysis of the video with the same title. While my focal point is the art of music video, it is important to distinguish the form and function of a song (as experienced without a visual accompaniment), with the form and function of a music video, which of course, will impact the meanings and sensations generated by the song. Since the terms promotional film and 'promo' are still used by many British directors,[22] I use this term where it seems appropriate. To avoid confusion, I use single quotes for promos ('Space Oddity') and music videos ('Heroes'), and double quote marks for songs ("Heroes"), italics for albums (*Heroes*), films (*The Image*), television series (*Quatermass*) and theatrical stage shows (*The Elephant Man*).

Screen-grabs are strategically positioned throughout the book to support my analysis of the videos. While these provide important visual accompaniment to the analyses, I encourage readers to watch the videos while you read. A link to a YouTube playlist is provided as a footnote at the beginning of each chapter. This

---

[22] Emily Caston, *British Music Videos, 1966–2016: Genre, Authenticity and Art* (Edinburgh: Edinburgh University Press, 2020).

enables readers to easily click through the videos in the order they are mentioned in the text. The following chapter outline shows how each chapter scaffolds chronologically from prior chapters.

Chapter one introduces my argument that Bowie played a key role in establishing and remediating music video as a collaborative artform. To support this argument, I step through an outline of relevant scholarship on music video and relate this to the concepts that frame my analysis of Bowie's videos. This chapter also includes an explanation of my multimodal analytical approach, and a three-phase outline of the key shifts in the industrial context underpinning the production of British music videos between 1965 and 1983. Some readers may wish to bypass the conceptual frame and move directly to chapter two.

Chapter two examines Bowie's traverse of stage and screen between 1967 and 1972, and situates this in relation to the broader process of remediation. I begin by establishing the cultural and collaborative context that shaped Bowie's artistic and commercial interests and fuelled his motivation to perform across stage and screen. Further context is provided by exploring Bowie's formative collaboration with Lindsay Kemp, and the inspiration he drew from mime, mask and the figure of Pierrot. The chapter then moves through an examination of selected promotional films directed by Malcolm J. Thomson, along with filmed performances for television shows such as *Hits a Go-go*, and *The Old Grey Whistle Test*.

Chapter three tells the story of Bowie's intensive collaboration with Mick Rock between 1972 and 1973. Delving into the essence of their working relationship, and tracing the development of Bowie's performance to camera, the chapter reveals how the two artists learnt much from each other, and shows how music video developed as a collaborative work of art. By exploring the specific affordances of painting, still photography and the moving image, I demonstrate how music video serves to remediate each of these mediums, while operating as a mobile, painted canvas.

Chapter four builds upon chapter three to demonstrate music video's remediation of painting and sculpture in relation to light. It does so by exploring the influence of visual music and painting upon Bowie's music videos from 1977 to 1979, which were directed by Stanley Dorfman, Nick Ferguson and David Mallet. The context is set by considering the impact of Berlin upon Bowie, and by exploring the creative process generated through the collaborative triumvirate of Tony Visconti, Brian Eno and Bowie. While suggesting the potential of music video as a vessel for the migration of gesture, close analysis also reveals the idiosyncratic aesthetic that specific directors contributed to Bowie's *oeuvre*, and to furthering music video as an artform.

Chapter five picks up where chapter four left off by examining the videos produced from Bowie's collaboration with Mallet from 1980 to 1982. Informed by insights gained from my interview with Mallet, further context is provided by considering the significance of Bowie's acting role in *The Elephant Man* (1980–1) and his approach to the album *Scary Monsters* (1980). With considerable space devoted to an analysis of 'Ashes to Ashes', the video is explored from various perspectives, including its remediation of 1920s surrealist film and *Commedia dell'arte*, along with Bowie's engagement with 'future nostalgia'. Progressing to an analysis of 'Wild is the Wind' (1981) and 'The Drowned Girl' (1982), I use the metaphor of metamorphosis to describe Bowie's response to personal tragedy.

Chapter six moves to the next phase of metamorphosis – 'eclosion'. This is where Bowie emerges from his cocoon as a colourful (tanned) butterfly, ready to spread his wings far and wide. Coinciding with the ascendance of MTV, Bowie's eclosion goes beyond his physical form. By examining the videos produced during this time, along with interview materials, we shall see that Bowie's eclosion is manifested through his revised approach to music video – as an artform for communicating anti-racist messages to a mass audience. Through an analysis of the videos for 'Let's Dance' and 'China Girl', this chapter examines Bowie's use of signifiers and gestures as an artistic strategy intended to cast light on racism and colonial oppression.

The book concludes with an epilogue, which reflects upon the key findings of my research, and then pivots towards the focus and scope for this book's forthcoming sequel – *David Bowie and the Transformation of Music Video (1984–2016 and Beyond)*.

I hope you enjoy the six-course meal that follows. While it was Bowie who set the menu, it took me some time to gather the ingredients and cook each dish with care, so as to satisfy the various tastes of our guests. Thankfully, I had some assistance in the kitchen and was able to consult the very best recipe books. The guest list includes a menagerie of personas, including artists and music video directors who collaborated with Bowie – all with fascinating stories to tell, so . . .

Take your protein pills and put your helmet on, commencing countdown, engines on![23]

---

[23] David Bowie, lyrics to 'Space Oddity', 1969.

1

The Art of Music Video

Video is there to be used as an artform as well as a sort of a commercial device for illustration and promotion. . . . I fell in love with video in the early seventies.

Bowie, 1981[1]

When Bowie confessed his love for the art of music video, the extent to which he had already shaped this artform was not well known.[2] In 1981, Bowie was lauded more for his status as a musician, but not so much for his visual art practice or for his contribution to the art of music video. There is now much greater awareness of Bowie's artistry across several mediums. This is largely due to the proliferation of his creative outputs via YouTube and other internet platforms, along with exhibitions such as *David Bowie Is* (2013–18), tributary performances, and documentaries, along with the publications mentioned in the preface. Despite this broad engagement with Bowie's art, there has not been a lot of attention given to the collaborative process and artistry of his music videos. More than forty years after Bowie expressed his love for video, his words resonate as I write this book. I too feel the need to state the obvious: music video is there to be used as an artform! While Bowie's videos communicate this idea in their own right, this book specifically explores how Bowie and his collaborators used the form as a canvas upon which they experimented with artistic possibilities. My hope is that this deep excavation of Bowie's videos will also help to demonstrate that music video is a collaborative artform with significant cultural value, and thus worthy of scholarship.

---

[1] Richard's David Bowie Channel, 'David Bowie 1981 interview'. YouTube video, 00.10.47, 15 February 2020, https://youtu.be/d7aJWFAu0Fo.
[2] A YouTube playlist for chapter 1 is available at https://tinyurl.com/mr3ps6p8.

This first chapter undertakes the important function of summarizing the literature on music video and providing an outline of the shifting industrial context that shaped the production of British music videos between 1963 and 1995. I then provide an explanation of the concepts and methods that frame my analysis of the videos. The terms 'loose continuity' and transmedia, worldbuilding and intertextuality are discussed in relation to Bowie's intermedial approach to art, all of which provides the context for the following chapters.

Music video scholarship

While this book owes much to the path-breaking research undertaken over the past decade, scholarship on music video was scant through the 1980s and 1990s. Where the form was given attention, it was considered as 'television fillers or postmodern flow', and typically perceived as a low priority in what Emily Caston has termed a '"hierarchy of screen arts" in film and television studies'.[3] Having developed my career across the disciplinary areas of screen media, art and cultural studies, I have witnessed first-hand almost three decades of such a hierarchy; music video has been relegated to a lower rung, despite its central role in generating representations and new configurations of old and new media, along with fine art and popular culture.

Will Straw and John Fiske were among those who explored music video in relation to a breakdown of singular truth systems. Writing in 1988, Straw downplayed the significance of music video's impact within the 'music-related industries',[4] a pessimistic viewpoint that he updated in 2018, only to bemoan its diminished cultural status due to YouTube's 'uncontrolled voraciousness and role as dumping ground for all kinds of minor cultural forms'.[5] This, he claims, led to a situation whereby music video 'has become little more than the sheathing in which the song is enclosed'.[6] More optimistically, Fiske announced in 1986 that 'Broadcast TV, approaching its half century has just developed its only original artform – rock video or MTV'.[7] While Fiske recognized music video's value as an

---

[3] Caston, *British Music Videos*, 2.
[4] Will Straw, 'Music Video in its Contexts: Popular Music and Post-modernism in the 1980s'. *Popular Music*, 7, no. 3 (1988): 248.
[5] Will Straw, 'Music Video in its Contexts: 30 Years Later', *Volume!* 14, no. 2 (2018): 1.
[6] Ibid., 1.
[7] John Fiske, 'MTV: Post-Structural Post-Modern', *Journal of Communication Inquiry* 10, no. 1 (1986): 74.

artform, such statements are indicative of the academic blind spot that obstructed scholars from realizing how the form developed as an original artform long before the launch of MTV in August 1981. Although this blind spot continues to eclipse the academic field of vision, over the past two decades music video has been explored from many different perspectives, with recent publications taking it more seriously as an artform with social and cultural significance.

While music video once appeared to function primarily as a commercial medium for popular entertainment, the form has recently been exposed by scholars as functionally diverse. Music video has been explored as a site for philosophical provocation, and as a stage for complex acts of representation,[8] performativity and personae,[9] worldbuilding, fandom and the development of participatory cultures.[10] According to my own audience research, music video may function as a suitably flexible form with which to provoke a therapeutic engagement with identity.[11] Unconstrained by the conventions of more literal or didactic modes of representation, music video affords an almost unlimited potential for provoking an imaginative engagement with memory,[12] for generating nostalgia and for vivifying spectres from the past.[13]

The prehistory of music video

Music video's capacity to connect us with the past seems obvious when we consider the form's rich prehistory, which has been traced even further back in time than the few decades preceding MTV. Those scholars who have traced the form's antecedents are quick to point out that 'music video has not just one, but several prehistories'.[14] Describing visual music films of the mid nineteenth

---

[8] Diane Railton and Paul Watson, *Music Video and the Politics of Representation* (Edinburgh: Edinburgh University Press, 2011).
[9] Philip Auslander, 'Framing Personae in Music Videos', in Lori A. Burns and Stan Hawkins (eds), *The Bloomsbury Handbook of Popular Music Video Analysis* (New York: Bloomsbury, 2019), 91–109.
[10] Lisa Perrott, 'The Animated Music Videos of Radiohead, Chris Hopewell, and Gastón Viñas: Fan Participation, Collaborative Authorship, and Dialogic Worldbuilding', in Lori A. Burns and Stan Hawkins (eds), *The Bloomsbury Handbook of Popular Music Video Analysis* (New York: Bloomsbury, 2019), 47–68.
[11] Perrott, 'Bowie the Cultural Alchemist': 528–41.
[12] Lisa Perrott, '"Accented" Music Video: Animating Memories of Migration in "Rocket Man"', *Music, Sound and the Moving Image* 13, no. 2 (2019): 123–46.
[13] Lisa Perrott, 'Moonwalking "Backwards into the Future": "Poi E," Music Video, and Documentary', in Mathias Korsgaard and Tomáš Jirsa (eds), *Travelling Music Video* (New York: Bloomsbury, 2023).
[14] Henry Keazor and Thorsten Wübbena, *Rewind, Play, Fast Forward: The Past, Present and Future of Music Video* (Bielefeld: Transaction Publishers, 2010), 21.

century as 'proto-music videos',[15] Saul Austerlitz (2007) charts the development of other antecedents to the form, such as Hollywood musicals, Soundies, Scopitones, Snader Telescriptions and the jukebox. This historical trajectory shows how audio-visual media underwent successive changes, while serving as precursors to the early promotional films (promos) of the mid-to-late-1960s.[16]

Emphasizing the multiplicity and intermediality of the form, Mathias Korsgaard (2017) explains how diverse media and intersecting audio-visual pathways eventually developed into a medium we now refer to as music video.[17] Throughout the twentieth century, the audio-visual-kinetic relations prefiguring music video underwent development through various mediums and performance modes. It is therefore vital to consider the role of antecedents to music video, such as visual music, silent cinema, theatrical performance modes, and avant-garde approaches to visual art, film and music, all of which form an important historical context for considering the artistry of the music videos examined in this book. The broad contours of these antecedents are outlined below.

Theatrical performance modes

Although scholarship on this topic is scant, various modes of stage and street theatre provide deep historical roots for the different types of performance depicted in contemporary music video. This is particularly relevant to several of Bowie's videos, which remediate performance traditions associated with mime, masking, *Commedia dell'arte* and *kabuki* theatre. While Bowie continued to draw upon these performance traditions throughout his career, he also strove to synthesize several media and literary forms to create a convergence of theatrical stage and screen artforms.[18] For this, he derived inspiration from another antecedent to music video – '*Gesamtkunstwerk*',[19] which has been translated as 'total work of art' or 'synthesis of arts'.[20] Exploring Richard Wagner's theories on

---

[15] Saul Austerlitz, *Money for Nothing: A History of the Music Video from the Beatles to the White Stripes* (New York: Continuum, 2007), 13.
[16] Ibid.
[17] Mathias Korsgaard, *Music Video After MTV: Audiovisual Studies, New Media, and Popular Music* (Abingdon: Routledge, 2017), 17.
[18] Although this can be observed as a recurring artistic goal throughout Bowie's career, it was most evident in the stage shows for *Ziggy Stardust* (1973), *Diamond Dogs* (1974), *Glass Spider* (1987) and *Lazarus* (2015).
[19] For more on this, see Lisa Perrott, 'Ziggy Stardust, Direct Cinema and the Multimodal Performance of *Gesamtkunstwerk*', in Dixon and Black (eds), *I'm Not a Film Star*, 25–51.
[20] Krisztina Lajosi, 'Wagner and the (Re)mediation of Art: *Gesamtkunstwerk* and Nineteenth Century Theories of Media', *Frame* 23, no. 2 (2010): 43.

Gesamtkunstwerk and theatre as an ideal medium, Krisztina Lajosi suggests the concept 'might also be rendered as "communal or collective artwork of the future"'.[21] Contemporary proponents of *Gesamtkunstwerk* strive for a multisensory synthesis of artforms, often involving the communal and/or integrated performance of music, literature, theatre, dance, painting, and sculpture.[22]

From visual music to audio-vision

This aim to engage multiple senses through a synthesis of media is also shared by the interdisciplinary tradition of visual music, a precursor and close relative of contemporary music video. Despite the tradition's dispersal across music, painting, still photography, film, animation, kinetic sculpture and installation art, it is loosely held together by a desire to explore the relations between sound, music, visual art, and the senses. Noting how visual music finds continuity in music video, Korsgaard describes it 'as the tradition of applying musical concepts or ideas (for instance, aspects of rhythm or techniques of counterpoint) to a form that is primarily visual – thereby "pushing visual art toward the condition of music"'.[23] Visual music artists aim to bring together visual and sonic media in ways that incite the experience of a direct relationship between sonic elements such as rhythm and timbre, with visual and sensory stimuli such as light, colour and the perception of movement. Proponents of the tradition explore audio-visual analogues and compositional strategies that provoke connections between the senses.[24]

Pioneering figures in the history of visual music include Wassily Kandinsky, František Kupka, Arnold Schoenberg and Mikalojus Konstantinas Čiurlionis. Building upon the work of these abstract painters, photographers and visual artists explored the relations between sonic and visual elements such as light, colour, and sculpture. This three-dimensional tier of visual music included artists such as Alfred Stieglitz, Zdeněk Pešánek, Francis Bruguière and Thomas

---

[21] Ibid., 46.
[22] Michael Goddard, 'Audiovision and *Gesamtkunstwerk*: The Aesthetics of First – and Second – Generation Industrial Music Video', in Gina Arnold, Daniel Cookney, Kirsty Fairclough and Michael Goddard (eds), *Music/Video: Histories, Aesthetics, Media* (London: Bloomsbury, 2017), 163–80.
[23] Korsgaard, *Music Video After MTV*, 21–2.
[24] Kerry Brougher, Olivia Mattis and Jeremy Strick (eds), *Visual Music: Synaesthesia in Art and Music Since 1900* (New York: Thames and Hudson, 2005).

Wilfred.[25] Those who practiced moving image methods for composing visual music added a kinetic dimension, contributing new approaches to abstract animation, experimental film and kinetic sculpture. Among these artists, Len Lye, Oskar Fischinger, Norman McLaren and Harry Smith were pre-eminent for their experimentations with audio-visual-kinetic relationships, which have inspired the practice of contemporary music video directors. For example, the principles and aesthetics of visual music underpin the choreography for Daft Punk's video 'Around the World' (1997), directed by Michel Gondry; for Björk's video 'Hidden Place' (2001), Inez and Vinoodh used extreme close-ups of sensory organs and body fluids to convey the experience of synaesthesia. As we shall see, Bowie's engagement with visual music is also apparent in his videos, as portrayed through his collaborations with artists such as Brian Eno and Stanley Dorfman, and by his persistent engagement with the relations between the sonic and visual arts.

While visual music may be the more obvious artistic tradition when considering the prehistory of music video, some of the most innovative and imaginative music videos of the past fifty-five years owe a debt to avant-garde strategies that were established by proponents of surrealism, Dada, Bauhaus, Situationism, Fluxus, punk, agit-prop, expanded cinema, experimental film and DIY audio-visual culture. These movements and cultures have provided artists and music video directors with sonic and visual languages and strategies for performing acts of subversion – a practice that has been explored by Kevin Donnelly,[26] John Richardson, Holly Rogers, Carol Vernallis and myself.[27] A prominent example of this strategic engagement with the avant-garde can be found in the Dada-inspired performance strategies used by Lady Gaga, which Michael Peters describes as 'Gagaism'.[28] In her video for 'Poker Face' (2008), director Ray Kay uses the technique of audio-visual glitch, which, according to Caetlin Benson-Allott, serves as a strategy for subverting the gendered ocular gaze established by Hollywood cinema.[29] Not only was Bowie a key source of

---

[25] Ibid.
[26] Kevin J. Donnelly, 'Experimental Music Video and Television', in Laura Mulvery and Jamie Sexton (eds), *Experimental British Television* (Manchester: Manchester University Press, 2015), 166–79.
[27] Lisa Perrott, Holly Rogers and Carol Vernallis, 'Beyonce's Lemonade: She Dreams in Both Worlds', *FilmInt*, 2 June 2016, https://tinyurl.com/rw6w5jrj.
[28] For more on this, see Michael A. Peters, 'On the Edge of Theory: Dadaism, (Ca-Caism), Gagaism', *Review of Education, Pedagogy, and Cultural Studies* 34, no. 5 (2012): 216–26; Goddard, 'Audiovision and *Gesamtkunstwerk*'.
[29] Caetlin Benson-Allott, 'Going Gaga for Glitch: Digital Failure @nd Feminist Spectacle in Twenty-First Century Music Video', in Carol Vernallis, Amy Herzog and John Richardson (eds), *The Oxford Handbook of Sound and Image in Digital Media* (Oxford: Oxford University Pres, 2014), 127–37.

inspiration for Lady Gaga and many other artists, he forged the path for music video as a meeting ground for popular music and avant-garde subversive strategies.

Surrealism

The avant-garde strategies at play in Bowie's videos may be better understood when considering the significance of surrealism as an antecedent to the development of contemporary music video. This lineage is explored by John Richardson, who highlights music video's suitability for experimenting with surrealist methods. Using the term 'neo-surrealism', he explains that an essential aspect of this idea of the neo-surreal is a principle expounded by the historical surrealists: 'the capacity of surrealist acts, performances or objects to bring about altered perceptions of the world – to help us to imagine afresh'.[30] Following Richardson, I have explored the neo-surrealist remediation of popular music video, showing how surrealist strategies converge with music video conventions and experimental animation techniques, thus operating to 'subvert the diametric boundaries drawn around popular and avant-garde, and "high" and "low" cultural forms'.[31] Chapters four and five extend upon this research to examine surrealist strategies within the context of videos such as 'Boys Keep Swinging' (1979) and 'Ashes to Ashes' (1980). Given the extent to which Bowie incorporated surrealist strategies into many elements of his creative process (including lyric writing, sonic and visual composition), an outline of the key tenets of surrealism may help us to understand the intent behind some of the more perplexing moments in his videos.

Although often relegated to the 1920s–1930s, the key tenets of surrealism pre-dated this period, and continue to provide conceptual and methodological tools for artists to generate subversive acts, or to release the creative potential of the unconscious psyche. Driven by a desire for artistic and literary freedom, the early surrealists aimed to create sensorially provocative art and literature through irrational juxtapositions of words and images and the estrangement of familiar objects. While Bowie's creative process underwent constant transformation, it

---

[30] John Richardson, *An Eye for Music: Popular Music and the Audiovisual Surreal* (New York: Oxford University Press, 2012).
[31] Lisa Perrott, 'Experimental Animation and the Neosurrealist Remediation of Popular Music Video', *Animation Practice, Process & Production* 8 (2019): 88.

was influenced by surrealist tenets such as: an urge to create art through play, experimentation, and chance occurrence; a desire to tap into the subconscious psyche, dream-states, archetypes, symbolism and mythology; an aim to transcend normative signifying systems (such as the codification of gender, sexuality, and identity per se); an intent to subvert 'rational' structuring devices (such as classical narrative, continuity editing and linguistic rules); an inclination to generate absurdist humour; and the provocation of an uncanny experience through estranging that which is familiar (for example, depicting a familiar beach scene with strange colours and inverted lighting). These broad tenets of surrealism underpin methods such as aleatory process, analogical composition, temporal dissonance, defamiliarization and *détournement* – concepts that will be explained in the following chapters. Proponents of the surrealist, Dada and Situationist movements used *détournement* as a strategy to interrupt conventional signifying systems by altering their familiar coding and re-routing their dominant or intended meanings.[32]

Remediation

Whether it be delving into the tenets of surrealism, visual music, *Gesamtkunstwerk*, silent cinema or experimental animation, the act of charting the prehistory of music video reveals a process of constant dialogue with antecedents to the form. While this may not always be explicit, close analysis reveals how these antecedents inform the work of artists and directors such as Floria Sigismondi,[33] Michel Gondry,[34] Stephen R. Johnson,[35] Mark Romanek, Jonas Åkerlund, Kahlil Joseph and Melina Matsoukas.[36] By engaging with the avant-garde, these directors

---

[32] These movements established a set of practices motivated by a desire to interrupt and defamiliarize linguistic and cultural conventions, enabling the playful reproduction of cultural forms, liberated from the perceived constraints of individual consciousness. Practices of *détournement* included using automatic writing methods, reworking and defamiliarizing texts and phrases, cutting up and rearranging their signifiers to achieve semantic discrepancy. For more on this see Jeremy Stubbs, 'Surrealism's Book of Revelation: Isadore Ducasse's *Poésies, Détournement* and Automatic Writing', Romantic Review 87, no. 4 (1996): 493–510; Guy Debord and Gill J. Wolman, 'Methods of Détournement', *Les Lèvres Nues* no. 8 (1956), Nothingness.org, https://tinyurl.com/yttkn8sm.
[33] Lisa Perrott, 'The Alchemical Union of David Bowie and Floria Sigismondi, "Transmedia Surrealism" and "Loose Continuity"', in Carol Vernallis, Holly Rogers and Lisa Perrott (eds), *Transmedia Directors: Artistry, Industry and New Audiovisual Aesthetics* (New York: Bloomsbury, 2019), 194–220.
[34] Richardson, *An Eye for Music*.
[35] Perrott, 'Experimental Animation and the Neosurrealist Remediation of Popular Music Video'.
[36] Perrott, Rogers and Vernallis, 'Beyonce's Lemonade'.

contribute a refreshed experience of historical artforms, and a reconfiguration of how we experience old and new media. Since Bowie and his collaborators were vanguards of this process of 'remediation', it is important to explain how this process works. Jay Bolter and Richard Grusin used this term to describe the process by which new media attain cultural distinctiveness by paying homage to, and refashioning earlier media such as painting, photography, film, and theatrical stage productions.[37] While they argue that 'remediation is a defining characteristic of the new digital media',[38] this concept is also useful when applied to promotional films and music videos that were made before the advent of digital media. Throughout this book, I show how non-digital film and video also attained cultural distinctiveness by incorporating the aesthetics, techniques, gestures and conventions of earlier media.

By defining 'remediation' as 'the representation of one medium in another',[39] Bolter and Grusin call attention to the affordances that distinguish mediums, while also suggesting how these might be modified through media convergence.[40] In addition to the act of *representation*, remediation involves a process of *alteration* of one medium by another, which may occur due to new technology, changing social, cultural, and economic conditions, shifting aesthetic preferences, and changes in the ways media is produced, distributed, received and reconfigured. Bolter and Grusin use the term 'visible remediation' to describe a process whereby a reworked artform, using newer media technologies and presented in a contemporary setting, 'becomes a mosaic in which we are simultaneously aware of the individual pieces, and their new, inappropriate setting'.[41] While this notion of remediation provides a tangible way to consider how mediums change, I would qualify this statement by noting that remediation is also a sonic and audio-visual phenomenon. Furthermore, a prime catalyst for remediation is the practice of experimenting with intersecting media, which is one of the ways in which Bowie developed the art of music video.

An understanding of remediation is vital for any study of music video as an artform undergoing transformation. Korsgaard (2017) provides an insightful reflection on the remediation of various antecedents to music video, arguing that

---

[37] Jay Bolter and Richard Grusin, *Remediation: Understanding New Media* (London: MIT Press, 2000), 44–50.
[38] Ibid., 45.
[39] Ibid.
[40] Ibid.
[41] Ibid., 47.

'music video enters into fundamental relations with other media, old as well as new, in incorporating, transforming, or repurposing their techniques, forms and aesthetics'.[42] He shows how the prehistory of music video plays an important part in shaping the ways in which new digital technologies, along with networking and file sharing capabilities, have enabled previously unconsidered production practices and collaborative assemblages. Korsgaard proposes that remediation can be viewed as 'a process of "historical reversal," where not only new media remediate old media but also the other way around'.[43] He observes how 'the audiovisual language of music video is based upon expressions and techniques known from elsewhere', and that 'music video transforms some of these expressions, thus gradually forming new ones that slowly feed back into the media from which the expressions first came'.[44] Music video is not only changed by other mediums, it may have a transformative impact on those mediums – and significantly – upon the way in which they are perceived by audience members. My close examination of Bowie's videos explores this facet of audience perception and reveals how his infiltration of music video with other mediums and traditions has not only shaped it as an artform but has also reconfigured and revitalized those mediums. From his first promotional films through to his final music videos, Bowie played an important part in experimenting with the intersection of several mediums, thus remediating stage theatricality, mime, dance, television, film, sculpture, literature, costume, painting and photography. Although comprising several other intersecting mediums, music video has distinct affordances and capabilities, each of which explain why the medium provides a suitable canvas for an artist like Bowie. Each of the affordances outlined below link together to build a modular framework for contextualizing and analysing the videos in this book.

Volatile audiovisuality

Music video generates rich analyses, partly due to the medium's volatile audiovisuality. Although this is often overlooked, the fecundity of music video's

---

[42] Korsgaard, *Music Video after MTV*, 41.
[43] Ibid.
[44] Ibid.

audio-visual relations provides fertile ground for practitioners and scholars alike. This topic has been extensively charted by Holly Rogers (2010, 2014, 2017), whose research is vital for understanding the productive dialogue between music video, visual music, audio-visual media, avant-garde film and video art.[45] Carol Vernallis has also contributed much to the study of music video and audio-visual media. In her book *Experiencing Music Video* (2004),[46] Vernallis argues that music video generates intensified experiences due to its capacity for producing unique relations between music, image, and moving bodies. This idea is further developed in her book *Unruly Media* (2013), where the term 'rhythmicize' is used to describe the heightened capacity of music video to kinesthetically engage the body of the viewer.[47] The topic of audio-visual media has been explored from a variety of perspectives by contributors to *The Oxford Handbook of New Audiovisual Aesthetics* (2013).[48] Building upon this research, Korsgaard (2017) provides an analytical framework for comprehending the audiovisuality of music video 'through the dual concepts of a visual remediation of music and a musical remediation of vision'.[49] He explains that 'audiovisual analysis explores how added value functions audiovisually, both in situations of *audio-viewing*, where sounds add value to images, and in the reverse situations of *"visio-audition,"* where images add value to sounds'.[50] By examining the multimodal space in which sounds and images collide, one can identify the generation of new meanings, unexpected audio-visual combinations, and intensified aesthetics. The seemingly alchemical collisions occurring within this space can be explored by employing a variation of the flexible analytical framework developed by Lori Burns (2019).[51] Using the term 'dynamic multimodality', Burns explains how her proposed analytical approach:

---

[45] Holly Rogers, *Visualising Music: Audiovisual Relationships in Avant-Garde Film and Video Art* (London: Lambert Academic Publishing, 2010); Holly Rogers, 'Twisted Synaesthesia: Music Video and the Visual Arts', in Germano Celant (ed.), *Art or Sound* (Venice: Fondazione Prada, 2014), 383–8.
[46] Carol Vernallis, *Experiencing Music Video* (New York: Columbia University Press, 2004).
[47] Carol Vernallis, *Unruly Media: YouTube, Music Video, and the New Digital Cinema* (New York: Oxford University Press, 2013), 159.
[48] John Richardson, Claudia Gorbman and Carol Vernallis (eds), *The Oxford Handbook of New Audiovisual Aesthetics* (New York: Oxford University Press, 2013).
[49] Korsgaard, *Music Video After MTV*, 63.
[50] Ibid.
[51] Lori Burns, 'Dynamic Multimodality in Extreme Metal Performance Video: Dark Tranquillity's "Uniformity," Directed by Patric Ullaeus', in Lori A. Burns and Stan Hawkins (eds), *The Bloomsbury Handbook of Music Video Analysis* (New York, Bloomsbury, 2019), 183–200.

...distinguishes the *spatial, temporal* and *corporeal* dimensions, as these cut across the expressive composite of word-music-image. This analytical approach yields multi-dimensional perspectives on the music video as the site of lyrical, musical, and visual expression, facilitating the analyst's exploration of how meanings are created in the audiovisual text.[52]

Since Bowie and his collaborators were often keen to experiment with the volatile audiovisuality afforded by music video, Burns' approach towards multimodal analysis offers an appropriate analytical model, which I have adapted for my analysis of Bowie's videos. Following Burns, I begin by excavating through the strata of each video to identify 'individual expressive channels',[53] such as lyrics, musical arrangement, framing, camera technique, lighting, colour, set-design, editing and performance, including mime, pose and gesture. Once I have undertaken an in-depth examination of each of these modes as individual layers, this analysis then forms the basis for exploring the volatile relations between them. As we shall see, this step-by-step method of analysis shows how a song or artform can take on new meaning when remediated as a music video. This process also reveals insights about collaborative and creative process, and the vivifying possibilities of audio-visual assemblage.

A transformative media configuration

Music video affords the capacity to be transformative: to transform other forms, to transform our experience of songs and identities, and to transform our perception of time and space. Not only does it have the potential to catalyse such transformation, music video is *in* transformation. While its forms and functions are constantly changing, so too is the way that music video is produced, exhibited and experienced. Like a living organism, it is in a constant state of flux and renewal; always brushing up against other cultural forms and forever drawing new connections amongst numerous intertexts. For Tomáš Jirsa and Mathias Korsgaard, music video is an 'ever-transforming media configuration which is both morphing and confusingly multifaceted'.[54] They define music video as a 'hybrid audiovisual configuration driven by the interaction of recorded sounds,

---

[52] Ibid., 187.
[53] Ibid.
[54] Tomáš Jirsa and Mathias Korsgaard, 'The Music Video in Transformation: Notes on a Hybrid Audiovisual Configuration', *MSMI* 13, no. 2 (2019): 113.

moving images, and lyrics; an intertextual space of perpetual remediations where one medium transforms the other'.[55] Building upon this definition, I describe music video as a collaborative artform (un)like any other. It is a mutable, time-travelling medium with the special ability to embody and mimic other artforms, mediums and traditions. Since the functional possibilities of music video have often been overlooked, I argue that it is not only a commercial artform with aesthetic and economic value, the form also has the capacity to be educational, insightful, subversive, relational, therapeutic and transportive.[56]

Music video TARDIS

Music video has the remarkable capacity to transport us across space and to particular moments in time, yet it may also be experienced as uncannily timeless. Through its travels, a video may resonate with diverse generations and communities, even when experienced in a completely different milieu from when it was created. This travelling affordance may be illustrated using the metaphor of the TARDIS, the time-travelling vessel used to explore the universe in the television series *Doctor Who* (1963–89).[57] As an acronym for 'Time And Relative Dimension In Space', the progenitors of the TARDIS drew inspiration from the science fiction idea of the time machine, which dates back to H.G. Wells' novels *The Time Machine* (1895) and *The Chronic Argonauts* (1888).[58] In *Doctor Who*, the TARDIS travels through time and space by rematerializing as it passes through the dimensional plane known as the 'time vortex'.[59] While the exterior of the TARDIS is usually represented as a British police box, it is fitted with a 'chameleon circuit', which (when operational) enables it to change form and camouflage itself, thus blending into whichever environment it may land. Just as this sci-fi logic provides a flexible metaphor for the mutability and time-travelling affordances of music video, the metaphor is particularly well-suited to an examination of Bowie's music videos. As we shall see, many of his videos serve as vessels for transporting storyworld components, myths and archetypes across

---

[55] Ibid., 117.
[56] Perrott, '"Accented" Music Video'; Perrott, 'Moonwalking "Backwards into the Future"'.
[57] *Doctor Who* (1963–89), BBC, United Kingdom.
[58] H.G. Wells, *The Time Machine* (London: William Heinemann, 1895); H.G. Wells, *The Chronic Argonauts* (London: Royal College of Science, 1888).
[59] For more on this, see David K. Johnson, 'Wormholes, the Time Vortex, and TARDIS: Time Travel and "Dr Who"', *Wondrium Daily*, 8 April 2021, https://tinyurl.com/yc3r2hv9.

time and space, including those derived from science fiction. By charting the travels of videos such as 'Space Oddity' (1969, 1972, 1979) and 'Ashes to Ashes' (1980), these videos appear as mobile palimpsests undergoing constant transformation.

Time is out of joint

By investigating the travelling affordance of music video, we become aware that the medium's particular configurations of sound, word and image have the capacity to refer us to the future and to the past. Musical and lyrical phrases may align with visual resonances to provoke nostalgia, and they can also trigger the sensation of being transported to another place or time. While this might be a pleasurable experience, it can also conjure an uncanny untimeliness, a sensation which has been characterized by the phrase 'the time is out of joint'.[60] This line from William Shakespeare's *Hamlet* was appropriated by Jacques Derrida in 1994 to describe a state of haunting whereby 'revenants' (spirits, spectres, ghosts) re-appear in a different time, giving rise to a sense of ontological uncertainty.[61] While Derrida coined the term 'hauntology' with reference to the apparitional workings of political discourse, this concept has since been developed as a means of examining how mediated cultural forms trigger a sense of temporal dissonance. Extending and refashioning Derrida's theory, Mark Fisher has demonstrated how music and screen media can produce a nostalgic engagement with the past and future, along with an eerie sense of dyschronia.[62] Propelled by Fisher's acute attention to the temporal and cultural affordances of music and audio-visual media, I have drawn on his notion of hauntological media as a means of understanding Bowie's persistent engagement with time travel, temporal dissonance, and nostalgia.[63] Since my earlier publications on this topic demonstrate the concept's utility as a tool for analysis of audio-visual media,[64] 'hauntology' is used in this book as a means for gaining insights about music

---

[60] Jacques Derrida, *Specters of Marx: The State of the Debt, the Work of Mourning and The New International* (New York: Routledge, 1994), 20.
[61] Ibid.
[62] Mark Fisher, *Ghosts of My Life: Writings on Depression, Hauntology and Lost Futures* (Alresford: Zero Books, 2014); Mark Fisher, 'What is Hauntology?' *Film Quarterly* 66, no. 1 (2012): 16–24.
[63] Lisa Perrott, 'Time is Out of Joint: The Transmedial Hauntology of David Bowie', *Celebrity Studies* 10, no. 1 (2019): 119–39.
[64] Ibid.

video's affordance for conjuring a sense of nostalgia for the past and future. The concept becomes particularly useful in chapter two, where we will begin to explore Bowie's rumination on 'future nostalgia' – a sense of yearning for a future that will not come to pass.[65] This is further elaborated in chapter five, thus demonstrating the continuity of this idea across Bowie's songs, films, and videos.

A collaborative artform

Music video is a fundamentally collaborative artform, which draws together a diverse array of skillsets and production processes. The productive aspect of this commingling is demonstrated in the following chapters, which open a window onto Bowie's collaborative relationships and creative processes. While revealing the collaborative nature of Bowie's approach to creativity, this examination highlights the surprising possibilities that emerge from the convergence of different skillsets, ideas and ways of seeing.

Between 1969 and 1983, Bowie's music videos emerged predominantly from collaborations with British practitioners. For this reason, Emily Caston's book *British Music Videos: 1966–2016* provides an important source for understanding the collaborative and industrial context in which Bowie's videos of this period were produced.[66] Caston argues that British music video has its roots in collaborative relationships, commercial contractual arrangements and audio-visual assemblages that emerge from industry settings.[67] By focusing on the creative contributions, technical innovations and collaborative process of industry practitioners, Caston challenges those scholars who privilege music video directors as auteur figures without fully acknowledging the complexity of collaborative assemblage. Her book is a useful source for my study, since it deconstructs other common misconceptions that linger in the literature on music video. Unpicking the common belief that music video was born in America after the birth of MTV, Caston shows that music videos were being produced, distributed and exhibited in Britain for at least seventeen years before the launch of MTV.[68] While these debunking arguments are reaffirmed by

---

[65] David Bowie, TeenageWildlife, 'David Bowie – Scary Monsters Interview, PART 1 (12" Promo 1980)', YouTube video, 00:07:51, 26 March 2009, https://tinyurl.com/yseam5yb.
[66] Caston, *British Music Videos*.
[67] Ibid.
[68] Ibid.

scholars such as Justin Smith (2019),[69] they gain further support from my research into the collaborative process behind the scenes of Bowie's pre-MTV videos.

Describing music video as 'an industrial product defined by a distinctive supply chain',[70] Caston defines music videos and promos as 'short films commissioned and released by record labels for mass audiences',[71] which 'comprise a copyrighted synchronised picture and audio track in which a percentage of the royalties accrue to recording artist or record label'.[72] This definition provides a useful pivot for reconsidering what counts as a music video, and who counts as director, practitioner, artist or co-author. While most of the videos discussed in this book were produced prior to the internet, not all of them meet the criteria outlined by Caston. For instance, some of Bowie's early promos were not initially released to the public, let alone a mass audience. Also, some of the videos recorded for television shows, and those re-edited by fans or produced through non-official processes, are outliers to the standardized practices around copyright and monetization. While such videos do not fit neatly into common-sense understandings of what counts as a music video, they are instructive for understanding how the form is dispersed across mediums, platforms, and authors.

Since music video is now experienced as a dispersed artform and is often viewed on YouTube alongside early promotional films, televised performances, concert footage, excerpts from long-form films and fan-made videos, I propose an expanded definition that accounts for alternative modes of production, authorship and reception. Music videos are collaboratively formed time-travelling vessels with porous skin, much like the permeability that enables documentary to morph into surprising forms. As I have argued elsewhere, music video and documentary share the characteristic of being mutable artforms, and their convergence is aptly demonstrated in Brett Morgen's film *Moonage Daydream* (2022).[73] Following this logic, I borrow from Bill Nichols's definition of documentary to argue that, with the form's 'permeable boarders' and

---

[69] Justin Smith, 'Absence and Presence: *Top of the Pops* and the Demand for Music Videos in the 1960s', *Journal of British Cinema and Television* 16, no. 4 (2019): 492–544.
[70] Caston, *British Music Videos*, 19.
[71] Ibid.
[72] Ibid.
[73] Lisa Perrott, 'Moonage Daydream: Brilliant Bowie Film Takes Big Risks to Create Something Truly New', *The Conversation*, 14 September 2022, https://tinyurl.com/3aecydm7.

'chameleon-like appearance',[74] the sense of something being a music video 'lies in the mind of the beholder'.[75] On the basis of this definition, this book extends beyond the analysis of official music videos, thus allowing some surprising outliers to share the stage with official videos.

Three phases of music video production

Since the production, reception and scholarship of music video has undergone transformation over the past fifty-five years, it is important to consider the social, cultural and technological factors that played a part in shaping the videos discussed in this book. Produced between 1969 and 1983, most of these videos resulted from collaborations with British directors. Therefore, Caston's book on British music videos provides a useful source for understanding the context in which these videos were produced and distributed. In the next section, the industrial changes identified by Caston are mapped onto three distinct phases; each demarking a shift in Bowie's approach to music video, along with a specific set of factors related to industry, technology, aesthetics, funding, distribution and reception.

Phase one (1963–74) is distinguished by the independent production of promotional films and provides a useful context for chapters two and three. The year 1963 was a revolutionary year for the emergence of a new wave of popular music. Just as Bowie left school in July of that year, the Rolling Stones were emerging on the touring circuit.[76] *Doctor Who* had just landed on British television screens, inspiring a generation of musicians with its sci-fi storyworld and electronic theme music. The next year was notable for the release of The Beatles' promo 'Can't Buy Me Love' (1964), along with their film *A Hard Day's Night* (1964), an eighty-seven-minute musical comedy shot in a *cinéma verité* style, which influenced other promo films of the 1960s, and was described by Stephen Glynn as having 'invented the pop music video'.[77] Launched in 1964, BBC's *Top of the Pops* became the primary means for British audiences to view promotional films.[78] This first phase was characterized by independent

---

[74] Bill Nichols, *Introduction to Documentary* (Bloomington: Indiana University Press, 2010), 33.
[75] Ibid.
[76] Geoffrey Marsh, 'Astronaut of Inner Spaces', in Broackes and Marsh (eds), *David Bowie Is*, 30.
[77] Stephen Glynn, *A Hard Day's Night: Turner Classic Movies British Film Guide* (London: Bloomsbury, 2005), https://tinyurl.com/2p94ct4u.
[78] Caston, *British Music Videos*, 2.

production, a non-organized industry with 'no institutionalized procedures or trade agreements', and by experimentation with cinematography.[79] Caston describes 1966 as the 'landmark year' in which bands began providing TV shows with 'specific "filmed inserts" which they had shot on location and edited independently'.[80] This shift in the production process released directors from their earlier ties with television production and opened the way for creativity to emerge from independent film production.[81] A relevant example of such liberated creativity is Michael Lindsay-Hogg's direction of The Who's promo 'Happy Jack' (1966), which remediated the comedic food throwing trope of English slapstick.[82] At this time, many directors owned their own technical equipment, enabling them to shoot and edit films at their own homes or through independent production companies.[83] This phase saw the rise of directors such as Lindsay-Hogg, Peter Whitehead and Peter Goldmann, along with the release of seminal promos by The Beatles, Bob Dylan, The Monkees, The Beach Boys, The Who, The Rolling Stones and The Kinks. These promos tended to be approached as either location films shot outside of the studio, such as The Beatles' 'Strawberry Fields' (1967) – or as studio performances with bands lip-syncing, for example, The Monkees' 'Daydream Believer' (1968). While production was prolific during the mid to late 1960s, it slowed down for most artists during the early 1970s. Referring to the British context, Justin Smith notes that:

> With some notable exceptions (e.g. Mick Rock's work with David Bowie) music video's development stalled during the early 1970s, in part because of television's rather conservative response to popular music, and in part because popular music itself fragmented and diversified in ways which made television (always only a utility medium for the transmission of pop) less important.[84]

Given this stalling in development, it is worth considering why Bowie and Rock were able to buck this trend by (arguably) creating some of the most path-breaking music videos of the seventies. Chapter two delves into the essence of this collaboration, demonstrating how significant it was for establishing music video as an artform within the few years of stalled development during this first phase.

---

[79] Ibid., 4.
[80] Ibid.
[81] Smith, 'Absence and Presence,' *Journal of British Cinema and Television* 16, no. 4 (2019): 492–544.
[82] Caston, *British Music Videos*, 148.
[83] Ibid.
[84] Smith, 'Absence and Presence', 539.

Phase two (1975–81) is the pre-MTV period which maps onto chapters four and five. During this phase, directors such as Bruce Gowers, Stanley Dorfman and David Mallet were beginning to develop a reputation based on their approach to cinematography, lighting and editing. While Dorfman and Mallet stand out for their collaborations with Bowie during this period, Gowers rose to prominence after directing Queen's 'Bohemian Rhapsody' in 1975. Due to its iconic low-angle lighting and previously unseen visual effects, many commentators have incorrectly described it as the first music video, thereby overlooking the significance of the previous decades in establishing music video as an artform.

During phase two, the capacity of directors to experiment with music video was supported by a combination of notoriety, institutional independence and increasing funds from the music industry, which was becoming more organized around recording companies as the primary source of funding. Record labels had increased economic power and were showing more interest in music video's value as a promotional tool and revenue generator. While videos were developing popularity on broadcast television, between 1976 and 1986 there was a 'period of conflict between music video filmmakers and established powers in the film and television industries – notably the BBC, the Musicians' Union (MU 1893–) and the Association of Cinematograph, Television and Allied Technicians (ACTT 1956–91)'.[85] One source of frustration was that both British and American broadcasters tended to impose rigid censorship, which obstructed the release of videos perceived to be offensive or transgressive. As discussed in chapter four, 'Boys Keep Swinging' (1979) serves as a pertinent example of the censorship imposed by broadcasters during this phase.

Phase three (1981–95) begins with the launch of MTV in August 1981, and concludes in 1995 when MTV began replacing music video content with animated and reality programmes. After this, music video began to decline both creatively and financially.[86] While these years of decline are relevant for understanding Bowie's approach to music video throughout the 1990s and 2000s, it is the first two years of this phase that provide the most useful context for the videos discussed in chapter six. This was a period that initiated what Korsgaard describes as music video's 'first golden age',[87] when 'music videos

---

[85] Caston, *British Music Videos*, 4.
[86] Korsgaard, *Music Video After MTV*, 18.
[87] Ibid.

exploded into the public consciousness following the launch of MTV'.[88] With its mass audience and endless running hours, MTV was thought to be able to make or break the career of a popular musician or band. While a three-minute video aired on MTV could be a catalyst for an artist's rise to stardom, it could also redirect them along a path toward the pitfalls of hyper-celebrity. Another less explicit issue was that although the platform delivered a seemingly endless flow of music and images to a broad audience, this was curated through a hegemonic lens of (white) American privilege, which of course, did not reflect the reality of MTV's audience. As elaborated in chapter six, Bowie was outspoken in calling out MTV's lack of inclusion and representation for artists of colour, and he attempted to tackle this issue through the use of pointed representational strategies in his music videos.

With its mass audience and commercial model, the rise of MTV led to increased budgets and higher production values. Although artists and directors needed to navigate the powers and pressures of a more commercial production environment, the higher budgets enabled new opportunities to experiment with technologies and artistic strategies. As a result, several videos produced during this phase demonstrate prolific innovation along with an engagement with historical art traditions. This point is aptly demonstrated by Peter Gabriel's video for 'Sledgehammer' (1986, Stephen R. Johnson), a remediation of neo-surrealist strategies and experimental animation techniques.[89] Another example is Michael Jackson's video for 'Thriller' (1983), which remediated the aesthetics of George Romero's horror films. 'Thriller' triggered an ongoing process of remediation as the dance movements reappeared in Taika Waititi's film *Boy* (2010) in the form of a 'Thriller Haka', a hybridized dance sequence that was further remediated in subsequent music video mashups.[90] As elaborated in chapter five, Bowie's video for 'Ashes to Ashes' (1980) pre-empted MTV's large budget innovation by experimenting with video technology to remediate 1920s surrealist film, along with the pre-eighteenth century theatre tradition of *Commedia dell'arte*.

These three phases provide a framework for considering the shifting context for the production, distribution, and reception of the music videos discussed in this book. Since a few disciplinary-specific terms are sprinkled throughout the book, I shall now turn to a definition of the terms 'loose continuity', 'transmedia', 'storyworld' and 'intertextuality'. Along with the already defined terms

---

[88] Ibid., 16.
[89] See Perrott, 'Experimental Animation and the Neosurrealist Remediation of Popular Music Video'.
[90] See Perrott, 'Moonwalking "Backwards into the Future"'.

remediation and hauntology, these concepts work together to provide a framework for my analyses. The following explanation is intended to provide tools for navigating the enigmatic changes and continuities across Bowie's music videos.

Transmedia through and beyond narrative

The continuity across Bowie's music videos can be usefully examined through the conceptual lens of transmedia. Much of the existing literature on transmedia is concerned with transmedia storytelling, particularly the way in which narrative elements travel across media, texts and platforms. David Bordwell and Henry Jenkins are amongst a handful of scholars who developed useful theoretical frameworks for considering the idea of transmedia storytelling, primarily in relation to film, television and franchise. Aware of the limitations of prioritizing film and franchise as central to the discussion on transmedia, Bordwell acknowledges that 'it's hard to think outside the franchise model, even if we want to denounce Hollywood for being stuck in an outdated commitment to the theatrical feature as foundational "content".[91] Encouraging researchers to consider the role played by fans in elaborating canonical storyworlds, Jenkins defined a 'transmedia story' as one that 'unfolds across multiple media platforms, with each new text making a distinctive and valuable contribution to the whole.[92] Arguing that 'worldbuilding' and 'seriality' are the 'aesthetic properties of texts that lend themselves to transmedia experience', Jenkins adds that transmedia texts 'rely on open ended and serialized structures', where the hope is 'for a certain level of integrity and continuity between the pieces which allows us to find the coherent whole from which the many parts must have once broken adrift'.[93] While Jenkins' definition has been predominantly applied to film, television and franchise development, its flexibility is most obvious when applied to a broader range of media, and may therefore provide a lens through which to examine the *oeuvre* of artists such as Bowie, whose work across mediums is not centred upon this triad. However, Bowie's 'story' is not quite as straightforward

---

[91] David Bordwell, 'Observations in Film Art: Now Leaving Platform 1' (2009), https://tinyurl.com/u38t62vd.
[92] Henry Jenkins, *Convergence Culture: Where Old and New Media Collide* (New York: New York University Press, 2006), 95–6.
[93] Henry Jenkins, 'The Aesthetics of Transmedia: In Response to David Bordwell (Part 3)', (2009), https://tinyurl.com/mrw6z8a6.

or as continuous as Jenkins's theory suggests, and the Depth of Field captured by the lens of 'transmedia storytelling' doesn't extend to the broad field of aesthetics, objects, archetypes and intangibles threaded through his music videos.

When we consider the trajectory of Bowie's creative outputs across five decades, it would appear to be marked by discontinuity. Seemingly borne out of a restless drive for experimentation, this discontinuity involved frequent chameleon-like changes in appearance, death and re-birth of personae, and shifts in musical style and visual aesthetic. However, his *oeuvre* is also distinguished by 'loose continuity', a concept developed by the painter Paul Klee to allude to 'those vague patterns, random encounters and tangential connections that are only revealed in hindsight after a long passage of time'.[94] For scholars and fans who have paid close attention to Bowie's work, what is revealed 'after a long passage of time' is a veritable toybox full of characters, archetypes and ideas, all of which provide threads of 'loose continuity'. As with the tropes of the puppet, the mask and the alien, the figures of Pierrot, Major Tom, Thomas Newton and The Thin White Duke exemplify resilient threads of continuity that persistently weave their way through and across mediums, texts, and time. In a similar vein, Toija Cinque *et al.* observe that Bowie's screen performances are 'loosely bound by a profound alterity – a signification of difference'.[95] While the particular signifiers of this difference are often conveyed through allusion, an obvious example would be Bowie's anisocoria – his differently-sized pupils. Ironically, this was one of the few signifiers that Bowie did not choose, borrow or appropriate, yet he learnt to use this sign of otherness in his videos and visual representations. Other signifiers threaded through his videos include vocal timbre, musical phrases, lyrics, feminized poses and subversive gestures, many of which Bowie foraged, synthesized and re-inflected with his own 'signature' style.

Bowie is distinctive as a transmedia artist partly because of this very paradox: his work across media simultaneously exhibits loose continuity and discontinuity. Just as he constructs imaginary world components that develop over time, their development is marked by incoherence, instability, transformation and temporal dissonance. If it is possible to discern a story unfolding across Bowie's *oeuvre*, it unfolds not with narrative coherence, but more akin to the surrealist subversion of conventional narrative achieved by the film *Un Chien Andalou* (Luis Buñuel and Salvador Dalí, 1929). Bowie's surrealist approach to transmedia doesn't fit

---

[94] William Boyd, 'William Boyd: How David Bowie and I Hoaxed the Artworld', *The Guardian*, 12 January 2016, https://tinyurl.com/jxbt4vmu.
[95] Cinque, Ndalianis and Redmond, 'David Bowie On-Screen', 126.

neatly into the framework already drawn around transmedia storytelling and worldbuilding, with its emphasis on narrative continuity and the coherency of canonical worlds.[96]

A transmedia navigator

It was Bowie's affinity for the tenets of surrealism and *Gesamtkunstwerk* that led to him being considered as a vanguard of transmedia,[97] or as Mehdi Derfoufi describes him, 'a star of the transmedia era'.[98] Such lofty evaluations find support from several scholars who contributed a range of perspectives on Bowie's navigational role across media to the book *David Bowie and Transmedia Stardom* (2020).[99] Even as early as 1976, Bowie was beginning to perceive himself as a transmedia navigator:

> I thought, 'Well, here I am, I'm a bit mixed up creatively, I've got all these things I like doing at once on stage ... I'm not quite sure if I'm a mime or a songwriter or a singer, or do I want to go back to painting again. Why am I doing any of these things anyway ...' and I realised it was because I wanted to be well known [...] I wanted to be the instigator of new ideas, I wanted to turn people on to new things and new perspectives ... I always wanted to be that sort of catalytic kind of thing.[100]

With this 'catalytic' impulse and his natural inclination to move across media, Bowie not only modelled his own transmedia practice, he also shone a torch on the many ways in which transmedia has been done in the past and how it could be done with a difference in the future. When interviewed in 1976, he suggested that one of these ways was to *become* a medium:

> I ... decided to use the easiest medium to start off with which was rock 'n' roll, and then to add pieces to it over the years and so that really by the end of it I was my own medium ... I mean hopefully that'll happen one day ... that's really why

---

[96] For more on this, see Mark Wolf, 'Transmedia WorldBuilding: History, Conception, and Construction', in Matthew Freeman and Renira Rampazzo Gambarato (eds), *The Routledge Companion to Transmedia Studies* (New York: Routledge, 2019), 141–7.
[97] Perrott, 'The Alchemical Union'.
[98] Mehdi Derfoufi, 'Embodying Stardom, Representing Otherness: David Bowie in "Merry Christmas Mr. Lawrence"', in Devereux, Dillane and Power (eds), *David Bowie: Critical Perspectives*, 160.
[99] Mendes and Perrott, *David Bowie and Transmedia Stardom*.
[100] David Bowie, interview extract from 'Changes' (1976), quoted in Kathryn Johnson, 'David Bowie Is', in Devereux, Dillane and Power (eds), *David Bowie: Critical Perspectives*, 9.

I do it ... to become a medium ... I guess I was one of the first to come out and say I'm using rock 'n' roll, it's not my life ... I'm only using it as a medium.[101]

Although the term 'transmedia' was not part of the lexicon in 1976, Bowie appears to be theorizing something akin to transmedia, which entailed using himself as a particular type of medium – a canvas. As he stated in another interview that same year, 'I'm using myself as a canvas and trying to paint the truth of our time on it'.[102] Just as a painter would apply different textures and hues of paint to a canvas, Bowie would apply different media to himself as a canvas, according to the specific affordances of each medium. Beyond expressing this as an abstract notion in interviews, Bowie reiterated this idea in his work so insistently that scholars are now able to reflect on his body of work and examine the figure of Bowie as a medium. For example, Katherine Johnson suggests that Bowie's creative process can be 'interpreted as part of the process of becoming a "medium"'.[103] In a similar vein, Will Brooker examines 'Bowie's work not as a linear evolution ... but as a matrix, a dialogue, a network of ideas that echo back and forth across the five decades of his career, interacting with each other and with the surrounding culture.'[104] Also understanding Bowie as a developing medium within a matrix, Dene October explores Bowie's identity as 'seriously instantiated through and across media'.[105] This notion of an artist's identity developing across media confounds those conceptions of authorship that rely on identity stability, and takes the concept of transmedia through and beyond the realm of storytelling. Reading Bowie's story 'through a transmedia lens', October observes how the character Thomas Newton 'survives the film *The Man Who Fell to Earth* (Roeg 1976) to appear in adaptations, music videos and the play *Lazarus* (2015). Like David Bowie he can be understood as a serial figure, one who exists as a series across media.'[106] Describing this phenomenon as the 'Bowie-Newton matrix', October shows how the serial figures of Bowie and Newton are medial agents interlocked in a dialogic relationship, serially weaving their way through

---

[101] Ibid., 14.
[102] Jean Rook, 'Waiting for Bowie and Finding a Genius Who Insists He's Really a Clown', *Daily Express*, 5 May 1976, https://tinyurl.com/bdddnhys.
[103] Katherine Johnson, 'David Bowie Is', in Devereux, Dillane and Power (eds), *David Bowie: Critical Perspectives*, 15.
[104] Will Brooker, *Forever Stardust: David Bowie Across the Universe* (London: I.B. Taurus, 2017), iii.
[105] Dene October, 'Transition Transmission: Media, Seriality, and the Bowie-Newton Matrix', *Celebrity Studies* 10, no.1 (2019): 104.
[106] Ibid., 104; *The Man Who Fell to Earth* (1976), directed by Nicholas Roeg, based on the 1963 book of the same title, by Walter Tevis. In this film, David Bowie acted as Thomas Newton, a humanoid alien who comes to Earth to get water for his dying planet.

texts and across media.[107] Beyond the examples mentioned above, intertextual references to Newton and *The Man Who Fell to Earth* appear in the music and cover designs for Bowie's albums *Station to Station* (1976) and *Low* (1977), in the music videos for 'Lazarus' (Johan Renck, 2015) and 'No Plan' (Tom Hingston, 2017), in the *Vittel* commercial (Andrew Douglas, 2003), and the duffle coat worn by Bowie/Newton in *The Man Who Fell to Earth*, which was provocatively referenced by *Doctor Who* actress Jodie Whittaker,[108] and emulated in the fashion of the Liverpool subculture known as the 'Football Casuals' during 1976–9. Examining the medial transit of Newton's duffle coat, Mairi McKenzie points out how 'Bowie reconfigured and advanced the meanings inherent in this material object, transcending the weight of its history, and activating a process of transmedial cultural transit'.[109] Music videos provide a particularly suitable vehicle for the cultural transit of such material objects and their convergence with other media. As we shall see, videos such as 'Space Oddity' (1979) and 'Ashes to Ashes' (1980) can be likened to a TARDIS, as they transport the characters of Major Tom and Newton across time and space. On that note, another particularly resilient strand of Bowie's transmediality can be examined through the lens of science fiction. Angela Ndalianis observes how Bowie's 'science fictionality' has 'contagiously filtered into popular culture, forming a logic of its own'. Through this process, Ndalianis adds, 'Bowie as science fiction has become a stable memetic complex, spreading its memes and becoming its own distinctive form of science fiction thinking'.[110] As will be elaborated, Bowie's songs, videos, and imagined storyworlds drew inspiration from the films of Stanley Kubrick, the literature of William Burroughs and George Orwell, and television series such as *Doctor Who* and *The Quatermass Experiment* (1953), along with numerous other sources of science fiction.[111] One of the ways in which Bowie actively spread memes across his songs, music videos, and other mediums was by the development and refashioning of complex storyworlds – a process Jenkins refers to as 'worldbuilding'.

---

[107] October, 'Transition Transmission', 104.
[108] Nick Reilly, 'Is Jodie Whittaker Channelling David Bowie in her "Dr Who" Reveal?' *NME*, 17 July 2017, https://tinyurl.com/3pku5jx9.
[109] Mairi McKenzie, 'Football, Fashion and Unpopular Culture: David Bowie's Influence on Liverpool Football Club Casuals 1976–79', *Celebrity Studies* 10, no.1 (2019): 38.
[110] Angela Ndalianis, 'Bowie and Science Fiction / Bowie as Science Fiction', *Cinema Journal* 57, no. 3 (2018): 140.
[111] Ibid.; Jason Heller, 'Anthems for the Moon: David Bowie's Sci-fi Explorations', *Pitchfork*, 13 January 2016, https://tinyurl.com/y3h78sea.

From storyworlds to intertexts

Throughout this book, the term 'world' is used to imply a type of imaginary vessel, which is both a creative assemblage and a dynamic 'system of relationships between individual existents'.[112] Considering the function of this vessel in relation to authorship, a 'world' is a useful signifying system as it contains various components, described by Marie-Laure Ryan as 'the social and historical setting typical of the author's works ... the major themes and recurrent images of this work ... and the author's general ideas and philosophy of life', what we might informally understand as a 'worldview'.[113] While a world might represent the essential qualities, philosophies and aesthetic attributes associated with an artist, it differs from a storyworld, which requires the components of a world to be narrativized and imaginatively interpreted by authors and audiences. Burns' framework for multimodal analysis provides a sense of how narrative elements bind stories to worlds. Borrowing from David Herman, Burns examines how a transmedia storyworld is materialized in and through narrative elements such as 'discursive context and situatedness', 'time course of specific events', 'events that disrupt the storyworld', and the subjective experience of the disruptive experience.[114] In conjunction with these elements, the concepts of storyworld and worldbuilding provide useful tools for framing my analysis of Bowie videos, since they offer a means to account for the mutability of characters such as Major Tom and Newton, as they travel through time and reappear in different videos.

Examining the serial and worldbuilding aspects of Bowie's music videos can be an enriching experience, particularly when considering each song and video as a text, interwoven with references to cultural, cinematic, literary and philosophical texts. The sheer density of such references across Bowie's *oeuvre* can generate a rewarding type of hypervigilance, a characteristic of transmedia texts that Jenkins calls 'drillability'.[115] This term is particularly relevant to Bowie's

---

[112] Marie-Laure Ryan, 'Story/Worlds/Media: Tuning the Instruments of a Media-Conscious Narratology,"' in Marie-Laure Ryan and Jan-Noël Thon (eds), *Storyworlds Across Media: Toward a Media-Conscious Narratology* (Lincoln: University of Nebraska Press, 2014), 30.

[113] Ibid., 30.

[114] Lori Burns, 'Interpreting Transmedia and Multimodal Narratives: Steven Wilson's "The Raven That Refused to Sing"', in Ciro Scotto, Kenneth Smith and John Brackett (eds), *The Routledge Companion to Popular Music Analysis: Expanding Approaches* (New York: Routledge, 2018), 97; David Herman, *Basic Elements of Narrative* (Hoboken, NJ: Wiley, 2009), 9.

[115] Henry Jenkins, 'Transmedia Education: the 7 Principles Revisited', *Confessions of an Aca-fan*, 21 June 2010, https://tinyurl.com/4pxh6ej4.

music videos, since it implies the satisfying process by which fans are drawn to 'drill deeper' through the layers of a video, to identify constellations of signs, symbols, myths and archetypes, along with previously unconsidered webs of dispersed authorship and assemblage.[116] These connections between texts and authors can be appropriately understood through the lens of Mikhail Bakhtin's interrelated concepts of intertextuality, dialogism, and heteroglossia.[117] Bakhtin argued that all texts are 'living utterances' and thus to some extent are in constant dialogue; 'having taken shape at a particular historical moment in a socially specific environment', a text 'cannot fail to brush up against thousands of living dialogic threads, woven by socio-cultural consciousness and around the given object of an utterance'.[118] In other words, just as living organisms undergo change when they brush past each other, texts alter their form in relation to other texts, accents, discourses, and socio-cultural affordances. Following Bakhtin, Julia Kristeva argues that a text is 'a permutation of texts, an intertextuality in the space of a given text' within which 'several utterances, taken from other texts, intersect and neutralize one another'.[119] From this standpoint, instead of studying a text (song or video) in isolation, a more holistic understanding can be gained by considering a text as a 'compilation of cultural textuality'.[120]

This idea can be metaphorically illustrated by Roland Barthes' notion of a text as 'a tissue, a woven fabric'.[121] If we imagine a text to be like a reconstituted garment, woven from the threads of former garments, created and worn by others, each garment and thread will be altered by the fray and residue of other times, cultures, and experiences. Proposing the suitability of a Bakhtinian framework for analysing songs and related forms, Caroline Ardrey asserts that the nature of heteroglossia is 'altered and enriched when collaboration crosses the boundaries between artforms and, in the case of song, the plethora of languages contained within each word is further refracted through the filter of music'.[122] In this respect, intertextual collaborations that cross the boundaries of sonic, lyrical and visual

---

[116] Ibid.
[117] Dennis Cutchins, 'Bakhtin, Intertextuality and Adaptation', in Thomas Leitch (ed.), *The Oxford Handbook of Adaptation Studies* (Oxford: Oxford University Press, 2017), 71–86.
[118] Mikhail Bakhtin, *Dialogic Imagination: Four Essays*, ed. Michael Holquist (Austin: University of Texas Press, 1981), 276.
[119] Julia Kristeva, *The Bounded Text. Desire in Language*, trans. Leon S. Roudiez (New York: Columbia University Press, 1980), 36–63.
[120] Graham Allen, *Intertextuality: The New Critical Idiom* (London: Routledge, 2000), 36.
[121] Roland Barthes, *Image-Music-Text* (London: Fontana, 1977), 159.
[122] Caroline Ardrey, 'Dialogism and Song: Intertextuality, Heteroglossia and Collaboration in Augusta Holmès's Setting of Catulle Mendes's "Chanson"', *Australian Journal of French Studies* 54, no. 2–3 (2017): 238.

media (such as songs and music videos) produce not only an enrichment, but a new configuration of voices and a layered refraction of authorship, thereby providing useful examples of how intertextuality works within audiovisuality. This dialogic conceptualization of intertextuality appropriately frames my analysis of Bowie's music videos. By viewing each video as a collaboratively authored text, woven from foraged materials, the concept enables us to identify the complex interlacing of references to a plethora of other texts and authors.

Entering the TARDIS

This chapter began by introducing my premise that Bowie played an important role in establishing music video as a collaborative artform. To provide readers with a lens through which to undertake a critical reading of this book, the chapter needed to take a deep dive into the scholarship on music video. Building upon Jirsa and Korsgaard's definition of music video as a 'hybrid audio-visual configuration', and their elucidation of the form as 'an intertextual space of perpetual remediations', I add that it is a collaborative artform (un)like any other. I argue that it is a mutable, time-travelling medium with the special ability to embody and mimic other artforms, mediums, and traditions. This definition forms a scaffold for the concepts of remediation, transmedia and intertextuality, which work together to frame my analysis of Bowie's music videos. Chapter two begins on a lighter note, transporting us to a minimalist London studio in 1969, where we find Bowie playing the clown...

2

Traversing Stage and Screen

What the music says may be serious, but as a medium it should not be questioned, analysed, or taken so seriously. I think it should be tarted up, made into a prostitute, a parody of itself. It should be the clown, the Pierrot medium. The music is the mask the message wears – music is the Pierrot and I, the performer, am the message.

Bowie, 1971[1]

When Bowie uttered these words in a 1971 interview, he was being typically allusive. His words might have been perceived as oblique, but he was providing a useful guide for anyone wanting to gain meaning from his songs and music videos.[2] Since he considered himself a performance medium, he should not be taken too seriously, and his work should not be taken at face value. Bowie also delivered this hint in his final address to camera at the end of the promo for 'Love You till Tuesday' (1969). After performing in an awkward manner one might associate with Anthony Newley or Frank Spencer, Bowie walks briskly into and out of the frame, then leans back into the shot, looks directly into the camera lens and says 'Well I might be able to stretch it till Wednesday.' His final facial expression says it all – 'don't take me seriously – I'm playing the clown!' (Figure 2.1).

The artifice with which Bowie presented himself throughout the twenty-nine minute compilation film *Love You till Tuesday* (1969) appears poles apart from the cool 'authenticity' and zany spontaneity that we see depicted of The Beatles

---

[1] John Mendelssohn, 'David Bowie: Pantomime Rock?' *Rolling Stone*, 1 April 1971, https://tinyurl.com/mushsbkp.
[2] A YouTube playlist for chapter 2 is available at https://tinyurl.com/49nejktt.

Figure 2.1 Bowie's final facial expression says it all. 'Love You till Tuesday' (Malcom J. Thomson, 1969).

in *Let it Be* (1970) and in *Get Back* (2022), both filmed in 1969.[3] It may be unfair to compare neophyte Bowie to an established band at the peak of their fame, but this comparison shows how he was moving against the grain of authenticity that characterized pop and rock music of the mid-late 1960s. While using the notion of artifice as a performance strategy, Bowie was also attempting to merge promotional film with pantomime and 'light entertainer' performance; in this way, he was undertaking a sort of experimental remediation. Although poorly directed and commercially unsuccessful, this experiment in blending mediums and performance modes provides important context from which to consider Bowie's subsequent music videos.

This chapter examines Bowie's traverse of stage and screen in relation to the broader process of remediation. In the first section, I establish the cultural and collaborative context that shaped Bowie's artistic and commercial interests and

---

[3] *Let it Be*, directed by Michael Lindsay-Hogg (1970, UK: Apple Corps); *Get Back*, directed by Peter Jackson (2022, UK and New Zealand: Apple Corps, Wingnut Films).

fuelled his motivation to perform across stage and screen. I then explore Bowie's formative collaboration with dancer and mime artist Lindsay Kemp, along with the continuous inspiration he drew from mime, mask and the figure of Pierrot. Although not all the examples discussed in this chapter are music videos, they demonstrate Bowie taking fledgling steps from stage to promotional film, followed by his initial performances on television shows. These different types of filmed performances provide an important context for understanding Bowie's part in remediating the music video form in relation to theatrical performance modes.

With this context established, the second part of the chapter examines selected promotional films that comprise *Love You till Tuesday* (1969). The film itself demonstrates a bold (if naïve) experimentation with blending theatrical stagecraft with the emergent genre of studio-shot promotional films. Bowie's transition from performing on stage to performing for the television screen is also explored via his first television performance with his band The Spiders from Mars, which was filmed in 1972 for *The Old Grey Whistle Test*. These early promos are best understood when considered within the context of the social and cultural upheavals occurring in the United Kingdom during Bowie's formative years.

The London boy

As with many of his artistic contemporaries, Bowie's outlook was shaped in part by the changes occurring in the United Kingdom during the post-war years, which took on a particular character in London.[4] After the Second World War ended in 1945, British citizens were struggling to adjust to the devastating consequences of war. They were experiencing a gradual process of readjustment to social, economic and political conditions, which was complicated by global instability brought about by the Cold War, the arms race and the Korean War, as well as the migration of refugees and workers. All these factors 'amplified the anxieties and fears of men and women already rendered vulnerable by the cumulative stresses of separation, injury and loss'.[5]

---

[4] For more on this see Marc Burrows, *The London Boys: David Bowie, Marc Bolan, and the 60s Teenage Dream* (Barnsley: Pen & Sword History, 2022).
[5] Mark Jackson (ed.), *Stress in Post-War Britain: 1945–85* (New York: Routledge, 2015), 1.

Bowie was part of UK's 'transitional generation', a generation of Brits who were born in the late 1940s and early 1950s, and so were confronted with a unique 'constellation of stresses and strains'.[6] Members of this generation experienced tension between changing expectations about gender roles and emerging opportunities for self-fulfilment and choice, which was generated by more progressive stances around education and career paths available to women.[7] According to Mark Jackson, while people of all generations were coping with memories of conflict, this transitional generation 'struggled to adapt to shifting patterns of work and home life, to adjust to the changing conditions of industrial labour and to re-establish relationships with their families that had been disrupted by the war'.[8] On top of these challenges, this generation had to adjust to rapid advancements in science and technology, including new developments such as space travel, television, pop music and the contraceptive pill, all of which 'posed new ethical dilemmas and threatened to overwhelm the capacity of post-war populations to cope with the accelerating pace and complexity of life'.[9]

This transitionary period took on a distinct character in London, largely due to the impacts of economic disparity, migration, urban reconstruction and offshore cultural influences. These locally specific experiences of the post-war period offered possibilities for a more cosmopolitan city, along with relaxation of traditional social structures, the emergence of diverse identities, and the development of new subcultures. All these factors, along with increased access to television and American media, provided conditions for London-based artists to experiment with popular music and related audio-visual forms.

In her book *British Music Videos,* Caston describes how such conditions contributed to the development of independent promotional filmmaking, which was centred in London during the mid-1960s. The ten-year period from 1966 to 1976 was characterized by 'haphazard independent production with no institutionalized procedures or trade agreements whilst artists and filmmakers made these clips'.[10] As a result of this emergent independent sector, between 1966 and 1968, 'British artists and their labels commissioned and created a hugely impressive corpus of music videos'.[11] Caston explains how these 1960s promos:

[6] Ibid., 3.
[7] Ibid.
[8] Ibid.
[9] Ibid.
[10] Caston, *British Music Videos,* 4.
[11] Ibid., 4.

...drew attention to the medium of film itself and to the authorship of the filmmaker.... The early promos were full of disjunctive edits and fancy effects. Directors such as Peter Whitehead, who shot pioneering clips for The Animals and Pink Floyd and directed a semi-documentary, *Tonite Let's All Make Love in London* (1967), about the 'swinging London' scene of the 1960s, were the new superstars of counterculture in Britain. The '60s promos were influenced by the 16mm cinematography and location shooting of the French New Wave.[12]

According to Caston, 'tens of thousands of music videos' were 'made by a British industry that grew in the back streets of Soho from the late 1970s onwards, with aesthetic roots in the promo clips of the so-called "British Invasion" (1964–6)'.[13] The 'British Invasion' was a mid-1960s cultural phenomenon, whereby rock and popular music acts from the United Kingdom became popular in the United States, and were significant to the rising 'counterculture' in both nations.[14]

Counterculture and subculture

The countercultural movement associated with the 'British Invasion', combined with London's experience of post-war recovery, provided the conditions for the generation of new approaches to sonic and visual composition and performance art, as evident in the emergence of genres such as industrial music and electronic music, along with the mod, hippy, and punk subcultures.[15] The mod subculture provided creative fodder for the young David Jones, who temporarily adopted its stylistic features, codes and poses, as evident on the album cover for *David Bowie* (1967). In his seminal research into the mod subculture, Dick Hebdige defines mods as 'working class teenagers who lived mainly in London and the new towns of the South and who could be readily identified by characteristic hairstyles, clothing etc.'.[16] According to Timothy Brown, the mod was 'stylish, dedicated to cultivating the right look; upwardly mobile, very likely the son or daughter of a worker moving up into the white-collar realm of the bank or advertising firm'.[17] He also perceived the mod as 'a music fan, obsessed with dancing to American

---

[12] Ibid., 4–5.
[13] Ibid., 2.
[14] James E. Perone, *Music of the Counterculture Era* (London: Greenwood Publishing Group, 2004), 22.
[15] For more on this, see: Goddard, 'Audiovision and *Gesamtkunstwerk*', 163–80.
[16] Dick Hebdige, 'The Meaning of Mod', in Stuart Hall and Tony Jefferson (eds), *Resistance Through Rituals: Youth Cultures in Post-war Britain* (London: Routledge, 1993), 86.
[17] Timothy S. Brown, 'Subcultures, Pop Music and Politics: Skinheads and "Nazi Rock" in England and Germany', *Journal of Social History* 38, no.1 (2004): 157.

soul music at all-night parties'.[18] While Bowie dabbled in mod style during the late 1960s, this was more of a playful foraging exercise than a ritualistic act of belonging. In 1972, he described how he would try on subcultures like novelty outfits: 'I spent all those formative teenage years adopting guises and changing roles. One moment I was a musician and performer, the next a mod, just learning to be somebody.'[19] Between 1967 and 1969, he found it easy to slide from mod into a bohemian-mod-thespian, and then into the style of a Bob Dylan-esque folk singer-songwriter with avant-garde sensibilities. While he didn't appear to be genuinely committed to any one subculture or style, with each stylistic transition his music and videos changed accordingly.

Bowie's flirtation with mod style is best understood when considering how 'the progenitors of this style appear to have been a group of working class dandies, possibly descended from the devotees of the Italianate style'.[20] Bowie may have initially presented as a mod, but the influence of dandyism is more evident as a sustained influence and artistic strategy. In his book *Future Nostalgia*, Shelton Waldrep devotes an entire chapter to discussing 'the persistence of the dandy' across Bowie's *oeuvre*.[21] Dandyism might be commonly thought of as superficial hyper-attention to detail – particularly expressed through clothing – and often referring to the aesthetics of a bygone time. For Bowie, however, dandy style was used as an artistic strategy of objectification. As Waldrep explains: 'the process by which artists become the shock troop of the avant-garde is through the dandy, specifically the transformation of the body into an uncommodifiable substance – an object so objectified that it becomes a subject'.[22] While the strategy of self-objectification is at play across many of Bowie's videos, performances and musical paratexts (such as album cover artwork), its manifestation via dandyish style is perhaps most overtly apparent in his video 'Be My Wife' (1977) and in his film *Love You till Tuesday* (1969). Music video and related audio-visual media may be understood as a stage for the performativity of dandyism. In his book *The British Pop Dandy* (2009), Stan Hawkins points out that 'pop dandies, after all, are constructions of a visual music culture, where repeated viewings of them not only form a spectacle of entertainment, but also a sense of familiarity that

[18] Ibid.
[19] Miles Neville and Perry Neville, *Bowie In His Own Words* (London: Omnibus Press, 1980), 13–14.
[20] Hebdige, 'The Meaning of Mod', 86.
[21] Waldrep, *Future Nostalgia*, 49.
[22] Ibid., 52.

perpetuates their myth'.[23] As we shall see, the promos discussed in this chapter contribute to the formation of the myth of the pop dandy.

From subculture to art and music

Geoffrey Marsh notes that the street in Bromley where Bowie grew up from 1955 to 1967 'was surrounded by avenues of larger inter-war semi-detached houses – with proper gardens, garages and indoor bathrooms. Apart from being the physical manifestation of the expanding middle-classes, this new suburban Britain imposed a rigid code of social, moral and dress conformity'.[24] He adds that while many who were raised in such identikit suburbs during the 1960s and 1970s 'came to rail against their perceived blandness.... Few rejected it as vehemently as Bowie, and only a handful broke through to become performance stars'.[25] Bowie's rejection of conservative suburbia converged with his attraction to the bohemian culture of Soho, and his fierce appetite for art and media of many forms. During his teenage years he began a lifelong pursuit of traversing and synthesizing the sonic, visual and performing arts. At the age of fifteen, his band David Jones and the King Bees recorded Bowie's first single "Liza Jane". In 1965, he released two more singles with his bands The Mannish Boys and Davy Jones and the Lower Third. While learning to play musical instruments, singing and generating marketing ideas for his bands, Bowie studied art and design at Bromley Technical High School. He then developed his promotional and branding strategies as a junior visualizer/paste-up artist for Nevin D Hirst Advertising.[26] Much deeper than a fleeting teenage attraction towards an exciting alternative lifestyle, Bowie's frequent commutes to his job in the heart of London provided a taste of the subversive opportunities of visual, musical and performance art. This sense of creative possibility expanded during his involvement with London's theatre scene, particularly through his tutelage with Lindsay Kemp, whom Bowie described as a 'major influence on my "cultural gestation" period'.[27]

---

[23] Stan Hawkins, *The British Pop Dandy* (Abingdon: Routledge, 2009), 17.
[24] Marsh, 'Astronaut of Inner Spaces', 27.
[25] Ibid., 27.
[26] Christopher Mcquade, '"I loathed it". What David Bowie Learnt from His Brief Spell in Adland,' *The Drum*, 11 January 2016, https://tinyurl.com/2p8u767s.
[27] David Bowie, *Moonage Daydream: The Life and Times of Ziggy Stardust* (London: Palazzo, 2002), 70.

Ushered onto the stage

> I taught David to free his body.
>
> Lindsay Kemp[28]

It was June 1967 when a mutual friend introduced Lindsay Kemp to Bowie. Kemp had been listening to the eponymously titled album *David Bowie* (1967) with much ardour, and Bowie responded to Kemp's theatrical performance with equal enthusiasm. During an interview in 1974, Kemp reflected on how they were drawn to each other in a collaborative spirit:

> Even before meeting, David and I had felt the need to work together. I'd identified myself with his songs, and he'd seen my performances and identified himself with my songs. I was singing the songs of my life with my body; he was singing the songs of his life – very fabulously – with his voice, and we reckoned that by putting the two together the audience couldn't help but be enthralled.[29]

Under the tutelage of Kemp, Bowie honed his skills in live stage performance, dance, and mime. Having survived Bowie to tell the story of their union in flamboyant detail, Kemp was keen to divulge what Bowie had learnt from him. In 2018, he asserted that what Bowie 'was learning all this time from me was stagecraft. How to be, how to look on the stage ... how to make an entrance, how to make an exit, and quite a few things in between'.[30] While journalists and biographers have had a field day speculating on the nature of the 'few things in between', this tabloid gossip diverts attention away from the specifics of the artform that Bowie was learning. When interviewed just after Bowie's death in 2016, Kemp proudly elaborated:

> I taught him to express and communicate through his body. I taught him to dance. I taught him the importance of the look – makeup, costume, general stagecraft, performance technique ... We talked about *kabuki*, avant-gardists, the world of the music hall, which we were both attracted to. We talked about Jean Genet.[31]

---

[28] Mick Brown, 'Lindsay Kemp: The Man Who Taught Bowie His Moves', *Bowie Wonderworld*, September 1974, https://tinyurl.com/59behzcb.
[29] Ibid.
[30] Michael Bonner, 'Lindsay Kemp on David Bowie: "I taught him how to make an entrance and how to make an exit"', *Uncut*, 25 August 2018, https://tinyurl.com/4d5r9j6d.
[31] Chris Wiegand, 'Lindsay Kemp: I Tried to Get David Bowie to do Puss in Boots', *The Guardian*, 12 January 2016, https://tinyurl.com/47ahtak8.

Bowie later described his immersion in the world of Jean Genet as a subconscious inspiration for the title of his song 'The Jean Genie' (1972).[32] Like a sponge soaking up all that his collaborators shared with him, Bowie absorbed specific techniques from Kemp, which would become useful strategies for bridging theatrical performance and music video. He applied everything he learnt about theatre, stagecraft, *kabuki* and the avant-gardists to the screen. Most distinctively, Bowie can be attributed with infiltrating promotional film with mime.

Kemp studied with Marcel Marceau, a twentieth-century French mime master who also influenced Bowie, particularly with regard to his use of the mask and masking more generally as a stage and screen performance tool. Given Bowie's interest in the filming of mime performance, it is significant to mention the parallels between Étienne Decroux and Marshall McLuhan, both inspirations for Bowie. Observing their 'parallel worlds', Wayne Constantineau writes that while McLuhan 'was fond of repeating that we could understand media through mime, Étienne Decroux (1898–1992), the founder of corporeal mime, spent sixty years investigating McLuhan's world of media'.[33] Decroux developed an approach he termed corporeal mime, which he described as 'making visible the invisible', an approach that would require a performer to explicitly use their body as a tool to communicate internal states.[34] Theatre actor and director Nicola Baylis explains Decroux's definition of the corporeal mime performer as 'one who possessed the body of a gymnast, the mind of an actor, but also the heart of a poet' – an approach to mime that may have resonated with Bowie.[35] Decroux's ideas 'were intrinsically bound in life, its passions, and its dreams. Ways of expressing thought, love, reverie, work, struggle, social relationships, and the divine are central to the practice of corporeal mime'.[36] Baylis observes that in the teaching of corporeal mime, 'movement concepts are expounded with references to the work of sculptors, painters, musicians, playwrights, philosophers, and poets, as well as to a diverse range of stories and legends'.[37] Given the intermedial and philosophical centrality of this approach, it's easy to see why Bowie was

---

[32] Chris O'Leary, 'The Jean Genie', *Pushing Ahead of the Dame*, 3 June 2010, https://tinyurl.com/yk8dykwz.
[33] Wayne Constantineau, 'Mime and Media: The Parallel Worlds of Étienne Decroux and Marshall McLuhan', *Dalhousie French Studies* 71 (2005): 115.
[34] Nicola Baylis, 'Making Visible the Invisible: Corporeal Mime in the Twenty-first Century', *Theatre Quarterly: NTQ, Cambridge* 25, no. 3 (Aug 2009): 274.
[35] Ibid., 275.
[36] Ibid.
[37] Ibid.

inspired by Decroux's version of corporeal mime, particularly given Bowie's fascination with combining philosophical and literary elements with intermedial performance. Transferring his musical and mime performance from stage to screen gave Bowie a taste for platform-crossing. In 1968, he acted as 'Cloud', performing alongside Kemp in the pantomime *Pierrot in Turquoise or the Looking Glass Murders*.[38] Initially staged at the London Mercury Theatre, the show was re-performed as a television short in 1970, enabling Bowie to consider the different affordances of theatre and televisual media and potential expansion of audience enabled by acting on screen.[39]

Bowie described Kemp as 'a living Pierrot. He lived and talked Pierrot. He was tragic and dramatic and everything in his life – theatrical. And so the stage thing for him was just an extension of himself'.[40] As noted by Alexander Carpenter, Bowie too could be understood as a living Pierrot. Ironically, 'the ambiguity between performer and person, or persona and person he ascribes to Kemp was, for many years, Bowie's defining characteristic as a pop performer'.[41] Persona, mime, mask and gesture were key modes of performance that played an important role in the early stages of Bowie's career, eventually becoming persistent threads of continuity across his *oeuvre*. Tying all these threads together was the figure of Pierrot.

The mask of Pierrot

A prominent stock character of the sixteenth century Italian performance troupe *Commedia dell'arte*, Pierrot was symbolically staged as a naïve fool and a sad clown. As an improvised dramatic form, *Commedia* was distinctive for its emphasis on artifice and 'self-conscious theatricality'.[42] More than simply a stock character, Pierrot is an archetype that has evolved across four centuries of European dramatic artforms. During this process, he became associated with

---

[38] *Pierrot in Turquoise or the Looking Glass Murders*, directed by Brian Mahoney. The play debuted on 28 December 1967 at the Oxford New Theatre. After modifications, it opened at the Rosehill Theatre, Whitehaven, before its proper run at London's Mercury and Intimate Theatres in March 1968.
[39] *Pierrot in Turquoise or the Looking Glass Murders*, directed by Brian Mahoney, filmed at the Scottish Television's Gateway Theatre in Edinburgh in 1969, aired 8 July 1970.
[40] Richard Cromelin, 'David Bowie: The Darling of the Avant Gard', *Phonograph Record*, January, 1972, *Rock's Backpages*, https://tinyurl.com/3axx4kv4.
[41] Alexander Carpenter, '"Give a Man a Mask and He'll Tell the Truth": Arnold Schoenberg, David Bowie, and the Mask of Pierrot', *Intersections* 30, no. 2 (2010): 15.
[42] Devereux, Dillane and Power, *David Bowie: Critical Perspectives*, 38.

character traits and visual signifiers that can be traced to specific performance traditions. With his naivety, clown antics, white face, and hat being established as part of *Commedia dell'arte*,[43] Pierrot evolved as a more complex and vulnerable character during the eighteenth century and then developed into a 'dandified persona amongst the nineteenth century Romantics'.[44] While this dandified Pierrot was visually represented in terms of melancholic beauty, 'Pierrot the clown' was often associated with pantomime.[45]

Having engaged with the figure of Pierrot via pantomime as early as 1968, Bowie used face paint to create versions of the distinctive Pierrot mask in many of his theatrical and film performances. By 1971, he was using the figure of Pierrot as a way to describe music, saying 'it should be the clown, the Pierrot medium. The music is the mask the message wears – music is the Pierrot and I, the performer, am the message.'[46] Expanding upon Marshall McLuhan's proclamation in 1964 that 'the medium is the message',[47] the young Bowie was dropping a significant clue about his use of Pierrot as a parodic medium and a form of performative masking. In doing so, he was also suggesting a distinction should be made between the performer (as message), and the mask (as Pierrot). In other words, Pierrot functions as a mask that mediates the performer's message, both as artifice and interface. According to Carpenter, the mask of the Pierrot provided Bowie 'the means for reflection upon the nature of art and the artist's relationship to both his art and the world at large'.[48] In other words, the mask wasn't just a performance prop for Bowie. It was a medium by which he could relate to his art and to the world. Taking the idea of the mask and Pierrot further and deeper than the application of face paint and the use of mime, Bowie drew from their philosophical basis in persona to create his own personae which were not divorced from his core identity, but intimately tied to his understanding of the multiplicity and fluidity of identity. While Bowie's exploration of mime, masking, and persona is apparent in several of his music videos, these forms are presciently articulated in 'The Mask (A Mime)', which features in the middle of *Love You till Tuesday* (1969).

[43] Richard Kurth, 'Pierrot Lunaire: Persona, Voice, and the Fabric of Allusion', in Jennifer Shaw and Joseph Auner (eds), *The Cambridge Companion to Schoenberg* (Cambridge: Cambridge University Press, 2010), 120–34.
[44] Devereux, Dillane and Power, *David Bowie: Critical Perspectives*, 38; Hawkins, *The British Pop Dandy*, 38.
[45] Hawkins, ibid., 38.
[46] Mendelsohn, 'David Bowie: Pantomime Rock?'
[47] Marshall McLuhan, *Understanding Media: The Extensions of Man* (Cambridge: MIT Press, 1964), 7.
[48] Carpenter, '"Give a Man a Mask and He'll Tell the Truth"', 5.

Love You till Tuesday – the promotional film as compilation

Bowie transferred his well-honed skills in mime and theatrical stagecraft to the medium of film for *Love You till Tuesday*, which was created to promote selected songs from the albums *David Bowie* (1967) and *David Bowie: The World of David Bowie* (1970). These promos include: 'Love You till Tuesday' (1967), 'Sell Me a Coat' (1967), 'When I'm Five' (1968), 'Rubber Band' (1967), 'The Mask (A Mime)' (1969), 'Let Me Sleep Beside You' (1967), 'Ching-A-Ling' (1968/69), "Space Oddity" (1969) and 'When I Live My Dream' (1967).[49] The film was directed by Malcolm J. Thomson and features performances solely by Bowie as well as group performances by his band The Feathers, a trio he'd formed with Hermione Farthingale and John 'Hutch' Hutchinson. Although producer Kenneth Pitt intended the film to be broadcast on television, it failed to inspire television broadcasters and did not reach a broad audience until 1984, when Pitt instigated its release on VHS and subsequently DVD. The film has since been derided by critics, and even serious fans have expressed distaste for the film's kitsch folk aesthetic, along with Bowie's light theatricality and awkward engagement with the camera. The film has also been criticized for its low production values and amateur film direction.

By making the film for a prospective television audience, Bowie and his collaborators were attempting something naïvely innovative at a time when television was beginning to be considered a venue for the exhibition of promotional films. Bowie was effectively experimenting with ways to do theatre within the televisual format, combining characteristics of the historic tradition of *Commedia dell'arte* with the technological and aesthetic affordances of the 'new' medium of television. In this respect, most of the promos in this compilation were staged and shot in a minimalist studio setting with a white background and few props. Bowie's contrived movements are choreographed to work within the constraints of the studio setting, with fixed cameras and studio lighting rigs. In the following passages, I undertake a close examination of four promos from *Love You till Tuesday*, each exemplifying a different facet of Bowie's transit from theatrical stagecraft to promotional film. Where appropriate, I have provided a preliminary discussion of the song's lyrical and sonic construction, which builds towards a multifaceted picture of the lyrical, sonic, visual and kinetic relationships produced by the promotional film.

---

[49] These songs were released on the albums *David Bowie* (1967) and *David Bowie – The World of David Bowie* (1970). For more on this, see https://tinyurl.com/ym84sv7f.

"Love You till Tuesday" – the song

> David's voice is almost an exact voiceprint of Anthony Newley's.... A singer, actor, songwriter, mime and dancer, Newley was the prototype of the star Bowie longed to become. 'I was Tony Newley for a year' he once admitted.
>
> Wendy Leigh[50]

Biographer Wendy Leigh aptly sums up the presence of Newley in many of the songs Bowie released in the late 1960s. Most strikingly, the song "Love You till Tuesday" bears a canny resemblance to Anthony Newley's vocal performance in 'Pack Up Your Troubles' (1961). Having first seen Newley perform in the 1961 stage show *Stop the World I Want to Get Off*, fourteen-year-old Bowie took immediate inspiration from his popularized theatricality.[51] He mimicked many of Newley's vocal idiosyncrasies, including his 'modified stage Cockney' accent and aspects of his light entertainer performance.[52] These traits were intertwined with his own dark sensibilities and storytelling style, for which he has been likened to Jacques Brel.[53] When interviewed by Paul Du Noyer in 1990, Bowie provided a retrospective assessment of the songs he produced during 1967:

> Aarrghh, God, that Anthony Newley stuff, how cringey. No, I haven't much to say about that in its favour. Lyrically, I guess it was really striving to be something, the short story teller. Musically, it's quite bizarre. I don't know where I was at. It seemed to have its roots all over the place, in rock and vaudeville and music hall and I don't know what. I didn't know if I was Max Miller or Elvis Presley. The Cheeky Chappy with a ... *hip*. [Laughs.] I don't know. It's quite funny.[54]

Describing "Love You till Tuesday" as 'catchy and rancid', Chris O'Leary adds that the song 'has a taste of desperation in its cheer. Bowie sings in an affected nasal tone, as if he's pretending that this track is from the cast recording of *Oliver!* and he oversells his mildly-clever lyric'.[55] Despite the song's lack of commercial success, Bowie's manager Kenneth Pitt arranged for it to be re-recorded and

---

[50] Leigh, *Bowie: The Biography*, 59.
[51] Ibid.
[52] Dave Laing, 'Listening to Punk', in Ken Gelder (ed.), *The Subcultures Reader* (London: Routledge, 2005), 451.
[53] Bonner, 'Lindsay Kemp on David Bowie'.
[54] Noyer, Paul Du, 'An Interview with David Bowie for the April 1990 issue of Q Magazine', *Q Magazine*, 6 February 1990, https://tinyurl.com/3cxbm6fw.
[55] O'Leary, 'Love You till Tuesday', *Pushing Ahead of the Dame*, 5 October 2009, https://tinyurl.com/nhbajxtb.

re-performed across several platforms, aimed at diverse audiences. In 1967, Bowie performed the song for the Dutch television show *Fenkleur* and for his first BBC radio session; in 1968, he performed it for the German television show *4-3-2-1 Musik Fur Junge Leute*, and as part of the London run of the pantomime show *Pierrot in Turquoise*. In preparation for what Pitt believed would be a German cut of the film *Love You till Tuesday*, a German language version of the song was recorded in 1969, with lyrics translated as 'Lieb' Dich Bis Dienstag'.[56] However, the German television producer lost interest in this plan once they saw the film.

'Love You till Tuesday' – the promo

Beginning with a stark white studio background and a bouncy comedic instrumental introduction, 'Love You till Tuesday' is intercut with the opening title and credit sequence for the film. Bowie enters the blank frame sporting a goofy smile, mod-style wig and grey suit with light blue embroidered lapels. This dandified image is completed by an old-fashioned blue scarf which matches the lapel detail. Bowie proceeds to deliver a perky performance, which at times verges on 'manic glee', exemplifying the vocal quality and light entertainer theatrical style he'd borrowed from Newley.[57] The high angle shot used throughout the clip contributes to the simplistic lilt of the music, portraying Bowie as childlike and not to be taken seriously. This tone is further reinforced by lyrics such as 'little me is waiting'. As though performing in a game of charades, Bowie uses bodily gesture to act out the lyrics, 'Who's that hiding in the apple tree, clinging to a branch! Don't be afraid it's only me, hoping for a little romance.' After enacting his 'hanging in a tree' pose, he drops seductively onto white cushions and sings invitingly into the camera at floor level (Figure 2.2).

With just a few gestures, he transforms from an awkwardly fey adolescent into a camp romancer attempting to be seductive. Towards the end of the promo, Bowie performs a move of playful flirtation with the camera. He walks into frame, sings into the camera, walks out of frame and then back in again, as though he's playing a trick on an audience of pre-school children. The song ends

---

[56] Pegg, *The Complete David Bowie*, 175.
[57] s.t., comment on O'Leary, 'Love You till Tuesday'.

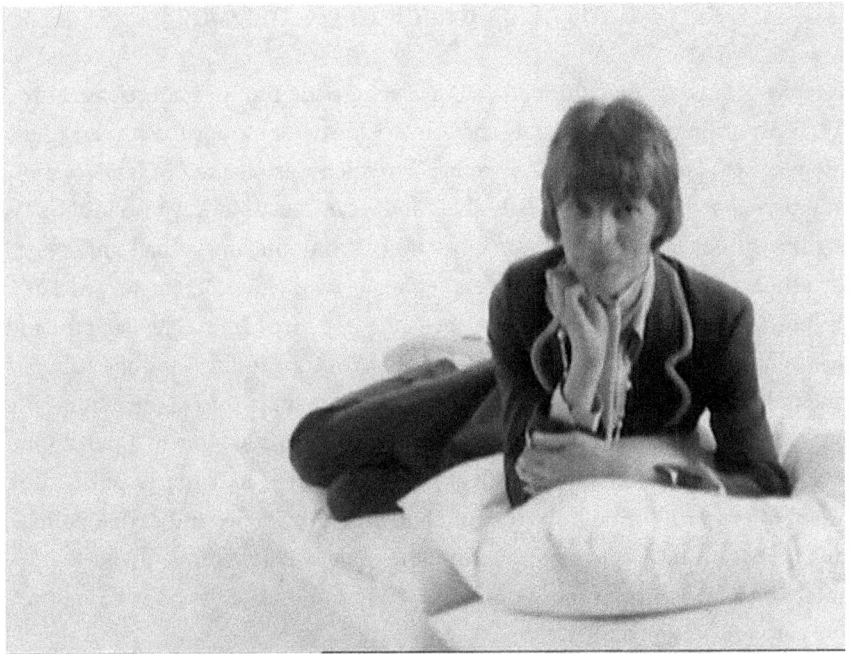

Figure 2.2 Bowie drops seductively to floor level. 'Love You till Tuesday' (Malcom J. Thomson, 1969).

with Bowie walking into and out of the white frame, singing 'Da-da-da-dum, da-da-da-dum', then leans back into the shot as though having an afterthought, and sings 'Well I might be able to stretch it till Wednesday'. Bowie combines bodily gesture and pose with trite lyrics and bouncy music to create a performance that is both childlike and camp. He appears to be performing the type of tongue-in-cheek silliness one might later associate with Frank Spencer, or with 'Yakety Sax,' the theme music for *The Benny Hill Show*.

As the opening piece of this compilation of promotional films, the theatrical artifice and tongue-in-cheek playfulness of Bowie's performance sets the tone for the compilation. Even at this very early stage of his career, Bowie was defying contemporary trends by creating a sense of untimely artifice, while evoking the bohemian spirit and cultural realities he'd experienced in London during the 1960s. 'Love You till Tuesday' enthusiastically runs against the grain of the authenticity of pop and rock music exhibited by British promotional films during 1964 and 1969. In doing so, 'Love You till Tuesday' sets the tone of gaudy artifice that lingers throughout the compilation.

"Let Me Sleep Beside You" – the song

Despite being recorded in 1967, "Let Me Sleep Beside You" was not released until 1970. According to O'Leary, the song was 'a bald attempt to ape the success of the Stones' "Let's Spend the Night Together"',[58] which was released in January 1967 and performed on *Top of the Pops* that same year.[59] "Let Me Sleep Beside You" is significant for marking Bowie's turn away from the music-hall influenced theatrics and eccentricity of his earlier material on the Deram record label. While the acoustic guitar drives the song forwards, the cello strings and restrained arrangement provide a refreshing contrast to the wind instruments and quirky musical arrangements that were prominent in the Deram album. The song was rejected by Decca for release as a single, possibly due to a perception that the title was too *risqué*.[60] While this might seem ludicrously puritanical, when interpreted through the lens of contemporary gender and sexual politics, an analysis of the lyrics might lead to more than raised eyebrows about Bowie's intention when writing the lyrics. Describing the song as 'a rake's come-on',[61] O'Leary breaks down the lyrics:

> The singer frames his seduction as being empowering, the rake merely serving as a means of liberation. He appeals to youth's vanity; he flatters his conquest with the promise of her alleged maturity: 'Brush the dust of youth from off your shoulder, because the years of threading daisies lie behind you now', Bowie murmurs, keeping a straight face. 'Lock away your childhood ... child, you're a woman now/your heart and soul are free.'[62]

Despite the manipulative air of these lyrics, when we see the hyper-hip-thrusting, guitar-swinging manner in which Bowie performs the song, 'its aim seems less about Bowie bedding the girl than Bowie wanting to convince the listener that he really *is* a seductive, charismatic rock star.'[63] Possibly with tongue in cheek, he later declared that the song 'might have been influenced by Simon and Garfunkel, but gone a little heavier ... I still thought I might have a chance of being a romantic songwriter, which never actually proved to be my forte.'[64]

---

[58] O'Leary, 'Let Me Sleep Beside You', *Pushing Ahead of the Dame*, 16 October 2009, https://tinyurl.com/yc2cckke.
[59] Dwaynepipe59, 'Rolling Stones Live – "Let's Spend the Night Together" TOTP '67', YouTube video, 10 July 2010, https://youtu.be/l61MFileuVM.
[60] Pegg, *The Complete David Bowie*, 157.
[61] O'Leary, 'Let Me Sleep Beside You'.
[62] Ibid.
[63] Ibid.
[64] Pegg, *The Complete David Bowie*, 157.

'Let Me Sleep Beside You' – the promo

Despite Bowie's claim that he was merely having a go at being a romantic songwriter, his performance in the promo betrays a less wholesome intent. Swinging a fake guitar and adopting exaggerated poses, it would seem likely that Bowie was either parodying, or trying very hard to emulate a hybrid 'Elvis-Jagger' figure (Figure 2.3).[65] There's plenty of support for O'Leary's assessment that Bowie was 'burlesquing the image of rock-star-as-sex-god, years before Ziggy'.[66] YouTube comments for this video include: '0:36 how is he moving literally every part of him in separate directions at the same time?'[67] 'Me, a teenager, listening to this song: "Oh, David! Take me now!" Me, a thirtysomething, listening to this song: "yOunG mAN, wHaT aRE yOuR inTenTiOns WiTh mY dAUgHteR?!"'[68] 'omg ... powerfully arousing ... that's a phenomenal video!'[69] 'oh man ... love this early stuff. So awkward yet so adorable at the same time. You can see classy later-Bowie in there trying to break free but he just ain't there yet.'[70] While many viewers find Bowie's performance in this promo to be arousing in one way or another, they're also quick to point out his lack of subtlety, which is emphasized by the camera directions and editing.

The technical quality appears rudimentary, especially when compared to modern music videos made with big budgets and the latest technology. However, when considering the conservative appearance of BBC studio productions of the time, Thomson has allowed for aberrations to the standardized (hidden) lighting, and has employed editing and camera techniques that break with studio recording and performance conventions. Just after Bowie enters the frame and the first guitar chords are heard, the camera pulls focus from the microphone to Bowie's upper body as he turns toward the camera. Then, the shot cuts quickly between frontal shots and point of view shots, thus violating the '180-degree rule' and creating a momentary sense of spatial disorientation.[71] Disorienting techniques occur several

---

[65] Ibid.
[66] O'Leary, 'Let Me Sleep Beside You'.
[67] Paige Crimp, comment on David Bowie, 'David Bowie – Let Me Sleep Beside You', YouTube video, 00:03:26, 2 August 2019, https://youtu.be/U_hX482pLbE.
[68] Anna, comment on 'David Bowie – Let Me Sleep Beside You'.
[69] Pavane Oliveiro, comment on 'David Bowie – Let Me Sleep Beside You'.
[70] ThinWhiteAxe, comment on 'David Bowie – Let Me Sleep Beside You'.
[71] The 180-degree rule or 'axis of action', is 'the invisible line that runs through the scene perpendicular to the camera. If the camera stays on one side of that line, characters will stay in a consistent spatial relation to each other. Character A will be on the left in every shot, Character B on the right – unless one of them walks to a different part of the setting. In other words, the axis creates consistent screen direction.' For more on this see Kristin Thompson and David Bordwell, *Observations on Film Art*, 25 May 2011, https://tinyurl.com/yc3swj92.

Figure 2.3 Bowie emulates a hybrid 'Elvis-Jagger' figure. 'Let Me Sleep Beside You' (Malcom J. Thomson, 1969).

times during the clip: a 'Dutch tilt',[72] rapid zoom-ins and zoom-outs, and jump-cuts that reiterate Bowie's dance moves. Breaching the conventions of 'continuity editing',[73] Bowie's eyelines are not matched between shots, and the background lighting appears discontinuous when shots are cut together from different directions. This breaking of 'verisimilitude' is also achieved by the lighting and set design.[74] The studio lights and their suspended rigs are unexpectedly visible. While they create flattering backlighting and a halo effect around Bowie's head and body, the lights are not plotted to move with the camera as it zooms in and out and changes angle. This results in the sense of an accidental stream of light shooting directly into the camera lens, which momentarily blows out the image and creates lens flares. The use of a circular framing device blurs the edges of the frame and draws further attention to

---

[72] The 'Dutch tilt' is a camera movement where the camera angle is slanted to one side. For more on this, see 'The Filmmaker's Handbook: What is a Dutch Tilt?' *The Take*, https://tinyurl.com/3sb3h8bk.

[73] Logan Baker, 'A Complete Guide to Continuity Editing in Film and Short Videos', *The Beat*, 9 September 2022, https://tinyurl.com/3m2vfxsf.

[74] 'What is Verisimilitude and How Does it Work inf Films?' Falmouth University, 1 December 2020, https://tinyurl.com/mrybwahw.

the mediating presence of the camera. The ample use of such techniques exemplifies Caston's observation that British promos of the late 1960s attempted to emulate the cinematography of the French New Wave – for instance, the way in which Jean-Luc Godard drew attention to the mediating presence of the camera by using direct address to camera and jump-cuts to break the fourth wall.[75]

'The Mask (A Mime)'

Although not set to music, 'The Mask (A Mime)' (1969) is classified on IMDb as a music video,[76] presumably because it is situated at the centre of a longer, music-based promotional compilation.[77] While devoid of music video conventions, this five-minute mime film exemplifies Bowie's attempts to remediate promotional film by merging it with mime and theatrical stage lighting. In keeping with the minimalist continuity established for *Love You till Tuesday*, 'The Mask' is shot with Bowie performing against a completely white studio backdrop. He wears white tights and a white Romantic-style shirt with puffed forearms and large ruffles. Completing this dandyish Pierrot look, his white face paint is accented by distinctive black eyebrows, eyeliner and tiny black diamonds painted under his eyes. The artifice of the costume, stage lighting and performance require the audience to interpret the piece as make-believe pantomime, but a slight sense of realism is created by the inclusion of diegetic sounds that produce a sense of a real-world environment.[78] We hear a door squeaking opening, the ding of a doorbell and the sound of a toy (or cat?) squawking when the protagonist stands on it. When Bowie mimes stepping outside the shop, the city street is suggested by an audio track layered with sounds of traffic, car horns and other street sounds. While these sounds establish a sense of location, other character's voices are introduced by Bowie's narration.

The film now stands out as a sibylline of Bowie's subsequent engagement with persona, masking, and the Pierrot figure, which were to become threads of 'loose continuity' throughout his *oeuvre*.[79] The film's prophetic quality was observed by

---

[75] Caston, *British Music Videos*, 4–5; for more about breaking the fourth wall, see chapter 3.
[76] 'The Mask (A Mime)', *IMDb*, https://www.imdb.com/title/tt9869108/.
[77] 'The Mask (A Mime)', directed by Malcolm J. Thomson (1969, London: Thomasso Film), YouTube video, 00:04:56, 22 September 2016, https://youtu.be/ss51eLEeJuY.
[78] Diegetic sounds are sounds that one would expect to occur as part of the story events. For more on this, see Filmsound.org, https://filmsound.org/terminology/diegetic.htm.
[79] Perrott, 'The Alchemical Union', 196.

the blogger Leonoutside, who refers to 'The Mask' as an example of '"a single early" work being a compact index of everything to follow'.[80] Through his mime performance, Bowie 'ominously depicts his future stardom and the subsequent near-madness it caused him', concluding with the demise of the mask-wearer.[81] The events depicted are communicated primarily by Bowie's mime movements along with his non-diegetic voiceover narration.[82] Bowie mimes his discovery of a mask; he tries it on, then furtively looks around to make sure he isn't seen pocketing the mask and leaving the shop without paying for it. After performing with the mask at concerts, the protagonist becomes corrupted by fame and cannot remove the mask. At his final show at the London Palladium, his spot-lit performance and arrogant gestures are met with applause (Figure 2.4), but after a silent struggle to remove his mask, he collapses and dies on stage. Bowie narrates: 'The next day, the papers made a big thing out of it "strangled on stage"

Figure 2.4 Bowie mimes arrogance. 'The Mask' (Malcom J. Thomson, 1969).

[80] Leonoutside, 31 August 2016, 2.43pm, comment on Chris O'Leary, 'The Mime Songs', *Pushing Ahead of the Dame*, 21 October 2009, https://tinyurl.com/3tnusm3s.
[81] O'Leary, 'The Mime Songs'.
[82] Non-diegetic sounds are sounds that are typically added onto a film and are not produced from events occurring within the story. For more on this, see Filmsound.org, https://tinyurl.com/3vdfyem8.

they said. Funny though, they didn't mention anything about a mask.' This morbid ending is interpreted by Carpenter as a statement about Bowie's sense that 'performer and mask were inseparable from the start. Pierrot was not merely dress-up, but rather the medium itself – an embodiment of music – through which the performer's message was conveyed.'[83]

Although 'The Mask' was shelved for several years along with the rest of *Love You till Tuesday*, its message seems mysteriously prescient. In hindsight, it would appear that Bowie was using the mask as a metaphor for his future relationship with stardom and celebrity. Eerily referencing the mime artist's demise in 'The Mask', on 3 July 1973 Bowie used his performance at the Hammersmith Odeon to put to rest the all-consuming Ziggy persona.[84] As we shall see, Bowie continued to use the mask, persona and the metaphorical death of the artist, as reiterated tropes threaded through his music videos.[85] A similar type of 'loose continuity' is also established by the evolving storyworld for "Space Oddity."

"Space Oddity" (1969) – the song

> "Space Oddity" shifts with the weather: it can be eerie, 'dated', tragic, yearning, young, time-blighted. It's a lost future for the present, a past for the future to discard or preserve. Where will it land in ten years' time? And as its composer said, where are we now?
>
> O'Leary, 2020[86]

"Space Oddity" has altered in tone and meaning with each landing, and in response to the *zeitgeist* of specific time periods. While it provides a perfect exemplar of the time-travelling possibilities of a single song, its numerous video accompaniments provide a fascinating case study of dispersed authorship.[87] Bowie is generally understood to be the original and sole author of the lyrics, but as noted by O'Leary, there have been some dubious claims to co-authorship of the song, including by the director of *Love You till Tuesday*:

---

[83] Carpenter, '"Give a Man a Mask and He'll Tell the Truth"', 17.
[84] For more on this, see Perrott, 'Ziggy Stardust, Direct Cinema'.
[85] See for instance, the following music videos: 'Life on Mars?' (1973), 'Look Back in Anger' (1979), 'Ashes to Ashes' (1980), 'Miracle Goodnight' (1993), 'I Can't Read 97' (1997), 'Love is Lost' (2013), 'Where Are We Now' (2013), 'Lazarus' (2015) and 'Blackstar' (2016).
[86] Chris O'Leary, 'Space Oddity at Half Century', *Pushing Ahead of the Dame*, 11 July 2019, https://tinyurl.com/4wk5p8fu.
[87] For more on this, see Lisa Perrot, *David Bowie and the Transformation of Music Video* (forthcoming).

Malcolm Thomson once said some of "Space Oddity" was communally written over a few nights when he and his assistant Susie Mercer visited Clareville Grove – we all produced lines. It was very much a spontaneous thing among a group of people – and Marc Bolan told Spencer Leigh that he'd written 'part' of the song.[88]

While it's entirely possible that Bowie drew inspiration from a variety of collaborators, in a 2003 interview for *Performing Songwriter* magazine, he explained that "Space Oddity" 'was written because of going to see the film *2001: A Space Odyssey*, which I found amazing . . . I was out of my gourd anyway, I was very stoned when I went to see it, several times, and it was really a revelation to me. It got the song flowing.'[89] Stanley Kubrick's films undoubtedly influenced Bowie's songs, videos and costumes, as did a broad array of science fiction literature and television shows. Although inspired by science fiction films and literature, "Space Oddity" was not buried when the space travel craze fizzled out. Its storyworld components developed lives of their own; like borer, they have persistently threaded their way through Bowie's songs, performances, and videos.

While the "Space Oddity" storyworld has developed across numerous videos, the tone of the song has altered along with vocal and instrumental differences that distinguish the various recordings of the song.[90] While partial 'demo' recordings were made as early as November 1968, the first full recording of the song was completed on 2 February 1969, a few days before its accompanying promo was shot for *Love You till Tuesday*. This version was conceived as a sort of duet, with Hutchinson singing the part of 'Ground Control' and Bowie as 'Major Tom'. According to O'Leary, this recording downplays the Stylophone, and is 'marred by leaden drumming and a wheezing Bowie ocarina solo'.[91] These issues were addressed by Bowie's subsequent demos of the song, resulting in the recording of a second version which was to become a hit. Recorded on 20 June 1969, this version was released as a single on 11 July, just days before the Apollo 11 moon landing on 20 July. This astute timing led to the BBC playing the song as part of their coverage of the event. While this helped Bowie to reach a broad audience, Tony Visconti had declined to produce the song, perceiving it as 'a cheap shot – a gimmick' to cash in on the excitement already generated by the impending moon landing.[92] Despite passing the production role over to Gus Dudgeon at that time, fifty years later Visconti produced a remixed version of the

---

[88] O'Leary, 'Space Oddity at Half Century'.
[89] Bill DeMain, 'The Sound and Vision of David Bowie', *Performing Songwriter Magazine*, September 2003, *Rock's Backpages*, https://tinyurl.com/44xs8dkv.

song using the immersive 'omni-directional' audio format called '360 Reality Audio', which enabled him to produce a more expansive sound.[93]

As it turned out, Dudgeon fully supported the vocal and instrumental changes Bowie wanted for the June 1969 recording.[94] The Stylophone was given a more pronounced role than in the earlier recording, which added a quirky science fiction character to the song. With Hutchinson no longer present to record vocals for this version, Bowie's voice was used for both 'Ground Control' and 'Major Tom'. The characters were differentiated by vocally shifting octaves and other studio production techniques which produced an imagined sense of space between the vocals for the two characters. This vocal narrativity is fused with densely layered instrumentation, including sonic resonances and harmonic language which are used as storytelling devices.[95] The narrative skill demonstrated in "Space Oddity" is also exemplified by the lyrics of other songs on the 1969 *David Bowie* album,[96] such as "Cygnet Committee" (1969), "Wild Eyed Boy From Freecloud" (1969), and "God Knows I'm Good" (1969). In all these songs, Bowie's use of allusion, tragedy and dialogue pulls us into the plight of identifiable characters that incite empathy and imagination.

The story of "Space Oddity" is told from two perspectives. The first is that of the Earth-based rocket controller who attempts to communicate with an astronaut as he is propelled into space. As though tempting fate, the controller tells him, 'It's time to leave your capsule, if you dare'. Following this suspenseful build-up, we hear the astronaut's perspective, reporting that he's 'stepping through the door'. As he orbits Earth, he experiences an existential crisis: 'the stars, look very different today'. Lost in space, he foresees a dystopian future for

---

[90] The first full studio recording of 'Space Oddity' was completed on 2 February 1969. In June 1969, a new arrangement of the song was recorded, which was produced by Gus Dudgeon. The February 1969 version accompanies the 'Space Oddity' promo included in *Love You till Tuesday* (1969).

[91] O'Leary, 'Space Oddity at Half Century'.

[92] Pegg, *The Complete David Bowie*, 256.

[93] Sam Richards, 'Watch Tony Visconti Discuss His New Mix of David Bowie's "Space Oddity"', *Uncut*, 15 November 2019, https://tinyurl.com/cp6atwsx.

[94] Dudgeon's production of 'Space Oddity' (June 1969) may have had some bearing on the 1973 release of Elton John's song 'Rocket Man' (also produced by Gus Dudgeon), which depicts the sense of alienation experienced by an astronaut character travelling through outer space. For more on this, see Lisa Perrott, 'Accented Music Video: Animating Memories of Migration in "Rocket Man"', *Music, Sound and the Moving Image* 13, no. 2 (2019): 123–46.

[95] For more on this, see O'Leary, 'Space Oddity at Half Century'.

[96] An album titled *David Bowie* was released on the Deram label in 1967. This album includes several songs featured in the 1969 film *Love You till Tuesday*. In 1969, an entirely different collection of songs was released on another album also titled *David Bowie*, on the Phillips label. In 1972, the songs on this album were re-released under the album title *Space Oddity*, on the RCA label.

his homeland: 'Planet Earth is blue, and there's nothing I can do.' This expression of ennui upon Major Tom's realization of a lost future is what Bowie later termed 'future nostalgia', noting that it had become a recurring tendency in his work.[97] Another reiterated theme – alienation – serves as both imaginative trigger and connective thread across the multiple 'Space Oddity' videos. Dispersed across time and authors, each video contributes a new temporal, spatial and cultural perspective towards alienation. Ironically, the very first promo for 'Space Oddity' is perhaps the least effective at visually communicating the theme of alienation, apart from by inducing awkward discomfort in the mode of Bertolt Brecht's 'alienation effect'.[98]

'Space Oddity' (1969) – the promo

'Quaint is probably the kindest description', offers Pegg,[99] while O'Leary describes it as 'tonally bizarre' and as a 'half-panto, half-borderline softcore short'.[100] For anyone who'd become touched by 'Space Oddity's' ennui and atmospheric complexity, stumbling upon the 1969 promo for this song after its release in 1984 may have felt like a strange let down. Directed by Thomson and filmed on 2 February 1969 at London's Morgan studios, while this promo is the excavated progenitor of a string of 'Space Oddity' videos, Bowie may have preferred this ancestor to have remained buried.

Unlike the other material on *Love You till Tuesday*, Thomson's promo for 'Space Oddity' follows a simple narrative and attempts to visually interpret the lyrics in an overly literal way ('put my helmet on' is accompanied with a shot of Major Tom putting on what looks like a souped-up moped helmet). In this first recording, it is Hutchinson who sings the vocals for Ground Control, but Bowie visually enacts both Ground Control and Major Tom. Noting the duality that underpins the song's arrangement, Glenn Adamson observes how 'a similar technological doubling occurs' in the filmed representation of Major Tom, where 'the background image is overlaid with a circular cut-out, the metaphorical

---

[97] Bowie, 'David Bowie – Scary Monsters Interview'.
[98] Brecht described the alienation effect as 'attempts to act in such a manner that the spectator is prevented from feeling his way into the characters. Acceptance or rejection of the characters' words is thus placed in the conscious realm, not, as hitherto, in the spectator's subconscious.' For more on this, see: Bertolt Brecht, 'On Chinese Acting', *Tulane Drama Review* 6, no. 1 (1961): 130.
[99] Pegg, *The Complete David Bowie*, 256.
[100] O'Leary, 'Space Oddity at Half Century'.

stand-in for the lens. Lest we miss the point, the first shot features Major Tom drifting into view and then reaching toward the camera, as if to adjust its settings.'[101] At the moment when Bowie reaches towards the camera, his eyes seem to accidentally make contact with the lens (Figure 2.5). It's as though he realizes at this moment, that by reaching toward the camera, he is breaking the invisible 'fourth' wall and making a direct connection with his audience. This gesture provides a meta-textual reference to science fiction films of the time, as do other not-so-subtle features of the set design.

As Adamson observes, 'the video ends with a further bit of meta-textual reference in the form of a space orgy; Jane Fonda's *Barbarella* had come out the previous year'.[102] Despite this loading of intertextual science-fiction references, Ground Control looks nothing like a rocket controller – rather an awkward teenager wearing over-sized Lennon-esque glasses and yellow pants. Just in case

Figure 2.5 Bowie's eyes accidentally make contact with the lens. 'Space Oddity' (Malcom J. Thomson, 1969).

[101] Glenn Adamson, 'Did David Bowie Invent the Music Video?' *Frieze*, 5 April 2018. https://tinyurl.com/4c5km77r.
[102] Ibid.

Figure 2.6 Bowie mimes floating in space. 'Space Oddity' (Malcom J. Thomson, 1969).

we don't register who Bowie is role-playing, the letters 'GC' are saliently displayed on his white tee-shirt and red cap. Major Tom also looks nothing like an astronaut. It is obvious who this character is, because of the label 'MAJOR TOM' stretched across the screen and applied to Bowie's shiny spacesuit. The promo is also beset with other obvious signposts, such as Bowie's attempt to mime floating in space, the souped-up helmet and the low-tech science-fiction set (Figure 2.6). Everything is literally spelt out for the audience. Given that Bowie has a long track record of favouring allusion and *not* spelling things out in a literal way, it's easy to see why fans might interpret this as one of Bowie's absurdist pranks. To be fair, televised science fiction aesthetics were usually very low-tech during the sixties. Just as series such as *Doctor Who* (1963), *Lost in Space* (1965), *UFO* (1969) and *Moonbase 3* (1973) became quickly dated, so too did the 1969 promo for 'Space Oddity'. Noting that 'low-tech space has always appealed',[103] Bowie retrospectively described this first promo as 'a funky little video' which had 'belaboured the no-budget factor'.[104] He added, 'this didn't really worry me, as

[103] Bowie, *Moonage Daydream*, 179.
[104] Ibid.

after the movie *2001: A Space Odyssey*, who wanted to compete with that dazzling and realistic hi-tech look?'[105]

While Bowie may not have been worried about this 'no-budget factor', many viewers did. YouTube comments range from absolute delight at Bowie looking like a gawky teenage version of Luke Skywalker or a character from the 1971 film *A Clockwork Orange*,[106] to comments such as 'he should have taken his protein pills' and 'luv you mr bowie but this looks like something I would make for a creative contest mini film in grade four'.[107] Critics also refer to the promo's clunky cinematic composition and to Bowie's awkward performance to camera. As discussed in the next chapter, Bowie's performance to camera is vastly different in the 1972 promo for "Space Oddity", which has a lot to do with his connection with director Mick Rock. Suffice to say, there is little evidence of Bowie having had a strong collaborative connection with Thomson.

Time travel and visual echo

The various recordings and videos emerging from the song "Space Oddity" provide a fascinating case study of time travel and dispersed authorship. As I have argued elsewhere, music video plays an important role in this process, by providing a vessel for the transit of a song across time, space, cultures and authors.[108] The concept of dispersed authorship is relevant when considering the way a text (song, video or piece of footage) travels through time, with several authors having represented it in different ways. The videos available on YouTube for different versions of "Space Oddity" exemplify this dispersal of authorship across time and space, showing how fans have elaborated the storyworld for this song, which Bowie himself modified across his *oeuvre*. This can be traced across five decades, beginning with the official videos directed by Thomson (1969), Mick Rock (1972) and David Mallet (1979).[109] Complementing these 'official'

---

[105] Ibid., 179.
[106] HONEEBEAR55, comment on David Bowie, 'David Bowie – Space Oddity', YouTube video, 00:03:46, 10 March 2019, https://youtu.be/tRMZ_5WYmCg.
[107] tobazko, comment on David Bowie, 'David Bowie – Space Oddity'.
[108] For more on this, see Perrott, 'Moonwalking "Backwards Into The Future"' and Perrott, '"Accented" Music Video'.
[109] David Bowie, 'David Bowie – Space Oddity', directed by Malcom J. Thomson, 1969, YouTube video, 00:03:46, 10 March 2019, https://youtu.be/tRMZ_5WYmCg; David Bowie, 'David Bowie – Space Oddity (Official Video)', directed by Mick Rock, 1972, YouTube video, 00:05:04, 10 July 2015, https://youtu.be/iYYRH4apXDo; Nacho Video, 'David Bowie . Space Oddity. Will Kenny Everett Ever Make It To 1980? Show. 31 December 1979', directed by David Mallet, 1979, YouTube video, 00:04:54, 1 January 2020, https://youtu.be/63qvJoQLumw.

music videos, several videos were created which document instances of "Space Oddity" being performed for various television shows. Following its use in the BBC's coverage of the moon landing in June 1969, filmed performances of the song were broadcast on the Dutch television show *Doebidoe* in August 1969, and on the BBC's *Top of the Pops* in October 1969. In November 1969, a video of Bowie performing "Space Oddity" was broadcast on the Swiss television show *Hits à Gogo* and on Germany's *4-3-2-1 Musik Fur Junge Leute*. A video also exists of Bowie performing "Space Oddity" at the Ivor Novello Awards in May 1970, where he received an award from the Songwriter's Guild for the song's composition.[110] As elaborated in chapter five, in 1979 two further 'Space Oddity' videos were created for television shows – one for Kenny Everett's *New Year's Eve* show and the other for Dick Clark's *Salute to the Seventies* show, which was broadcast on US NBC. This dispersal across time, space and authors is extended further with several fan-made videos,[111] including Commander Chris Hadfield's performance of the song which was shot on board the International Space Station (2013),[112] an acapella cover version directed by Soren Lundvall Danielsen (2017),[113] a tribute video directed by Tim Pope (2019),[114] an interpretation of the song performed by the Kingston University Stylophone Orchestra (2019),[115] and a digital youth chorale performance by the Silverlake Conservatory of Music Choir (2020).[116]

To this collection of authors and intertexts, fan editor Nacho contributed his own re-edited version of the 'Space Oddity' video that was originally screened on *Hits à Gogo* in 1969.[117] The initial broadcast of the video was at that time accompanied by the June 1969 recording of the song, but the existing copy of this television show suffers from poor sound quality. Aiming to address this issue, Nacho re-edited the footage to sync up to the 2019 Tony Visconti album mix of the

---

[110] Pegg, *The Complete David Bowie*, 258.
[111] For more on this, see Perrott, *David Bowie and the Transformation of Music Video*.
[112] Rare Earth, 'Space Oddity', recorded by Chris Hadfield, produced by Evan Hadfield, 2013, YouTube video, 00:05:30, 13 May 2013, https://youtu.be/KaOC9danxNo.
[113] DunkelDirks, 'Space Oddity acapella cover', YouTube video, 00:03:59, 23 August 2017, https://youtu.be/gLA5URPoWNo.
[114] David Bowie, 'David Bowie – Space Oddity (2019 Mix) [Official Video]', directed by Tim Pope, 2019, YouTube video, 00:04:43, 21 July 2019, https://youtu.be/ptVbk7r4IcA.
[115] KUSO, 'Space Oddity (Cover) – Kingston University Stylophone Orchestra', directed by Leah Kardos and Tony Visconti, 2019, YouTube video, 00:04:54, 17 December 2019, https://youtu.be/LzejkGiK64A.
[116] Silverlake Conservatory of Music, 'Silverlake Conservatory Youth and Master Youth . . . still bringing on the music!' YouTube video, 00:04:35, 22 April 2020, https://youtu.be/qMtMkZOoRQE.
[117] Nacho Video, 'David Bowie, Space Oddity (2019 Tony Visconti Full Length Mix), 1969', YouTube video, 00:05:19, 19 November 2019, https://youtu.be/PbNsWll5ufw.

original 1969 version of "Space Oddity", thereby creating what he describes as a 'marriage of the two sources'.[118] The original video has a gothic feel, due to its cobweb-laden set and dry ice rising up from dark steps. The video is remarkable for its stark lighting and monochromatic contrast, which has the effect of completely blacking out Bowie's face for much of his mimed performance. This seems like an odd approach, especially considering the dominance of Bowie's face in subsequent videos, but the strange lighting creates a sense of mystery, much in the way that enigma is created by the wearing of a mask. The use of top and back lighting with minimal front light throws Bowie's figure into silhouette. This filmed performance is projected onto the background screen, which produces a reiterated visual echo of Bowie's silhouette; an effect that provides a fitting visual analogue to the duplicity of the vocals and the layered assemblage of the song.

Although not classified as 'official' music videos, these filmed performances for television shows are now situated alongside 'official' and fan-made videos on YouTube, and are often viewed without much differentiation. Since these non-official videos play an important part in demonstrating Bowie's contribution to the art and remediation of music video, I have included them alongside my examination of 'official' videos. The set of videos created in 1972 for *The Old Grey Whistle Test* document Bowie's shift from stage to television performance at the moment when he was beginning to shed the awkwardness of his fledgling attempts at performing in front of the camera. While this transition is apparent on the *Whistle Test* videos for 'Oh, You Pretty Things' and 'Queen Bitch', these shifts in Bowie's performance are best exemplified by the *Whistle Test* video for 'Five Years'.

"Five Years" – the song

> The time is five years to go before the end of the Earth. It has been announced that the world will end because of lack of natural resources. Ziggy is in a position where all the kids have access to things that they thought they wanted. The older people have lost all touch with reality and the kids are left on their own to plunder anything. Ziggy was in a rock 'n' roll band and the kids no longer want rock 'n' roll. There's no electricity to play it.
>
> Bowie, 1974[119]

---

[118] Ibid.
[119] Craig Copetas, 'Beat Godfather Meets Glitter Mainman', *Rolling Stone*, 28 February 1974, republished at *Rolling Stone*, https://tinyurl.com/b8hf7c7f.

This was one of many occasions when Bowie alluded to his tendency to cogitate a sense of nostalgia for a lost future, a point that I elaborate in chapter five.[120] Perhaps more than any other song, "Five Years" stands out for its authentic expression of despair about a future which will not come to pass. In contrast to the optimism of the early 1960s, a pessimism about the future became a defining characteristic of the UK *zeitgeist* of the late 1960s and early 1970s. Themes of dystopia and apocalypse were prevalent in literature, television series and films of the time, such as Michael Moorcock's novel *Alien Heat* (1972), Alan Garner's novel *Red Shift* (1973), Roy Ward Baker's film *Quatermass and the Pit* (1967) and the associated *Quatermass* BBC serial which Bowie has pointed to as being influential during his formative years.[121] Describing such texts as British expressions of a type of nostalgia for a lost future, Mark Fisher explains that:

> The disappearance of the future meant the deterioration of a whole mode of social imagination: the capacity to conceive of a world radically different from the one in which we currently live. It meant the acceptance of a situation in which culture would continue without really changing, and where politics was reduced to the administration of an already established (capitalist) system. In other words, we were in the 'end of history' [as] described by Francis Fukuyama.[122]

Across several publications, Fisher explores how this *zeitgeist* of demoralization is manifest via popular music and audio-visual forms of the late 1960s and early 1970s, proposing that 'what haunts the digital cul-de-sacs of the twenty-first century is not so much the past as all the lost futures that the twentieth century taught us to anticipate'.[123] Well before the presence of digital media, Bowie's musical exploration of dystopia tapped into the sense of despair that the progressive future many had imagined, would not eventuate. This is particularly apparent in the vocal expression and lyrics to his song "Cygnet Committee" (1969), which combines a yearning for a future of love, life, and hope 'where money stood, we planted seeds of rebirth', with a sense of despair that it will never eventuate, culminating in a prescient awakening to the sounds and visions of a dark future: 'And I open my eyes to look around, and I see a child laid slain

---

[120] The influence of the *Quatermass* storyworld is apparent in 'Space Oddity', 'Five Years' and 'Ashes to Ashes'; for more on 'future nostalgia,' see chapter five.
[121] Heller, 'Anthems for the Moon'.
[122] Fisher, 'What is Hauntology?' 16; Francis Fukuyama, 'The End of History?' *The National Interest* no. 16 (1989): 3–18.
[123] Fisher, 'What is Hauntology?' 16.

on the ground. As a love machine lumbers through desolation rows, ploughing down man, woman, listening to its command.'[124]

By the time "Five Years" was released on the album *The Rise and Fall of Ziggy Stardust and the Spiders from Mars* (1972), the sense of despair in Bowie's lyrics had reached the point of resignation that the 'end of history' was nigh. Although lyrically focused on the loss of the future, the song is sonically haunted by ghosts from the past, as are other songs on this album. Abundant with haunting traces of a menagerie of star performers such as Jacques Brel, Lou Reed, Iggy Pop, Fats Domino and Jerry Lee Lewis, several songs on this album conjure the visual imagery, sensory associations, and spirit of 1950s rock'n'roll. Setting the tone for the rest of the album, "Five Years"' ghostly traces of 1950s America are estranged by the dystopia of Bowie's emotionally prescient lament for a lost future.

We hear visually evocative lyrics such as 'I think I saw you in an ice cream parlor, drinking milkshakes cold and long.' The tightly woven lyrics combine with the musical arrangement to evoke images and sensory associations of a particular time, place, and attitude. But just as these associations converge to construct a familiar sense of 1950s American youth culture, this sense of nostalgia for a more optimistic time becomes strangely defamiliarized by references to alienated states and alternate gender identities. The lyrics conjure images of a dystopian storyworld set in a market square, where a series of bizarre scenarios unfold. Characters include a weeping 'news-guy', a deranged girl hitting 'tiny children', a 'soldier with a broken arm', and a cop kneeling to 'kiss the feet of a priest', the latter inducing a 'queer' to throw up 'at the sight of that'. Bowie then sings of 'all the fat-skinny people', 'all the tall-short people', 'all the nobody people', and 'all the somebody people', all of which makes his 'brain hurt like a warehouse'. As Pegg observes, '"Five Years" drips with implication.'[125] When Bowie sings 'It was cold and it rained, so I felt like an actor', not only are we given a visual image of the song's protagonist walking in the rain, we are also likely to recall the miserable sensation of being stranded in the rain, wet and cold.

The sense of despair expressed in the lyrics is mirrored in the musical arrangement. Woodmansey's drumbeat introduces a sense of despondency, and then continues as a heartbeat of demoralization underpinning the entire song. While he described it as putting 'hopelessness into a drumbeat',[126] O'Leary

---

[124] David Bowie, 'Cygnet Committee' (1969).
[125] Pegg, *The Complete David Bowie*, 93.
[126] Chris O'Leary, 'Fifty Ziggy 50', *Pushing Ahead of the Dame*, 16 June 2022, https://bowiesongs.wordpress.com/.

unpacks this idea, explaining that the sound is generated by a 'kick drum and closed hi-hat, in 3/4 time, with a snare hit (flutter) on the third beat, then (wham!) on the downbeat'.[127] This drumbeat became such an iconic signifier of hopelessness that it served as an instantly recognizable moment of self-quotation when it reappeared as the outro to Bowie's song "You Feel So Lonely You Could Die" (2013), another song in which despair for a lost future is expressed instrumentally, lyrically, and vocally. While the drumbeat provides an underlying sense of hopeless plodding, Ronson's piano chords contribute a pronounced gravitas until the middle of the song, when the piano shifts into a syncopated rhythm. O'Leary aptly observes how 'the verses of "Five Years" seem like they will never end, until, after curling into a ball, they become a doomsday pub singalong refrain'.[128] The diatonic chord progression is then set against the gravitas of a full string section that builds in concert with the desperation of Bowie's vocals, eventually dismantling into a sonic cacophony at the song's climax. Similar to the urgent swirling sound of wasps swarming in multidirectional unison, this sound conjures the discordance of Krzysztof Penderecki's string composition "Polymorphia" (1961), which provides the creepy iconic tone to horror films such as *The Exorcist* (1973) and *The Shining* (1980).[129] Penderecki's music has been described as 'anxiety-inducing', due to its inclusion of 'chaotic sound masses which build in volume and unpredictability giving an absolutely unsettling feeling'.[130] Topping off the anxiety induced by this cacophony, Bowie's overwrought vocal has a way of cutting through one's emotional defences, much in the way that John Lennon's tortured vocal does in his song "Mother" (1970), which exemplifies Lennon's experimentation with Arthur Janov's 'primal scream' therapy.[131] While Bowie recorded a cover of 'Mother' in 1997, there is no suggestion that he underwent Janov's therapy, although he did use a guttural 'almost scream' in "It's No Game (Part 1)" (1980). According to Dennis MacKay, who worked as an engineer on the production of "Five Years", 'Bowie's screaming and what you hear on that song, the emotion is for real. I was in shock because he was also hitting every note spot on'.[132] By the song's end, the authentic trauma

---

[127] Ibid.
[128] Ibid.
[129] Jordan Sheppard, 'Penderecki and the Sound of Horror', *The Artifice*, 14 June 2019, https://tinyurl.com/kpv3mmxs.
[130] Ibid.
[131] Arthur Janov, *The Primal Scream: Primal Therapy, The Cure for Neurosis* (New York: Dell Publishing, 1970); Jordan Potter, 'How John Lennon Gave Primal Scream Their Name', *Far Out*, 11 January 2022, https://tinyurl.com/5n8ke7ux.
[132] O'Leary, 'Fifty → Ziggy ← 50'.

transmitted by Bowie's cracked voice as he repeatedly cries out 'five years!' is enough to leave a lump in the throat of the most stoic listeners.

'Five Years' – the TV promo

The musical arrangement described above is based on the first recording of "Five Years," which was completed in November 1971 and subsequently included on the *Ziggy Stardust* album in 1972. A few months later, on 7 February 1972, the song was performed for *The Old Grey Whistle Test* at the BBC Television Centre in London. According to Nacho, 'other than Bowie's live vocal, the band are miming to the Bowie/Ken Scott-produced backing track from the Ziggy album, minus the strings and other touches'.[133] For this reason, the musical arrangement for this promo is significantly pared back. Devoid of the full string section, this recording lacks the cacophony heard on the original recording. Despite the simpler instrumental sound, a sense of despair is conveyed by Bowie's impassioned vocal performance and Woodmansey's drumbeat. Further gravitas is provided by the impeccable placement of Mick Ronson's piano chords and Trevor Bolder's bass. Whether miming or not, the band deliver a tight performance with no apparent mishaps. Bowie's live-to-air vocal is also impressive, despite a minor lyrical error. Instead of the oxymoronic 'fat-skinny people' and 'tall-short people', he sings 'so many people' and 'short-fat people', but manages to hide the mistake well.

The promo is lit with a complementary colour palette. The first shot is of Woodmansey, lit by a single red light as he plays his distinctive drum intro. The first strum of the acoustic guitar triggers a white front light to be turned on, distinguishing Bowie from the Spiders, who are each lit with a red front light and a narrowly focused white top light. The band are separated from the studio background, which is lit with a wash of green. With coloured light used to distinguish the background, midground and foreground, Bowie stands out as the salient frontman – ironically the only member of the band whose skin colour looks 'natural'. This is one of many factors that contribute to Bowie appearing unusually 'authentic'. Perhaps for the first time in a promo, we see Bowie dropping his artifice in favour of an impassioned performance that, although controlled,

---

[133] Nacho, 'David Bowie – Five Years – HD Restored – The Old Grey Whistle Test –7 February 1972', *Nachos Videos*, 00:05:01, https://www.nachosvideos.com/bowie-videos.

Figure 2.7 Bowie drops his artifice in favour of an impassioned performance. 'Five Years' (Michael Appleton & Rowan Ayers, 1972).

portrays a sense of emotional integrity and a rawness that we might expect from a live performance (Figure 2.7).

This shift away from artifice is also apparent by the emphasis given to the acoustic guitar and visibility of the overhead lighting rig, cables and musical equipment in the background of the studio. With natural hair colour, unpainted face and wearing his newly tailored Droog costume, Bowie had only just begun the process of reinventing himself. This was indeed a pivotal moment for Bowie. Ziggy and the Spiders from Mars were a brand new entity, having just performed their first gig a week before at the Aylesbury Friars. The *Whistle Test* was the first time "Five Years" had ever been performed.[134] The fact that the video was captured in only one take adds another facet of 'authenticity' to the performance.

For many fans, this video was first seen when it was released in 1993 as an extra on the *Bowie Video Collection* as an extra.[135] Stumbling across the video amongst this curated collection of mostly 'official' videos, Tom Taylor experienced

---

[134] Ibid.
[135] *Bowie: The Video Collection* (United Kingdom: PMI, 1997), DVD.

it as 'an unearthed gem that heralds in the arrival of a future hero', adding that Bowie's 'full-blown celestial potential may not have been fully realised, but his mercurial magic is clearly in its budding spring and it is just about to burst into bloom'.[136] This comment aptly describes the significance of the *Whistle Test* video for 'Five Years' as an indicator of Bowie's future music video performances.

Denouement

This chapter began by providing a rough sketch of the social and cultural milieu which shaped Bowie during his formative years. As a member of Britain's transitional generation, the teenage David Jones experienced a particular confluence of stresses and strains related to his family life, along with profoundly changing social and cultural norms. This context is instructive when considering his approach to song writing, performance, promotional films and music videos. Bowie's early embrace of the visual, sonic and kinetic arts helps to explain his performance across stage and screen, and his subsequent interweaving of these artforms within the broader process of remediation.

By tracking Bowie's transit from theatrical stage performance to screen performance, we see his remarkable capacity to adapt across performance modes, while also melding mediums and genres to create a new hybrid form. This is particularly apparent by the way *Love You till Tuesday* incorporates mime and mask and other theatrical modes alongside cinematic strategies more suited to the screen arts. While Bowie's artifice and fledgling awkwardness may be perceived by some viewers as discomforting, this collection of promos documents significant moments in which Bowie can be seen experimenting with subcultural style, gesture and the merging of performance modes.

In the three years that followed, Bowie underwent a transitory period of musical development, along with maturation as a performer. By February 1972, his live-to-air performance on the *Whistle Test* portrays a capacity to drop the artifice in favour of a more authentic performance. While the material discussed in this chapter enacts considerable moments of discomfort, these are significant moments in which Bowie was taking his own advice to:

---

[136] Tom Taylor, 'Watch Rare Never Broadcast Footage of David Bowie Performing on the *Old Grey Whistle Test* in 1972', *Far Out*, 12 April 2021, https://tinyurl.com/yw3c3jtf.

> Always go a little further into the water than you feel you're capable of being in. Go a little bit out of your depth. And when you don't feel that your feet are quite touching the bottom, you're just about in the right place to do something exciting.[137]

It was this tenet that would propel Bowie to explore the artistic possibilities of music video, while preparing him for his next step. This would begin the following month, through a chance encounter with a kindred spirit.

---

[137] Bowie from *Inspirations*, directed by Michael Apted (1997); BOWIElover, 'David Bowie Inspirations', YouTube video, 00:20:21, 16 May 2011, https://youtu.be/pDmb_aR_OnY.

3

Opening the Third Eye

David thinks you see him the way he sees himself.... You see him through his eyes.

Tony Defries, talking to Mick Rock, 1972[1]

It was March 1972, and Bowie's manager Tony Defries passed on the good news to Mick Rock. Bowie had expressed this thought about Rock's vision after having cast his eyes on the results of one of Rock's earliest photo sessions with him. Perfectly encapsulating his comment, one image stands out for the way it represents the unique essence of Bowie's collaboration with Rock.[2] In this photo, Bowie is looking directly at Rock and at us, but his look is mediated through a mirror and the camera lens. Captured at Bowie's Haddon Hall home, the images produced from this session became iconic records of his fledgling Ziggy Stardust persona. The photos from this session have been published and exhibited in multiple mediums and sites, including the magazines *Club International* and *Playboy*, the *Space Oddity* album cover, and publicity posters for the 2022 film *Moonage Daydream*.[3] Viewing the photos for the first time, Bowie was struck by what he perceived as Rock's ability to 'see him' the way he saw himself. By verbalizing this thought to Defries, Bowie was embarking on one of his most significant collaborative relationships – one that would not only enable him to relax in front of the camera but would also provide the safety and confidence he needed to open up and perform for the camera. This relationship also provided a positive model for collaboration – one based on trust, friendship and a shared enchantment with literature and its capacity to be visualized. It was a model of

---

[1] Mick Rock, *Moonage Daydream: The Life and Times of Ziggy Stardust* (UK: Doppelganger, 2002), 45.
[2] A YouTube playlist for chapter 3 is available at https://tinyurl.com/mw3nbfc7.
[3] *Moonage Daydream*, directed by Brett Morgen (2022, United States, BMG).

symbiotic collaboration that provided Bowie with a template for his future experiences with music videos directors. Up until this point, Bowie hadn't experienced that special 'click' with a photographer or film director. By clinching an arrangement with Rock to be Ziggy Stardust's official photographer, Bowie activated a pivotal moment in his career – one that opened the door for him to master the art of performing to camera.

For twenty months, Rock lived and breathed Ziggy Stardust. This was photography by total immersion, and it led to an extensive catalogue of still photographs documenting the on- and off-stage performance of Ziggy. Revealing insights about the creation and demise of a persona, the photos tell the story of a little-known stage character who develops into an alien-rock-messiah – a living work of art.[4] By closely examining Rock's photos, we can see Bowie becoming increasingly fused with the identity of his creation. While fulfilling the form and functions of documentary photography, Rock's images have blurred the conventions of this genre, migrating across musical paratexts, the popular press, documentary photography, art photography, portraiture, live performance and music video. They have been published and exhibited in magazines, books, art galleries, websites and album cover art for prominent glam and rock artists of the 1970s.[5] Rock's role as Bowie's personal photographer from 1972 to 1973, then provides an important context for my examination of the videos he directed.

Described by Rock as a 'funny little collage video of live footage',[6] 'Moonage Daydream' was the first moving image film he made with Bowie. This film was shot in April and May 1972 to publicize the release of the album *The Rise and Fall of Ziggy Stardust and the Spiders from Mars*. Despite its promotional purpose, the film has receded into obscurity. Even so, the film's title has become synonymous with Rock's documentation of Ziggy Stardust, in the form of his 2002 book *Moonage Daydream*. The song title again burst into the spotlight in 2022 upon the release of Brett Morgen's documentary film *Moonage Daydream*, which includes much of Rock's work.

Rock went on to direct official videos for 'John, I'm Only Dancing' (1972), 'The Jean Genie' (1972), "Space Oddity" (1972) and 'Life on Mars?' (1973). Through a close analysis of these videos, my primary intention is to learn how each video contributes to establishing music video as an artform. I also hope

---

[4] See Rock, *Moonage Daydream* (2002), and mickrock.com, https://tinyurl.com/2cefdw3e.
[5] Such as album covers for, Bowie (*Space Oddity*, 1972; *Pin Ups*, 1973), Lou Reed (*Transformer*, 1972; *Coney Island Baby*, 1975), Queen (*Queen II*, 1974), Cockney Rebel (*The Psychomodo*, 1974) and Steve Harley (*The Candidate*, 1979).
[6] Rock, *Moonage Daydream*, 49.

that these videos may reveal some insights about the special collaboration between Bowie and Rock, and the creative process behind the sonic and visual construction of each video. It is therefore important to delve into who Rock was and discover what made him click so well with Bowie.

Mick Rock

> I am not in the business of documenting or revealing personalities. I am in the business of freezing shadows and bottling auras.
>
> Mick Rock[7]

Michael David Rock was born (as Michael Edward Chester Smith) in Hammersmith, London, on 21 November 1948. Although born only twenty-one months after David Jones and in a neighbouring suburb of the Jones's home in Brixton, Rock's upbringing led him along a different path – one of esteemed scholarship in the literary arts rather than practical artistry in the sonic and visual arts, as one might expect to be the case for a photographer with such a keen eye for visually representing musical performers. The biographical documentary *Shot! The Psycho Spiritual Mantra of Rock* (2016) provides insight into what underpins Rock's approach as a photographer.[8] In this film, Rock reflects that despite being 'born of extremely modest means',[9] he was propelled by the manifest affirmations of his mother to experience a privileged education. In doing so, he says, his mother taught him about projection, the art of making something happen through imagining it to be so. It was only due to the sheer strength of her projections that he was accepted into Cambridge University, where he graduated with a degree in Medieval and Modern Languages. Beyond this literary schooling, Rock went on to use his knowledge of the power of projection – in conjunction with the camera – to project talented musicians into musical icons. In this way, he was an ideal collaborative partner for Bowie, who was beginning a process of projecting himself into stardom by developing the Ziggy Stardust character as 'the Leper Messiah'.[10]

---

[7] Mick Rock, 'About Mick', *Mickrock.com*, https://www.mickrock.com/mick-about/.
[8] Mick Rock, *Shot! The Psycho Spiritual Mantra of Rock*, directed by Barney Clay (2017, USA: Vice Studios).
[9] Ibid.
[10] Lyrics to David Bowie's song 'Ziggy Stardust' (1972).

Bowie was drawn to collaborating with artists who were excited about the correlations between sonic and visual art. While Brian Eno and Stanley Dorfman come to mind here, Rock was also of this ilk. He once said, 'there's definitely a synchronicity between music and photography. There certainly is in my case.'[11] Not only did Rock share Bowie's enthusiasm for musical and visual analogues, but Rock was also fascinated by the synchronicity he saw between musicians and the great literary figures he studied at Cambridge. He recalls, 'that's where I got my head filled up with all those great poets zoomed out of their brains, coming up with great art.'[12] Through learning about the lives of the symbolists, the English Romantics and the American Beat poets, Rock developed a romanticized idea of the possibility of experiencing a heightened intensity of perception. When interviewed in 2020, Rock explained the intersection of his enchantment with the lives of poets and his experimentation with LSD:

> My brain was filled with symbolist poets who write about getting wacked-out on absinthe, sex and drugs. You know, something happened when I took the LSD: I began to *see*. There was no vision sense in the household I grew up in, my parents were lovely people, but they were more book oriented.[13]

Although underplaying the significance of his literary upbringing, Rock's immersion in literature and symbolist poetry may well have primed him to untap his 'vision sense'. His literary dexterity enabled him to articulate the idea that 'the lysergic experience opened up my third eye, you might say'.[14] Referring to his first experience of LSD, Rock recalled 'once it kicked in, the entire universe rushed through my body. I saw everything'.[15] The drug 'intensified all the colours, it intensified the frame, it intensified everything. The altered state was something that was there, it had become part of me.'[16] This experience coincided with stumbling upon a camera at his friend's house, and being in the intimate presence of a willing photographic subject. As Rock recalls:

> Photography wandered idly into my life. . . . There was a chemical experience, a chemical overload. Well, I got the excitement of the 'ptchew' every time I pressed that shutter. It was like an explosion. It looked different every time I clicked it. So there was this world of entertainment in the camera.[17]

---

[11] Rock, Mickrock.com.
[12] Rock, *Shot!*
[13] Scott Fishkind, 'The History of Rock: An Interview with the Iconic Mick Rock', *As If*, 22 July 2020, https://www.asifmag.com/story/interview-with-mick-rock.
[14] Rock, *Shot!*
[15] Ibid.
[16] Ibid.
[17] Ibid.

Despite later discovering that he'd been clicking away with no film in the camera, Rock remembers this psychedelic experience as the moment when the 'magic started to get into my mind'.[18] Subsequently, Rock undertook a brief period of tuition at the London Film School. This led him to work with the graphic design company Hipgnosis, and to writing articles for *Rolling Stone* magazine. While photography developed into his greatest passion, this became intertwined with what would become a life-long discipline of yoga.[19] These intersections between Rock's formal education and his intense life experiences help to explain his approach to his photography practice. For Rock, photography was a mind-body-spiritual practice that heightened his perceptual experience of a person, place, or moment in time. Describing it as a synaesthetic experience, he says, 'I smell pictures more that I see them. And I hear them more than I smell them. It's very habit forming.'[20] Such habits involved routinely practicing yoga and other bodily techniques that put him into what he calls a 'psycho-spiritual' perceptive state – a state that would enable him to *see* (and then photograph) the aura of his subject. He explained that, 'a soul is a little more difficult to get out. People's souls are very mysterious – but the aura is not. I want that certain kind of mystical energy.'[21] Rock's description of his art practice as 'freezing shadows and bottling auras' is entirely metaphysical and apparently devoid of a scientific basis. However, given the relationship between his photographic work and other forms of art, it's important to consider the literature focusing on photography and the 'aura'. This term was used by Walter Benjamin 'to encompass that which the painting has but the photograph lacks – the aura is all the contexts a thing gathers since its inception'.[22] He argued that, as a means of mechanical reproduction, photography was responsible for the decline of the aura of the traditional artwork. However, Benjamin complicates this notion by developing an alternative concept of 'aura', 'one which transcends fixed historical or technological categories through the model of an imaginary encounter between viewer and image'.[23] For Benjamin, photographs are able to embody '"the spark of contingency" with which the aura of the past shines in the

---

[18] Ibid.
[19] Rock, MickRock.com.
[20] Ibid.
[21] Daisy, 'Mick Rock – Beyond the Velvet Rope RIP', 18 November 2021, *My Punk Rock London Life*, https://tinyurl.com/ycxvvs92.
[22] Laura Thain, 'Walter Benjamin on Photography and Film', n.d., *Viz*, https://tinyurl.com/3cedm9u9.
[23] Carolin Duttlinger, 'Imaginary Encounters: Walter Benjamin and the Aura of Photography', *Poetics Today* 29, no. 1 (2008): 79.

present'.[24] Rock's use of the term 'aura' challenges Benjamin's initial argument, while also finding basis as a 'spark of contingency' and an imaginary encounter between photographer and image. His phrase 'bottling auras' describes an imaginary practice of materializing the immaterial and making visible the invisible. This practice is underpinned by his broader philosophy of psycho-spiritual projection, an idea that also fascinated Bowie.

Mismatched eyeballs

> It was all so very unlikely; the carrot coloured hairdo and the jumpsuit. The red plastic boots and the mismatched eyeballs. No seasoned betting man would have backed this one. But I knew what I liked and that was enough to make the first move.
>
> Rock, 2016[25]

That 'first move' involved turning up unexpectedly at Bowie's dressing room after photographing his show at the Birmingham Town Hall on 17 March 1972. Rock was able to chat with Bowie and take some behind-the-scenes photos to add to his collection of performance shots. Although these images don't exhibit the perceptual magic of the Haddon Hall photos, they provide a record of one of the first public outings of the newly-born Ziggy persona, complete with freshly-minted Droog costume. Rock recalls that first meeting:

> I remember that night I peeked around his dressing room door. 'I like your name. It can't be real' he told me. There and then he invited me back to his house and we stayed up all night and talked about all kinds of things. There was a certain awareness of being with that level of intelligence in the room. The pictures got elevated, they acquired this other quality.[26]

Excited by the idea that a connection of minds could somehow materialize into photographs, Rock returned to Haddon Hall for further photo sessions and interviews with Bowie. After Bowie had seen the results, his comment to Defries indicates that he also perceived the 'elevated' quality that Rock saw in the images. In 2017, Rock reflected on the initial connection he experienced with Bowie:

---

[24] Tim Dant and Graeme Gilloch, 'Pictures of the Past: Benjamin and Barthes on Photography and History', *European Journal of Cultural Studies* 5, no. 1 (2002): 5.
[25] Ibid.
[26] Ibid.

I think that was what sealed the deal with us because, one, he seemed to like the photos. But two, we got to exchange ideas and philosophies – there was a brain connection as well.... There's one photo in particular ... Bowie in the mirror ... and that was the session where he said to his manager 'Mick sees me the way I see myself'.[27]

It's possible that Bowie was referring to this photo of himself reflected in the mirror; perhaps he saw his aura reflected back at him. Whatever the case, Bowie appeared to trust Rock's vision enough to embrace him as both friend and professional photographer. This was the beginning of a creative adventure that enabled Rock to work alongside Bowie across several mediums. Over the next twenty months, Rock produced over 6,000 still images, numerous hours of 16mm footage and several recorded interviews for publication.[28] His role as music video director emerged as a spontaneous extension of his photography role. This was a logical progression, since he was a loyal and trusted collaborator who offered Bowie a crucial step up from the type of directorial relationship he had experienced with Malcolm Thomson. Throughout the filming of *Love You till Tuesday* (1969), Bowie's performance to camera was distinctively cheeky and provocative, yet awkwardly fey. Although playing up to the camera, Bowie appeared uncomfortably self-conscious. He had yet to learn how to take control of his screen representation.

While Kemp trained him in the art of moving on stage, it was Rock who unlocked Bowie's skill for performing in front of the camera. Some credit for this must also go to Keith MacMillan, Brian Ward and Brian Duffy, who collaborated with Bowie as he learnt the art of posing for the photographs that feature on his album covers from 1970 to 1973.[29] In the context of music video, it was Rock who enabled Bowie to take control of the cinematic gaze. As we shall see, Bowie's intensity of address to camera is a striking feature of all four videos Rock directed for Bowie. Although moving between still photography and moving image presented new challenges, Rock built upon his skillset as a photographer of glam and rock musicians. Using music video as an ideal form for packaging diverging

[27] Mick Rock, 'Mick Rock Talks Bowie, Iconic Photographs', interview by King 5 News Desk, YouTube video, June 29, 2017, https://youtu.be/cf89gEmzSuk.
[28] Rock, *Moonage Daydream*, 9.
[29] Bowie's skill in posing for the camera is evident in the photos used for the front cover of the following albums: *The Man Who Sold the World* (1970), shot by Keith MacMillan; *Hunky Dory* (1971), shot by Brian Ward and recoloured by Terry Pastor; *The Rise and Fall of Ziggy Stardust and the Spiders from Mars* (1972), shot by Brian Ward and recoloured by Terry Pastor; *Space Oddity* (1972), shot by Mick Rock; and *Aladdin Sane* (1973), shot by Brian Duffy, with makeup by Pierre Laroche.

tones, subcultures and gestures, Rock communicated a distinct attitude in each video. As with his photos, Rock's music videos capture the rebellious spirit that was fermenting in the UK during the early 1970s. The documentary basis of his work is discernible by the occasional glimpse of authenticity amidst the artifice, and by the inclusion of restless camera movement, unconventional editing and use of incidental footage. These attributes contribute an edgy feel to Rock's first official music video, which perfectly complements the sonic attitude of Bowie's song "John, I'm Only Dancing" (1972).[30]

"John, I'm Only Dancing" – the song

As Pegg outlines, there has been much debate about which recording of "John, I'm Only Dancing" came first, and which version might be considered 'best'.[31] For the sake of clarity, the following section focuses only on the version that accompanied Rock's official music video. This recording took place on 26 June 1972 at Olympic Studios, two months before its video-accompanied UK release.[32] Following its release, the song achieved success in the UK charts, but was perceived to be 'too alarming' by RCA and consequently remained unreleased in America until 1976.[33] While particular elements of the video were deemed to be disturbing to some, much has been said about the song's provocative lyrics, which have triggered a variety of responses. For instance, they have been interpreted as a homosexual or queer man declaring to his partner that he is 'only dancing' with a woman, and alternatively as a heterosexual man's assurance to another man that he is 'only dancing' with the man's female partner. There is also an unlikely rumour that the words 'John, I'm only dancing' may be a response to a derisive comment made by John Lennon, about Bowie's sexual ambiguity.[34] Offering a useful contextualization of the controversy around the song's lyrics,

---

[30] 'John, I'm Only Dancing', David Bowie (1972, UK: RCA Victor).
[31] Pegg, *The Complete David Bowie*, 143.
[32] Pegg notes that another version of 'John, I'm Only Dancing' was recorded six months later, during recording sessions for the *Aladdin Sane* album, and was released as a single in 1973. Known as 'the sax version', this second recording has a faster tempo and includes saxophone played by Ken Fordham. During recording sessions for *Young Americans* in 1974, an entirely re-worked funk version of the song was recorded and released in December 1979, with the title 'John, I'm Only Dancing (Again)'.
[33] Pegg, *The Complete David Bowie*, 143.
[34] Henry Hrebien, 'What Was David Bowie's Song "John, I'm Only Dancing" About?' Quora, https://tinyurl.com/2p5c2cua.

Chris O'Leary suggests that they work together with the video's imagery to conjure intertextual references to specific texts within the realms of gay and queer culture:

> 'John, I'm Only Dancing' is a vague, shadowy and unreadable performance; its promo video ... features a writhing male-and-female pair of dancers, while Bowie and the Spiders look like they've stepped out of Kenneth Anger's *Scorpio Rising*. If anything, 'John' is basically *Son of Suffragette City*, its lyric again (as in 'Queen Bitch', too) depicting a man in a possibly gay relationship flirting with a woman and trying to make excuses.[35]

These lyrical provocations to gay and queer culture fuelled rumours that Bowie had already planted about his sexuality. Although possibly contributing to US censors overly zealous restrictions, the rumours ultimately increased Bowie's notoriety amongst the less conservative music subcultures of the time. The *risqué* tone of the song is not only a result of the lyrics, but also of the musical arrangement, which according to O'Leary, 'mainly belongs to the Spiders'.[36]

> Mick Ronson's verse riff updates Eddie Cochran, while he offers a siren wail in the chorus and his coda solo ends with Ronson using the toggle switch on his guitar to create staccato bursts of feedback.... The rhythm section is also inspired.... And Trevor Bolder's bassline is one of the track's main hooks, especially in the chorus, where he starts with a slow rise-and-fall and then shifts to bars of octave-jumping runs.[37]

Pegg reiterates O'Leary's observation about the song's R&B inspiration, noting how the 'opening guitar strum is an R&B standard, perhaps coming to David via Sonny Boy Williamson and The Yardbirds' 1963 recording of "Pontiac Blues",'[38] while suggesting that Ronson's electric guitar riff might be 'poached from the saxophone intro to Alvin Cash's 1968 single "Keep on Dancing"'.[39] These R&B musical references merge with proto-punk aesthetics, posture, and attitude to create a culturally hybrid video.

---

[35] Chris O'Leary, 'John, I'm Only Dancing', *Pushing Ahead of the Dame*, 27 May 2020, https://tinyurl.com/muecc592.
[36] Ibid.
[37] Ibid.
[38] Pegg, *The Complete David Bowie*, 143.
[39] Ibid.

'John, I'm Only Dancing' – the video[40]

> The John, I'm Only Dancing promo is the very moment the modern idea of a video was born.
>
> Leslie Conway 'Lester' Bangs[41]

Rock's 'first promo film',[42] 'John I'm Only Dancing', was produced and directed with a budget of £200.[43] Most of the footage was shot during rehearsals of the stage show *David Bowie at the Rainbow*, which took place on stage at the Rainbow Theatre, London, between 19 and 25 August 1972.[44] Inspired by Bowie's long-held desire to create a 'total work of art',[45] the show combined a set by Ziggy and the Spiders with avant-garde dance performance by Annie Stainer, Jack Birkett and Lindsay Kemp. These performances provided concert footage for Rock to incorporate into the film's final edit. For the Rainbow show, Bowie's entrance on stage was accompanied by a projected slide-show of Rock's photographs – a montage of extreme close-ups of Bowie's eyes, mouth, hair and fingertips.[46] These images are early indicators of Rock's skill at engaging the audience through the projection of haptic imagery, as would become apparent with the intimate framing of Bowie's hair, mouth and eyes in his 1973 video for 'Life On Mars'. While he also shot such extreme close-ups for 'John, I'm Only Dancing', only a few of these made it into the final edit of the video, which mostly comprised mid-shots and long-shots. The wider shots are purposeful, since they provide enough space to show Bowie mimicking the gestural traits of Hollywood starlets. Gazing pleadingly into the camera, he lowers his eyelids alluringly, signalling that he is an object to be gazed at. Turning away from the camera, he crosses his forearms across his chest and clasps his throat (Figure 3.1).

These examples of feminized self-touching are consistent with the gestures that Bowie adopted for the 1971 *Hunky Dory* album cover photo shoot, which

---

[40] David Bowie, 'David Bowie – John, I'm Only Dancing' (Official Video), YouTube video, 19 July 2015, https://youtu.be/lmVVyhpuFRc.
[41] Nick, Leslie Conway 'Lester' Bangs, 'David Bowie, John, I'm Only Dancing (Nacho Edit with Unreleased Footage)' *David Bowie News*, 3 March 2017, https://tinyurl.com/ybmjw54c.
[42] Rock, *Moonage Daydream*, 85.
[43] Pegg, *The Complete David Bowie*, 143.
[44] Rock, *Moonage Daydream*, 85.
[45] For more on this, see Perrott, 'Ziggy Stardust, Direct Cinema'.
[46] Rock, *Moonage Daydream*, 69; '"John, I'm Only Dancing", by David Bowie – Promo Video', Thinwhiteduke.net, https://tinyurl.com/2p24tttv.

Figure 3.1 Bowie mimes the gestural traits of Hollywood starlets. 'John, I'm Only Dancing' (Mick Rock, 1972).

were inspired by photos of Marlene Dietrich and Gretta Garbo.[47] As we shall see, Bowie continued to use these specific gestures as part of a broader repertoire of bodily movement, reiterating them in subsequent videos, various stage performances and photo shoots. In 'John, I'm Only Dancing', these gestures enhance the allure of Bowie's gendered ambiguity, as does the tiny anchor painted on his left cheekbone. Many years later, Bowie explained that when he watched the television series *Bewitched* in the 1960s, 'for some strange reason Samantha occasionally wore tiny tattoos on her face. I thought it looked really odd, but inspired, so I used a little anchor on my face for the 'John, I'm Only Dancing' video'.[48] Despite this wholesome source of inspiration, the anchor tattoo became recontextualized in this video alongside a complex mixture of masculine and feminine codes. In this context, the anchor tattoo connotes a

---

[47] Brian Ward's photographs for the *Hunky Dory* album cover were influenced by a Marlene Dietrich book that Bowie took with him to the photo shoot. Images from the photo shoot include close replicas of the poses adopted by Dietrich and other female starlets.
[48] Rock, *Moonage Daydream*, 86.

fledgling punk-rock attitude. Whether through makeup, gesture or ocular address, Bowie performs as an object to be gazed upon. From the outset of the video, his sexually ambiguous gestural performance is fused with proto-punk posturing. Complete with spiky orange hair, black leather jacket, and staunch bodily pose, he steps into a singular shaft of blue light with arms drooped and guitar slung across his back.

What makes Bowie's entrance even more effective is that the preceding guitar riff establishes the expectation that we may see an R&B musician playing guitar in sync to the sound, as was conventional in promotional clips of the time. Rather than playing guitar as might be expected, Bowie uses the guitar merely as an attitudinal prop to reinforce his staunch pose, thus subverting the conventions of R&B music videos. This proto-punk attitude is also mirrored by the gritty sound of Mick Ronson's and Trevor Bolder's guitars. While Bowie and the Spiders provided the raw ingredients for this audio-visual tonal convergence, it was Rock's special connection with Bowie that enabled him to draw out the visual attitude, which appears as a fusion of UK and American counterculture codes. Such a fusion may have been gleaned from UK bands such as The Who and The Kinks, American bands such as The Velvet Underground and The Stooges, and Kenneth Anger's film *Scorpio Rising* (1963).[49]

As with his other videos, Rock employs the camera to accentuate a sense of theatricality, which plays out amidst a sparse *mise-en-scène*. This dramatic effect is largely achieved by using low-key, minimalist stage lighting, which obscures the background clutter of the busy Rainbow Theatre. The primary light source appears from the side, with some secondary backlighting, achieving a mysterious but flattering rim-light which clings to the contours of Bowie's figure, facial features and spiky mullet. Heightening the salience of his orange hair, low-key lighting provides a complementary colour scheme of blue, pink, orange and green light filters. This dramatic lighting design casts Ziggy as a sexually ambiguous enigma lingering in the shadows – an image consistent with Bowie's tabloid sexuality.

According to Rock, it was his capacity to see through his 'third eye' that attuned him to the dramatic interplay between Bowie, the Spiders, and the other 'characters' in the video – the coloured shafts of light. Edited to the rhythm of the song, these 'characters' form a visual interplay that alternates between full body shots of Bowie standing in a singular shaft of light, medium-close-ups with

---

[49] *Scorpio Rising*, directed by Kenneth Anger (1963, New York: Puck Film Productions).

Bowie in the foreground and the rim-lit Spiders in the background, close-ups of Bowie that accentuate his eye-acting, wide shots of writhing dancers, and lone shots of each of the Spiders playing their instruments. Although the dancers were shot on another day under different lighting conditions, this cross-cutting method creates the spatial illusion that they were in the same room with the band. Midway through the video, disorienting jump-cuts rupture the illusion of spatial continuity by violating the 180-degree editing rule. Unexpected shots of Bowie *not* lip syncing also breach verisimilitude, puncturing the suspension of disbelief established by continuity editing. With the sudden subversion of this convention, Bowie performs open-mouthed bewilderment as we hear his voice continue to sing 'she turns me on' without a visual sync. This audio-visual dissonance and breach of music video conventions works in conjunction with the rebellious attitude imparted by Bowie's gestural performance, all of which contributed to the video's impact as an act of cultural subversion.

'John, I'm Only Dancing' introduces Bowie's Ziggy persona as rebelliously *risqué*, staunch yet sexually alluring, masculine yet feminine, gritty yet glam and proto-punk yet with overtones of R&B, folk and metal. Armed with this ambiguous blurring of cultural codes, Bowie and Rock consciously play into the controversy that erupted only seven months earlier, when Bowie strategically declared himself as gay.[50] The video was not aired in the USA, and the BBC's *Top of the Pops* chose instead to accompany the song with alternative visual material,[51] acts of hyper-censorship that fuelled the enigma around both the video and Bowie's sexuality. For those who might view music video primarily as a marketing tool for economic success, it may seem unwise to have produced such an iconoclastic video at this time, knowing the content would be deemed too *risqué* for a broadcast audience. However, as Bowie reflected upon his collaboration with Rock during the early 1970s, he explains how he and Rock shared a prescient sense of the non-commercial value of music video:

> Although MTV and its kind did not yet exist, and there were few outlets for showcasing rock video, Rock and I had long decided that to film certain songs was an excellent way of broadcasting and making indelible and concrete representations of the attitude implied by them.[52]

---

[50] Michael Watts, 'Oh! You Pretty Thing', *Melody Maker*, 22 January 1972, quoted in 'Bowie: "I'm gay and always have been"', *The Bowie Bible*, 27 August 2018, https://tinyurl.com/bd4jh8h5.
[51] '"John, I'm Only Dancing" by David Bowie – Promo Video'.
[52] Bowie, *Moonage Daydream*, 152.

In this sense, 'John, I'm Only Dancing' is a pertinent example of the value that Bowie and Rock foresaw in music video. Despite not reaching a broad audience upon its initial release, this video survived as a record of a crucial moment in Bowie's emergent career – one in which he was taking control of both camera and gaze, becoming Ziggy, and using sexual ambiguity to cultivate enigma. The video, and its attitude, signpost a juncture of cultural change and emerging subcultural rebellion in London and other parts of the UK during the early 1970s. The video's nascent proto-punk aesthetic took inspiration from earlier expressions of cultural rebellion, but it also provided inspirational material for the development of the punk movement that reached fruition only a few years later. Bowie is cited as influencing several key figures of this movement, including Poly Styrene, Sid Vicious, Johnny Rotten, Vivienne Westwood, Malcolm McLaren and the Sex Pistols.[53]

Having played an influential countercultural role during the seventies, 'John, I'm Only Dancing' continues to inspire new cultural forms. In 2019, Bowie fan and YouTube re-editor Nacho, created a re-authored video using previously unseen outtakes culled from Rock's master reel footage for 'John I'm Only Dancing'.[54] Nacho's edit is notable for the absence of the green-lit, fishnet-clad dancers. Devoid of these cut-away shots, Nacho gives much more screen time to Bowie and his band members, the Spiders. His video also includes significant moments of rhythmic editing and audio-visual correlation.[55] While Nacho's video presents us with an example of re-authoring, it might also be considered a form of collaborative authorship – that is, Rock directed the performance and shot the footage that Nacho later edited. This was not collaboration in the sense of knowingly working together as Nacho and Rock never met or communicated with one another, but the final product is the result of creative decisions made by Rock, Bowie and eventually Nacho, with footage and ideas provided by Nacho's video editor colleagues. In this sense, there is an element of collaboration in the creative process, even if it is unsolicited – and although two of the authors are no longer alive to share that sense of collaborative authorship. Rock and Bowie may have been interested to see that the final shot of Nacho's video revealed a long-forgotten piece of footage that perfectly expresses the proto-punk attitude and subversive humour that they shared (Figure 3.2).

---

[53] Jason Heller, 'David Bowie Gave the Punk Movement Both Fuel and Fire', 27 January 2016, *AV Club*, https://tinyurl.com/4cbvek5j.

[54] Nacho Video, 'David Bowie | John, I'm Only Dancing | Promo | Unreleased Mick Rock Outtake Footage Re-edit | 1972', YouTube video, 00:02:43, 5 March 2017, https://youtu.be/adhFZr6VDes.

[55] For more on this, see Perrott, *David Bowie and the Transformation of Music Video*.

Figure 3.2 Bowie expresses proto-punk attitude in this out-take shot. 'John, I'm Only Dancing' (Mick Rock, 1972; Re-edited by Nacho, 2017).

"The Jean Genie" – the song

Having collaborated with Bowie in London to create an indelible record of early 1970s attitude, Rock's next step was to relocate the proto-punk aesthetic and meld it with the playful antics of an Americana street-rebel oozing with sexual liberation. Rock would again strive to create a visual analogue to the sonic attitude imparted by "The Jean Genie". Drawing inspiration from American rock and blues, this song documented a fundamental cultural and psychic shift for Bowie – a shift brought about by Ziggy and the Spiders' 1972 tour of the United States. It was during the first three weeks of this tour that the musical baseline for the song was conceived 'somewhere between . . . Memphis and New York',[56] in the back of a tour bus and in hotel rooms. With minimal time for rehearsal, the song was recorded at RCA's New York studio on 6 October, mixed a month later in Nashville, and then released as a single on 24 November 1972.[57]

[56] O'Leary, 'The Jean Genie'.
[57] David Bowie, 'The Jean Genie,' released as a single by RCA on 24 November 1972, and then later on the album *Aladdin Sane* (1973).

As with many Bowie songs, "The Jean Genie's" lyrics are visually evocative and literally perplexing. 'Small Jean Genie' is a gnomic character who sneaks around 'spaced out on lasers and slashed-back blazers',[58] much like the twisted antics of "The Laughing Gnome" (1967). Even more disturbing than this chortling bed-fellow, the 'poor little Greenie' eats all the razors and 'keeps all your dead hair, for making up underwear'.[59] Exemplifying the seriality of character-based song writing, these lyrics also demonstrate the workings of a surrealist songwriter, one who uses absurdist humour to tweak the imagination. One imagines a cosmic genie character sleeping in a space capsule by day and prowling around the city streets by night, collecting human hair and knitting it up into underwear. Providing some clarity as to the genesis of this mischievous character, O'Leary explains:

> Many have called "Jean Genie" a portrait of Iggy Pop as an authentic American Primitive, though Bowie told an interviewer in 2000 that the song's more about 'an Iggy-type character ... a white-trash, kind of trailer-park kid thing – the closet intellectual who wouldn't want the world to know that he reads'.
>
> He's also claimed that the obvious pun on Jean Genet wasn't intended, blaming his subconscious.[60]

A couple of years later, Bowie confirmed that the title was 'of course, a clumsy pun upon Jean Genet, Lindsay Kemp's favourite playwright', and that 'its central character was based on an Iggy-type persona'.[61] He added that the song 'started out as a lightweight riff thing I had written one evening in NY for Cyrinda's enjoyment', and that he'd 'developed the lyric to the otherwise wordless pumper and it ultimately turned into a bit of a smorgasbord of imagined Americana'.[62] Effectively Bowie's version of American 'swamp blues', the song is a slightly modified version of a standard blues riff with an increased tempo and some additional notes. One possibility is that the blues riff was ripped from Bo Diddley's song 'I'm a Man'. Both songs feature a harmonica and a maraca or tambourine-like rhythm accompaniment. O'Leary observes how '"Jean Genie" is fused from pieces of older rock and roll records, from the "I'm a Man" riff to the Mod harmonica'.[63] Of the rattlesnake harmonica sound that appears toward the

---

[58] Ibid.
[59] Ibid.
[60] O'Leary, 'The Jean Genie'.
[61] Bowie, *Moonage Daydream*, 146.
[62] Ibid.
[63] O'Leary, 'The Jean Genie'.

end of the song, Bowie acknowledged that he 'wanted to get the same sound the Stones had on their very first album'.[64] He added that despite not getting as close as he wanted to that sound, 'it had a feel that I wanted – that sixties thing'.[65] The next challenge for Bowie and Rock was to create that 'sixties feel' and 'imagined Americana' in the form of a video.

'The Jean Genie' – the video

With the intention of promoting the single in the US and in the UK, the video for 'The Jean Genie' was quickly conceived and shot in San Francisco on 27 October 1972, just in time for the song's release the following month.[66] Although 'reaching no higher than number 71' in the US charts, the song rose to number 2 in Britain.[67] This is despite the video being designed as a strategic move to grab the attention of the US audience. Aiming to 'locate Ziggy as a kind of Hollywood street-rat',[68] Bowie found a suitably gritty street location and cast model Cyrinda Foxe as a Marylin Monroe-esque playmate for Ziggy (both in the video, and in real life). Foxe's flirtatious characterization is perfectly paired with Bowie's James Dean-style charisma, another strategy for achieving Bowie's aim for the video – to transport Ziggy into American popular culture. When Rock was reviewing the location shots and studio footage he'd shot the previous day, he decided that more material was needed, but he had already used the entire budget of US $350. He recalled:

> Somehow I got more dollars off Defries to rent an Arriflex camera – a silent one – and I shot all the live stuff myself the next night, because David did two nights at the Winterland. So, I filmed him singing the Jean Genie that night, processed overnight and, because there was no time, edited in one ten-hour rush. I had to chop it up a lot to keep everything in sync with his live performance.[69]

Rock stitched together pieces of the concert footage he had shot at Winterland with the outdoor street shots and studio footage of Ziggy and the Spiders.[70] In

---

[64] David Bowie, quoted in Pegg, *The Complete David Bowie*, 139.
[65] Ibid.
[66] Ibid., 140.
[67] Ibid.
[68] Bowie, *Moonage Daydream*, 140.
[69] Mick Rock, 'David Bowie | The Jean Genie | Live in California | October 1972', by Nacho Video, YouTube video, 00:04:01, 20 October 2022, https://youtu.be/5X8PwHaGIYU.
[70] Ibid.

contrast to the low-key lighting of 'John, I'm Only Dancing', the long shots of the band posing and performing in the studio are illuminated with high-key lighting and shot against a minimalist white background. Rock intercut these sequences with shots of Foxe dancing playfully in the street along with his signature shots – extreme close-ups of Bowie's eyes and facial features. As we shall see, this distinctive characteristic of Rock's lens art was to become a salient and recurring feature across Bowie's subsequent videos.[71] Rock's rough shot-list for the studio session includes the notes: 'Cyrinda doing her Marylin bit – CU's of David – eyes – lips, hair, hands. Band performing songs. BCU of mouth singing, winking eyes. David doing his mime actions to the words.'[72] These actions include Bowie framing his eyes with his hands to form a picture frame, and a mask-like eye-framing gesture, which he often performed on stage and later described as the 'Ziggy-finger-mask' (Figures 3.3 and 3.4).[73]

Figure 3.3 Bowie frames his eyes with his hands. 'The Jean Genie' (Mick Rock, 1972).

---

[71] See, for instance, 'Space Oddity' (1972), 'Life on Mars?' (1973), 'Heroes' (1977), 'Space Oddity' (1979) and 'Valentine's Day' (2013).
[72] Rock (shot list notes for 'The Jean Genie'), *Moonage Daydream*, 148.
[73] Bowie, *Moonage Daydream*, 126, 159.

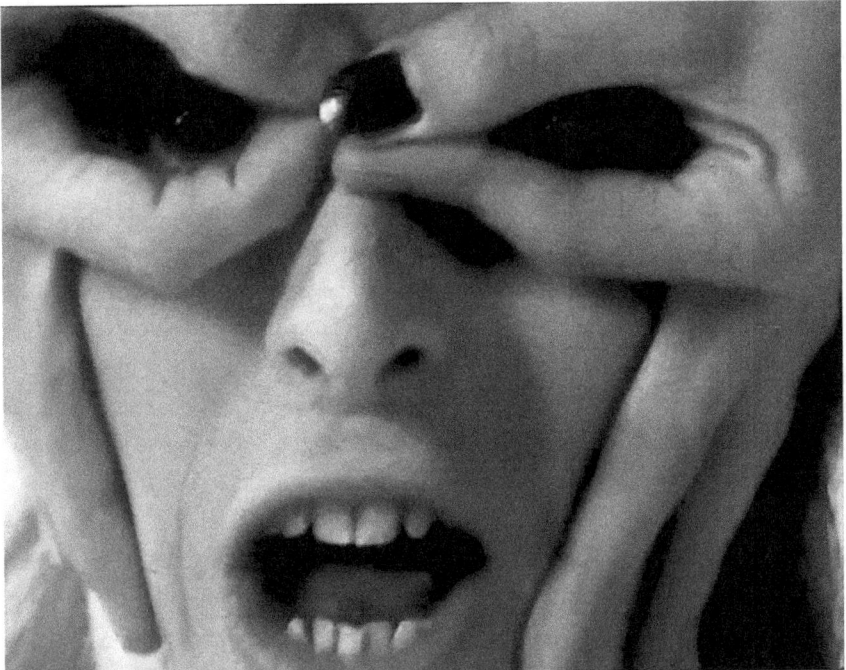

Figure 3.4 Bowie performs the 'Ziggy-finger-mask'. 'The Jean Genie' (Mick Rock, 1972).

Having shot a variety of different types of footage for this promo, Rock's editing strategy was to create an attitude of playful rebellion through constant movement. This frenetic movement is also accentuated by the way in which shots from multiple locations are cut to the beat of the song. *Cinéma vérité* style concert footage is intercut with stylized studio shots that jump 'to-and-fro between full face and CU of mouth', with Bowie's eyes directly working the camera.[74] The contrasting high and low keys of stage and studio lighting create drama across the intercut sequence of shots, which are punctuated with naturally lit external street shots that situate the video in time and space. With sharp wit, Rock wrote in his rough shot-list notes, 'Cosmic degenerate Bowie leaning on street corner – watching Cyrinda as she walks past'.[75] Ironically, what actually happens is a reversal of the plan for Bowie to be 'degenerately' enacting the male gaze, since he becomes the object of the gaze. Cyrinda tries to attract Bowie's attention as she dances provocatively on a gritty street corner, while Bowie poses in the foreground, dragging on a cigarette and

[74] Rock, *Moonage Daydream*, 148.
[75] Ibid., 157.

acting too cool to notice. In the next shot, the Mars Hotel sign is prominent within the frame, a subtle reference to the 'cosmic rocker' enigma that Rock intended for Bowie, and a prescient signpost to the 'Life on Mars?' video that Rock wanted to direct.[76] As though posing for a fashion shoot for American rocker jackets, Bowie leans against the external wall of the Mars Hotel with thumbs in pockets, wearing the very same 'James Deanish jacket' he'd worn for 'John, I'm Only Dancing'.[77] Bowie said he'd arranged for the jacket to be sent from London especially for this shoot, ,as it was 'perfect for the "American" Ziggy's video'.[78] As a loaded signifier linking the two videos, this jacket connotes different flavours of cultural rebellion, depending on how it is situated in relation to other cultural codes and how it is worn. In 'The Jean Genie', the jacket is unzipped to expose much more of Bowie's chest than was visible in the earlier video. The combination of punk-rock metal choker and masculine thumbs-in-pockets pose imparts a flavour of heterosexual masculinity, as opposed to the sexual ambiguity suggested by the synthesis of gender codes in 'John I'm Only Dancing'. These elements of costume and pose go some way to melding the proto-punk attitude of the former video with the rebellious Americana attitude that characterises 'The Jean Genie'. This strategic repackaging of Ziggy – first for a British audience and then for the American market – seems to have been successful. 'The Jean Genie' has been credited for broadening Bowie's base, particularly in America, and amongst the working class in the UK.[79]

The song benefited from bolstered promotion due to a televised studio performance broadcast on *Top of the Pops* in January 1973. Although the performance had been recorded, the tape was subsequently wiped, which was at that time a standard procedure for re-using tape. So, the video hadn't been seen until it was rediscovered and broadcast by the BBC on 21 December 2011. The finding of the tape was announced on the *Top of the Pops* Christmas special, along with the following caption:

> Former BBC cameraman John Henshall recently discovered this lost footage amongst his own collection of master tapes. As the operator of the fish-eye lens camera used in this footage, Henshall had made his own copy ... lucky as the BBC wiped the original tape! From January 1973, a spine-tingling *TOTP* treat of Bowie in his pomp playing live.[80]

---

[76] Ibid., 161.
[77] Ibid., 140, 160.
[78] Bowie, *Moonage Daydream*, 140.
[79] O'Leary, 'The Jean Genie'.
[80] GrabMore, 'David Bowie's Lost 1973 Top of the Pops Performance of The Jean Genie', YouTube video, 00:04:35, 22 December 2011, https://youtu.be/yEmGQYCuc6M.

Apart from the obvious excitement about the discovery of such long-lost footage, the video is notable for the brightly colourized pop art effect that complements Bowie's energized harmonica playing, and for Henshall's use of the fish-eye lens, which was viewed as an innovative broadcast effect in 1973. While these effects must have appeared magical to the 1973 audience, only a few weeks before this televised performance, Bowie had been sitting in an American 'space shuttle' of sorts – making magic with Rock.

"Space Oddity" (1972) – the video

As demonstrated by the previous two videos, Bowie and Rock shared an understanding of music video's capacity to communicate a song's attitude to a broad audience. Although slower to recognize this, recording company strategists were impressed by the impact of 'The Jean Genie', an early indication that music video was a form that could increase Bowie's cross-continental popularity and thus provide a revenue stream. Buoyed by the US re-release of *Space Oddity* and *The Man Who Sold the World*, RCA considered it timely to fund a new music video to promote the upcoming re-released single for "Space Oddity".[81] RCA were astonished by the monetary cost of Ziggy's American tour and were quick to see the potential cost benefits of shooting a minimalistic video set in a recording studio. Such a video would not only be cheap to produce, it could be screened on cable television networks, reducing the need for expensive tours. Despite smelling the prospect of financial success, RCA were not forthcoming with funding for this promo. As it transpired, these budgetary limitations may have ignited Rock's capacity for creating beautiful work on the smell of an oily rag. As it turned out, all he needed was the use of RCA's recording studio for two days, along with Bowie's performance to camera. When reflecting on this 1972 promo shoot in 2002, Bowie recalls his lack of enthusiasm for this RCA-inspired project:

> Rock pretty much just set his camera up, popped on a couple of really red lights and shot away as I sang. I only had a few hours for him as I hadn't yet finished packing the huge trunk that accompanied me on my nautical travels. I really hadn't much clue why we were doing this, as I had moved on in my mind from

---

[81] '"Space Oddity": 10 December 1972', *The Ziggy Stardust Companion*, 6 January 2019, https://tinyurl.com/2bdtreba.

the song, but I suppose the record company were re-releasing it again or something like that. Anyway, I know I was disinterested in the proceedings and it shows in my performance. Mick's video is good, though.[82]

Bowie's self-observation was right. Despite being exhausted after his whirlwind tour of the states, he was excited by the new culture and music he had been exposed to, along with the songs he'd been writing in response to this. Having moved on from the song, he was weary about plans emerging from the recording company, but as it turned out, Bowie's less energized performance and moody aura may have been just what his fans needed to see at this point. Rock managed to 'bottle' his aura right at the moment when his guard was down, thereby generating 'flickers of authenticity' that cut through layers of artifice.[83] Jane Roscoe first developed this idea to describe a moment in reality TV shows, in which participants unexpectedly let down their guard to show rare moments of emotional authenticity.[84] This momentary 'flicker' breaks with their coded performance, which often involves acting as though they are unaware of the 'camera's presence'. In this sense, 'flickers of authenticity' are moments in which 'the mask of performance falls away from the Reality TV contestant/participant'. Recalling Benjamin's writing about photography's 'spark of contingency', Barthes' notion of the 'punctum' and Brecht's 'alienation effect', these 'flickers' can be used as strategies of performative defamiliarization by actors and directors of both stage and screen.[85] While Bowie and Rock used such strategies in subsequent videos, in 'Space Oddity' (1972), Bowie's 'flickers of authenticity' have an inverse, de-alienating affect.

This glimpse into Bowie's internal state of malaise may not have been Rock's intention, but he had a vision for the promo and it served a purpose that Bowie was unable to see at the time of shooting. The promo was filmed in five hours in RCA's New York recording studio on 10 December 1972, just hours before Bowie sailed back to England. As Rock recalls, 'The next day I went back to film the oscilloscope and other studio equipment. I viewed the studio as Major Tom's "tin can"'.[86] This vision of the recording studio as a metaphor for Major Tom's space capsule became actualized as an enduring image of a musical astronaut. Devoid

---

[82] Bowie, *Moonage Daydream*, 179.
[83] Jane Roscoe, 'Real Entertainment: Real factual Hybrid Television', *Media International Australia*, 100 (2001): 9–20.
[84] Ibid.
[85] Derek Paget and Jane Roscoe, 'Giving Voice: Performance and Authenticity in the Documentary Musical', *Jump Cut: A Review of Contemporary Media* 48 (2006), https://tinyurl.com/nhfycu5b.
[86] Rock, *Moonage Daydream*, 177.

of eyebrows, Bowie certainly looks the part: wearing a tight metallic top with shoulder embellishments, his angular cheekbones and spikey orange hair are set alight by the low-key red glow omitted from the side light. This combination of moody atmosphere, no-budget spontaneity and the tin-can metaphor proved to be a brilliant antidote to the overly literal visual interpretation and low production values of Thomson's 1969 'Space Oddity' promo. The recording studio as space capsule is imaginatively alluded to by the oscilloscope imagery, which visually interprets the instrumental intensity and sonic space of this second recording of the song. This visual interpretation of sonic elements is also manifested by the layering of film footage, thus producing a visual duality that is analogous to the vocal harmonies (Figure 3.5).

Unlike his earlier videos, Bowie is seated and his body language betrays his end-of-tour exhaustion. Seeing him run his fingers through his hair and lower his forehead into his hand, one can't help but feel empathy for his obvious state of psychic fatigue (Figure 3.6). He manages a few other well-placed gestures, such as pointing toward the camera, a familiar trope of Bowie's performance to

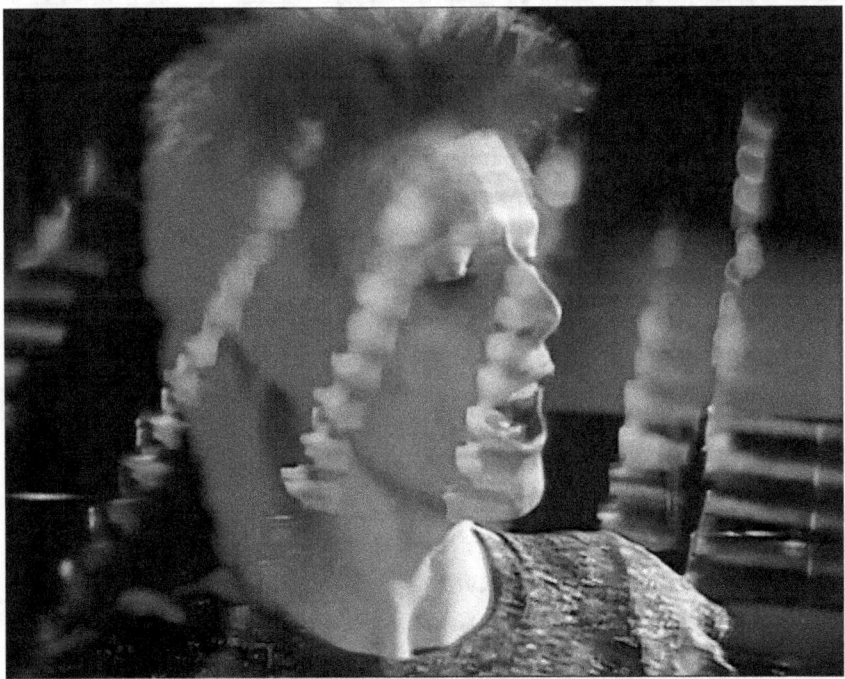

Figure 3.5 The visual interpretation of sonic elements is manifested by the layering of film footage. 'Space Oddity' (Mick Rock, 1972).

Figure 3.6 Bowie's body language betrays his exhaustion. 'Space Oddity' (Mick Rock, 1972).

camera, but his point towards space at the moment of 'lift off' reveals a feeling of lack-lustre. Despite this low energy performance, Rock energizes the promo by shooting Bowie in a way that draws out the intensity of his optical connection with the camera. While Rock's extreme close-ups highlight the alien-like quality of Bowie's mismatched eyes, they also exploit his newfound ability to connect with his audience by gazing intensely into the camera lens. While an established feature of the earlier two promos, in this video, Bowie's direct address to camera appears more authentic, perhaps due to the unplanned, slightly haphazard feel of the filming process. His look into the lens is sustained for longer than a comfortable eye-to-eye connection (Figure 3.7); to reinforce this sense of slight discomfort, Rock lets the shot linger, long enough for Bowie to look away for a moment, then look back into the camera again. This alternation between direct and indirect address may have been unplanned, but this is one of the first videos in which we see Bowie beginning to control the gaze by alternating between performing as an object to be looked at and a subject looking directly at his

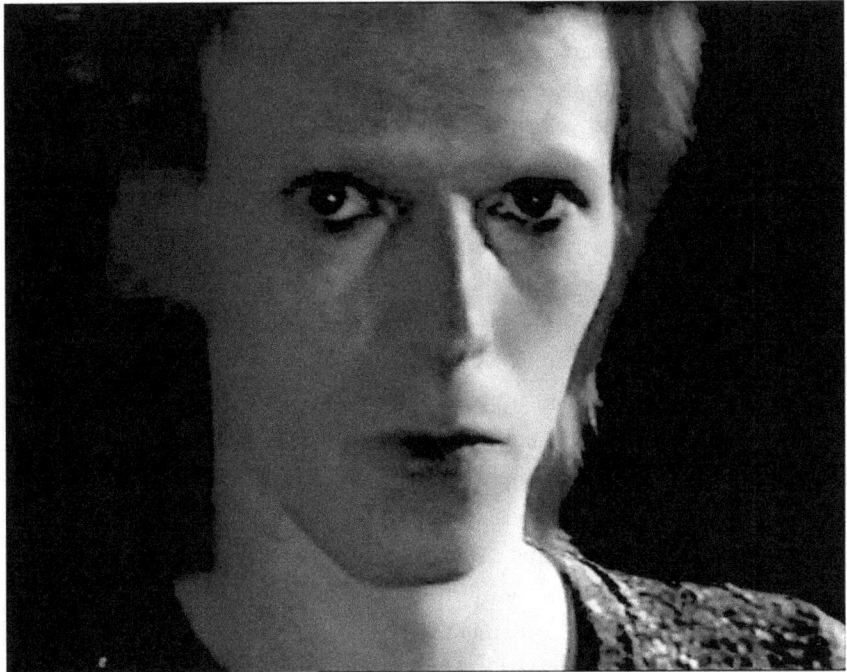

Figure 3.7 Bowie's direct address to camera portrays authenticity. 'Space Oddity' (Mick Rock, 1972).

audience. In this way, Bowie was taking an important step towards managing his connection with the audience in future music videos.

Other strategies Bowie used to take control of the gaze include the careful management of movement, stasis and 'frontality' for the camera. James Naremore describes 'frontality' in terms of the film actors' practice of maintaining an acute awareness of the spatial parameters within which they can extend their performance. He explains that 'Movie actors therefore learn to control and modulate behavior to fit a variety of situations, suiting their actions to a medium that might view them at any distance, height or angle and that sometimes changes the vantage point within a single shot.[87] In other words, this spatial awareness is necessary to remain within the borders of the cinematic frame. It is also a valuable tool for an actor who wishes to command object salience within the shot. Bowie and Rock's collaboration enabled a form of artistic empathy that will

---

[87] James Naremore, *Acting in the Cinema*. Berkeley: University of California Press, 1988, 41; David Bordwell, Janet Steiger and Kristin Thompson, 'The Classical Hollywood Cinema – Cap 5', *Leyendocine*, 1 May 2007, https://tinyurl.com/2nm6krzd.

have undoubtedly enhanced both artist's understanding of these strategies for performing for the camera, framing the performance and controlling the gaze. As we shall see, these strategies flowed through to subsequent videos, such as 'Heroes' (1977), 'Space Oddity' (1979), 'Wild is the Wind' (1981) and 'Valentine's Day' (2013). Positioning Bowie as the static central feature of an otherwise frenetic video establishes object salience and imbues him with gravitas. However, in 1972, when Bowie performed for the 'Space Oddity' video, he was apparently too exhausted to move from his chair, let alone employ acting strategies such as 'frontality'. It is Rock who can be credited for making a feature of Bowie's lacklustre stillness and complementing this with a constant sense of movement. Frenetic energy is produced by frequent cutting between alternately framed shots of Bowie and the hand-held camera exploring the studio, some of which is sped up. A sense of movement is also created by the camera's 360-degree arc shot of Bowie's head,[88] and by the lens as it pulls focus and rapidly zooms in and out in sync with the song's rapid chord changes and hand-claps. The tin-can metaphor is reinforced by the roaming shots of recording knobs, dials, controllers, screens and other technical equipment. This replicates the sense of weightlessness associated with floating inside a space capsule. The lighting, framing, camera movement and editing create a visual interpretation of the song's atmospheric quality, including its spatial and vocal duality.

Just as Rock's first two promos are memorable for visually creating the attitude conveyed by the songs, this is equally true for 'Space Oddity' (1972). Rebellion gives way to ennui, an attitude that imbues the song with new meaning and points towards the 1979 acoustic recording of "Space Oddity" and its ongoing storyworld development. Bowie's lack-lustre performance turned out to be an ideal expression of Major Tom's ennui – 'planet Earth is blue and there's nothing I can do'.[89]

"Life on Mars?" – the song

Despite having retired Ziggy during the six months between shooting 'Space Oddity' and 'Life on Mars?' there is continuity between the two videos. Apart

---

[88] An 'arc shot' is where the camera orbits around a usually static subject in an arc pattern, often using a dolly or Steadicam. For more about this, see Kyle Deguzman, 'The Arc Shot – Examples and Camera Movements Explained', *Studio Binder*, 23 May 2021, https://tinyurl.com/5a4rfs4n.
[89] David Bowie, 'Space Oddity' (1969).

from the continuity of the orange mullet and the androgynous mannerisms, the melancholic lyrics of both songs allude to a cosmic storyworld. Both songs were recorded at least two years before the videos were made and both can be traced to a prehistory littered with inspirations drawn from other artists. If you listen very carefully to "Life on Mars?" you might hear the remnants of the chord structure for "My Way". Though Sinatra can be credited for popularizing this song in 1969 (with lyrics adapted by Paul Anka), its musical elements derive from the French song "Comme d'habitude", composed in 1967 by Jacques Revaux, with lyrics by Claude François and Gilles Thibaut.[90] While Bowie retained a semblance of the initial chord structure, he employed aleatory methods to transform this 'borrowed' structure into his own song, trademarked by his visually poetic lyrics and emotionally-charged melody. As a result, traces of "My Way" are barely audible in this transformed song structure. Perhaps subliminally, we can hear the trace of those familiar chords from a song that became overused to the point of cliché. Although the chord structure for "My Way" and "Comme d'habitude" provided the transformative impulse for Bowie to create a new song, these barely perceptible origins are outshone by the compositional experimentation and enigmatic lyrics that distinguish "Life on Mars?" as a distinctively "Bowie" song. Just as "My Way" became synonymous with Sinatra, "Life on Mars?" is considered by many to be one of Bowie's signature songs. Bowie did "My Way" *his* way, and according to his recollection, it was as easy as a walk in the park:

> This song was so easy. Being young was easy. A really beautiful day in the park, sitting on the steps of the bandstand. 'Sailors bap-bap-bap-bap-baaa-bap.' An anomic (not a 'gnomic') heroine. Middle-class ecstasy. I took a walk to Beckenham High Street to catch a bus to Lewisham to buy shoes and shirts but couldn't get the riff out of my head. Jumped off two stops into the ride and more or less loped back to the house up on Southend Road.... I started working it out on the piano and had the whole lyric and melody finished by late afternoon. Nice.[91]

Having given up on his shopping expedition to get a riff out of his head, Bowie concluded his beautiful day with skeleton lyrics to a song that would eventually receive numerous plaudits, covers and tributes.[92] Much has been written about the lyrics to "Life on Mars?" particularly their capacity for conjuring visual images

---

[90] 'Comme d'habitude' (1967) composed by Jacques Revaux, with lyrics by Claude François and Gilles Thibaut. For more on this, see https://tinyurl.com/3aruaxxc *and* https://tinyurl.com/3daxx9tz.
[91] David Bowie, 'Life on Mars? Yesterday and Tomorrow', *DavidBowie.com*, 22 June 2014, https://tinyurl.com/5n8astap.
[92] Pegg, *The Complete David Bowie*, 163–4.

and emotional responses. Playing on the words '*mousy* hair' and '*mice* in their million hordes', the surreal lyric 'Mickey *Mouse* has grown up a cow' engenders an absurd cartoon image, possibly implying a subversive dig at American popular culture. At the other end of the emotional spectrum, 'she walks through her sunken dream' evokes sadness for the song's protagonist. Drawn into the song by the plight of this 'anomic heroine',[93] it's easy to feel empathy for (if not allegiance with) this teenage girl and her sense of tedium and isolation amidst a world of conservative adults and unreliable friends. The visceral phrase 'she could spit in the eyes of fools' triggers sensory empathy by alluding to body organs and fluids. Bowie's lyrics capture a sense of teenage dejection and angst – the yearning for transcendence that seems possible when you have the youthful levity to be transported by the flickering cinema screen to a magical world. Not only do the lyrics paint colourful images, they transport us to a place – 'to the seat with the clearest view' – and immerse us in a setting and a situation, where 'she's hooked to the silver screen'. The lyrics also tap into our cultural memories and screen histories to recall shared moments in time or mediatized images of 'sailors fighting in the dancehall' and of a 'lawman, beating up the wrong guy'. While skilfully composed, the word arrangement is often analogical, including esoteric references ('my mother, my dog and clowns') and semantic ambiguity (is it Lenin, or Lennon 'on sale again'?). Just as the lyrics do a masterful job of conjuring visual imagery, the sonic arrangements bring these words to life. O'Leary's analysis of the song explains how the lyrics are propelled by the sonic elements:

> The song becomes the screen, its pre-chorus is an extended trailer – soaring strings, thunderous piano, ascending chords – for the refrain, one of the most shameless, gorgeous melodies he ever wrote . . . the song also captures a teenager's ability to suddenly and completely lose themselves in art, to a degree we can never quite do again. It's what happens in the song as well. Bowie constructs an 8-bar bridge designed to build anticipation in the listener – the strings, the pounding piano, the rising chords in each new bar – and then makes good on his promise: the chorus, with Bowie vaulting nearly an octave to a high B-flat and ending with another high Bb, held for a brief eternity.[94]

O'Leary is not alone in interpreting "Life on Mars?" as a lyrical and musical masterpiece, and as one of Bowie's most epic songs. Describing the song as 'an elegant coming-together of found images, and one of Bowie's great pieces of

---

[93] Ibid.
[94] O'Leary, 'Life on Mars?' *Pushing Ahead of the Dame*, 23 March 2010, https://tinyurl.com/5ffajsds.

bricolage.'⁹⁵ Pegg reminds us that the song is a great example of collaboration between Bowie and virtuoso musicians Rick Wakeman and Mick Ronson:

> The finished lyric, and David's performance of it, are among his finest ever, while Wakeman's virtuosity and Ronson's operatic arrangement help to elevate a great piece of songwriting to classic status, from the plaintive opening piano chord to the climactic *Also Sprach Zarathustra* timpani roll at the beautiful false ending.⁹⁶

So, the song must be understood as a collaborative work of art, with Wakeman credited for the piano composition and Ronson for the string arrangement. Woodmansey points out that for the final recording session, 'we had a whole string section at Trident with the proper BBC session players'.⁹⁷ This session was completed on 6 August 1971, just in time for the song to be released on the *Hunky Dory* album. Described as enigmatic, allusive and cinematic, the song has been considered a masterpiece with the power to conjure visual imagery. It is perhaps no wonder that it existed for two years without an accompanying video. Despite this, the 'Life on Mars?' video directed by Rock in 1973 now seems indelibly fused to the song.

'Life of Mars?' – the video

> It wasn't so much an idea as a moment in time. I wanted to do something a little bit like a painting.
>
> Mick Rock, 1998⁹⁸

If the song is considered to be a collaborative work of art, the video for 'Life on Mars?' could be understood as an audio-visual palimpsest, woven by multiple authors who collaborated to achieve something 'like a painting'. This stratified aspect of the promo's construction is complicated further by the existence of several re-edited versions. The following analysis is focused on the version edited by Mick Rock that is the most publicly available to view, since this is widely perceived as the 'official' version.⁹⁹ For the sake of comparison, I will briefly discuss the other versions at the end of this section.

---

⁹⁵ Pegg, *The Complete David Bowie*, 163.
⁹⁶ Ibid, 162.
⁹⁷ Ibid.
⁹⁸ Ibid., 163.
⁹⁹ David Bowie, 'David Bowie – Life on Mars? (Official Video)', YouTube video, 00:04:09, 10 July 2015, https://youtu.be/AZKcl4-tcuo.

'Life on Mars?' was filmed and directed by Rock on 13 June 1973, in time to accompany the single release nine days later. London's Blandford West Ten Studio provided the perfect conditions – essentially a blank white canvas – enabling Rock to apply cinematic brush strokes and high-key lighting, thus creating a minimalist aesthetic.[100] Illuminated with abundance, the foreground, midground and background appear as a two-dimensional image. There is no attempt to create the illusion of perspective or to sculpt Bowie as a three-dimensional object, as conventional cinematic lighting tends to do. With its high-key lighting and two-dimensional pop art aesthetic, 'Life on Mars?' feels like an inverse companion to the equally epic yet minimalist video for 'Heroes' (1977), with its low-key sculptural lighting. Accentuating the pictorial quality of 'Life on Mars?' the light exposure fluctuates throughout the video, with some shots exposed to emphasize texture and colour, and others so over-exposed that Bowie's whitened face blends into the background.

'Life on Mars?' stands apart from all other music videos for the way it imparts a sense of '*Shibui*', a Japanese term that describes the qualities of ethereal simplicity and tranquillity, which are imbued by works of art such as paintings, architecture, raku pottery and gardens.[101] This minimalist aesthetic is due to the simplicity of the video's *mise-en-scène*, as well as the film having been subjected to a bleaching process. The resulting blown-out look reinforces the idea of 'Bowie-as-alien' and enhances the unique ethereal quality that was already apparent in the raw footage. Manifesting Rock's desire to create a video 'like a painting', the white background serves as a canvas, upon which he has applied hues of orange, teal and red. The result is a haptic moving painting, resembling Japanese paintings of the Edo period known as *Ukiyo-e* (pictures of the floating world), which use minimalist aesthetics to depict a transient world in two dimensions. Bowie later said that 'Rock burnt the colours right out so that it had a strange, floaty pop-art effect'.[102] This pop-art effect is also achieved by limiting the colour palette and by using multi-directional light sources, thus reducing contours and flattening the image so as to appear two-dimensional. The white studio provides a canvas for the colours and textures of Bowie's hair, the vibrant *geisha*-like makeup applied by Pierre Laroche, and the exquisitely tailored ice-blue suit designed by Freddie Burretti.[103] This stylized look

---

[100] Rock, *Moonage Daydream*, 257.
[101] Johanna van Gogh, 'Shibui', *The Painters Keys*, 20 May 2008, https://painterskeys.com/shibui/.
[102] Pegg, *The Complete David Bowie*, 163.
[103] This suit became a transmedial fashion phenomenon that would develop a mimetic life of its own, escaping the bounds of music video and leaping onto catwalks, fashion magazines and even adorning the bodies of television newsreaders.

has become so iconic that, along with the fan art replicating this imagery in a pop art style (exemplified by my painting on the cover of this book), the ice-blue suit has also experienced a resurgence, being worn by model Kate Moss for the 2003 issue of British *Vogue*,[104] and by costume designer Sandy Powell as a statement of androgyny at the BAFTAs.[105] Also showing the potential of music video aesthetics to reverberate across time and mediums, in 2022 Mattel released a second female Bowie Barbie doll named 'Glam Rock in Blue', which replicates the costume, shoes, hairstyle and makeup worn in 'Life on Mars?'[106] Springing from an intermedial lineage stretching across music video, fan art and fashion, Bowie Barbie assures future generational continuity of this iconic look across five decades and multiple mediums. While it is interesting to track the way music video can be a vehicle for the transit of a signifying system made up of costume, hairstyle and makeup, it is also important to acknowledge the various artforms that lent inspiration to the look and feel of this video.

Mask, mime, gesture and gaze

Bowie's use of mask, mime and gesture eschews the authenticity expected of rock music and of music videos of the time. While these aspects of 'Life on Mars?' portray Bowie's ongoing fascination with *Commedia dell'arte*, they also signal his interest in Japanese performance modes. Gleaned from vastly different cultures and time periods, these inspirations merge with pop art aesthetics to create an otherworldly depiction of androgynous beauty. Although the mask painted by Laroche for this video recalls the Pierrot face paint worn in Bowie's 1969 film 'The Mask', it was largely inspired by the *kabuki* tradition of theatrical face painting. In fact, actual *kabuki* powder was used to create the white foundation that formed a base for Bowie's eye and lip paint. Recalling Laroche's artistic contribution to this video, Bowie said, 'when I brought all the *kabuki* powders back from Japan, he went crazy with them and for weeks my stage persona went all *geisha*'.[107] When framed in a series of extreme close-ups, this bleached-out mask of face paint and powder offers the audience an experience of 'haptic

---

[104] 'Shoot Footage: Bowie's Blue Suit', 19 February 2016, *Show Studio*, https://tinyurl.com/4nctdnj4.
[105] Olivia Lidbury, 'Sandy Powell's David Bowie homage was one the best looks at the Baftas', *The Telegraph*, 15 February 2016, https://tinyurl.com/yp7eb9j4.
[106] '"Glam Rock in Blue", David Bowie Barbie Doll 2', Mattel Creations, https://tinyurl.com/mr3xn7ex.
[107] Bowie, *Moonage Daydream*, 256.

visuality'. This concept is described by Laura Marks as a cinematic viewing experience where 'the eyes themselves function much like organs of touch'.[108] Marks describes 'haptic cinema' as a particular approach to filmmaking that 'encourages a bodily relationship between the viewer and the video image'.[109] This is achieved by employing techniques such as over-exposure and camera blur. Other strategies include emphasis on film grain, videotape degradation or digital pixels, extreme close-ups and projected imagery of intimate body parts or sensory organs such as the eyes, mouth, nose and ears. In 'Life on Mars?' haptic visuality is generated by the extreme close-ups of Bowie's vibrantly-coloured hair and facial features, which are offset by his powdered skin (Figure 3.8).

This haptic effect is even more apparent when viewing extracts of this video on a large cinema screen, as became possible with the 2022 release of Brett Morgen's film *Moonage Daydream*.[110] When watching 'Life on Mars?' on a large

Figure 3.8 Rock's close-framing lingers on Bowie's mismatched eyes. 'Life On Mars?' (Mick Rock, 1973).

[108] Laura Marks, 'Video Haptics and Erotics', *Screen* 39, no. 4 (1998): 332.
[109] Ibid.
[110] For more on this, see Perrott, '*Moonage Daydream*: Brilliant Bowie Film Takes Big Risks'.

screen, the sense of watching a moving painting is punctuated with moments of bodily gesture that remind us of Bowie's tuition in the art of mime. He uses his hands like a signer, almost as though he is attempting to help us understand the enigmatic lyrics. Singing 'Mickey Mouse has grown up a cow', Bowie mimes with his hands the notion of growing from small to tall (Figure 3.9). His fingers scuttle across the screen to signify 'mice in their million hordes' scurrying 'from Ibiza to the Norfolk Broads'.[111] Forming a delightfully light coda to such an epic song, Bowie mime-plays the (invisible) piano to Rick Wakeman's distant piano notes.

Bowie's attitudinal gestures are filmed and edited in a way that signposts pronounced sonic and lyrical moments. Visually reinforcing the intense sonic drop of the strings, Bowie turns dramatically from one camera to another, shooting a solemn stare at the audience. He closes his eyes while tossing his head back, this sharp gesture of indignation aptly conveying the attitude of wanting to 'spit in the eyes of fools' (Figure 3.10). This could be described as a kind of reverse

Figure 3.9 Bowie mimes 'Mickey Mouse has grown up a cow'. 'Life on Mars?' (Mick Rock, 1973).

[111] David Bowie, 'Life on Mars?' (1971).

Figure 3.10 Bowie gestures 'spit in the eyes of fools'. 'Life on Mars?' (Mick Rock, 1973).

'visual onomatopoeia', where the extreme close-up images of eyes and hair imitate their mention in the lyrics. This also occurs with the close tracking shot of Bowie's hair at the start of the video, which attaches visual texture and hue to the lyric 'the girl with the mousy hair'. This is ironic, since the hair we see is far from mousy, and the face is not that of a girl but of an androgynous-looking man. At one point, Bowie tips his head back with closed eyes and slightly open mouth, creating an image that might be associated with sexual satisfaction (Figure 3.11). Conjuring the attitude of this 'anomic' teenage girl, Bowie performs a flirtatious feminized leg kick to accompany the lyrics 'as she's lived it ten times or more'. Having drawn us in with his attitudinal gestures, Bowie then makes a direct and confronting connection with his audience by pointing upwards into the hovering camera lens (Figure 3.12).

As well as pointing towards the camera lens, Bowie was also mastering an even more effective way to connect with his audience via music video. Rock's close framing lingers on Bowie's mismatched eyes, which look directly into the camera as he sings. His intense look into the camera breaks the 'fourth wall' by meeting the gaze of his audience and drawing attention to the presence of the

Figure 3.11 Bowie performs a gesture of sexual satisfaction. 'Life on Mars?' (Mick Rock, 1973).

Figure 3.12 Bowie makes a direct connection with his audience. 'Life on Mars?' (Mick Rock, 1973).

camera (Figure 3.8).[112] Asserting an empathetic connection with his audience, Bowie maintains control over their gaze by occasionally lowering his eyelids and looking away. Adopting feminized gestures codified via Hollywood starlets and Orientalized *geisha* in Western cinema, Bowie performs as an exquisitely painted object to be gazed at – much like a painted porcelain doll. Bowie and Rock work together in their final video collaboration, both complicit in playing with the gendered codification of the cinematic gaze. Their awareness of this – from both ends of the lens – enabled them to master this act of representation, thus constructing Bowie as an ambiguously-gendered enigma. 'Life on Mars?' provides a pertinent example of Rock's capacity to respond artistically to Bowie's songs. Rock has responded to this epic song, not by presenting literal depictions of the lyrics, but by creating a moving painting that evokes simplicity and balance – a response that doesn't compete with the song's capacity to conjure its own imagery. In 2016, Rock reflected on the significance of 'Life on Mars?' as a minimalist work of art that stands apart from all other music videos

> I had an amazing subject and an amazing song – this was the song that had turned me on to David – so what else did I need? David never looked like this at any other time. He never wore that suit again, never had that makeup on again. He never looked more amazing – like a *space doll*. When his videos got inducted into the Museum of Modern Art in New York, this was the one that everyone stood for – there were no distractions, no dancing girls, just David.[113]

'Life on Mars?' – other versions

While I have focused my analysis on the 'official' version of the 'Life on Mars?' video (LOM2), several different versions of the video exist. Of the three versions shot and edited by Rock (LOM1, 1973; LOM2, 1973; LOM3, 2016),[114] the first of these versions was restored and re-released by Nacho Video (LOM4, 2021).[115]

The first video to be released with the single in June 1973 was the original 'unbleached' version (LOM1), which includes cut-aways of fans at a live

---

[112] For more on this, see Carmen Bonasera, 'Estrangement, Performativity, and Empathy in Bo Burnham's Inside (2021)', *Between*, 12, no. 23 (2022): 93–116.
[113] Michael Hann, 'Watch the Reworked Video for David Bowie's Life on Mars', *The Guardian*, 4 November 2016, https://tinyurl.com/zhjusdyp.
[114] Nick, 'David Bowie – Life on Mars? 2016 Mix Re-edit Mick Rock', *David Bowie News*, 4 November 2016, https://tinyurl.com/5fdbxkmj.
[115] Nick, 'David Bowie – Life on Mars? (Original Unedited Version, Remastered by Nacho)', *David Bowie News*, 17 December 2021, https://tinyurl.com/2p89ka5s.

performance. This version disappeared from public access and was at some point replaced with a re-edited, bleached version (LOM2),[116] in which the crowd scenes were removed and some of the detail and colour bleached out.[117] Both the bleaching process and the redaction of fan footage were enhancements, since they stripped away excess and thus contributed to the video's *Shibui*. However, fans who knew the original unbleached version existed wanted to see it. When Nacho was gifted a master tape of the original version (LMO1) plus outtakes, he restored the footage and recorded it to HD quality. He also synced it to a high-quality audio track, one that included the original unedited, unfaded longer ending. Outtakes from the 'Life on Mars?' video shoot were used to fill the additional running time.[118] Nacho's remastered video has had a revelatory impact for fans, since it includes previously unseen outtakes along with the accidental ending that had only existed on the original recording of the song.[119] In Nacho's video, the epic song concludes, only to be followed by Bowie gesturing disappointment and Ronson verbally cursing; both expressing frustration at the prospect that the recording had been ruined by the sound of the phone ringing in the back of the recording studio. Nacho's inclusion of these audio and visual outtakes reveals moments of spontaneity and humour, giving the video a *vérité* feel that was not present in the 1973 versions of 'Life on Mars?'

A few months after Bowie's death, Rock released a tributary version (LOM3), which was restored and re-edited with the inclusion of outtake footage.[120] When interviewed about this in 2016, Rock recalled that 'at the time' of the video's release in 1973, 'it was hardly seen at all, and it gathered some serious moss'.[121] He explained:

> In the late 90s, David gave me the copyrights for the four videos I had made for him, because I had never been paid for them – not that I had looked for any money. So, when Parlophone contacted me about re-editing it I said: absolutely. I had a little gem and I wanted to polish it into a state where it was absolutely perfect. I had the black and white segments, and when I came across that very last bit after the music stopped, I thought it was a little gift, so I made it into an epilogue. People like the original video, but I think this version takes it to another

---

[116] David Bowie, 'David Bowie – Life on Mars? (Official Video)'.
[117] Nick, 'David Bowie – Life on Mars? (Original Unedited Version, Remastered by Nacho)'.
[118] Ibid.
[119] For more on this, see Perrott, *David Bowie and the Transformation of Music Video*.
[120] Nick, 'David Bowie – Life on Mars? 2016 Mix Re-edit Mick Rock'.
[121] Rock, 'Watch the Reworked Video'.

level. The scenes really add a new flavour for it. I'm really happy with it, and I'm interested to see what the fans make of it.[122]

In comparison with the 'official' version, Rock's 2016 HD re-edit looks crisper and the colours are significantly more vibrant. With every frame having been 'polished', the shine of the makeup pops and the overall image has more depth. The constant shifting between colour and greyscale breaks the continuity of the video, having the effect of making the viewer more aware of how the colours characterize the video with a pop art aesthetic. The inclusion of outtakes reveals Bowie making mistakes in his performance, laughing and breaking out of performance mode (Figure 3.13). These additions add 'flickers of authenticity' that momentarily rupture the artifice of Bowie's performance, and of the video. The illusion that was achieved in LOM2 – of watching a perfectly-rendered moving painting – is broken, but this sense of broken virtuosity is replaced with revelation. As is the case with 'Space Oddity' (1972), Rock has broken the shell of

Figure 3.13 The outtakes reveal 'flickers of authenticity'. 'Life On Mars?' (Mick Rock, 1973; remastered by Nacho, 2021).

[122] Ibid.

artifice so that we may get to see the interior authenticity of Bowie. Beyond the alien artifice, we get to see a real human.

Denouement

As a photographer and director of music videos, Rock had a unique talent for composing within the frame and for playing with the illusion of depth. The sense of movement and stasis produced by the camera highlights Rock's artisanal capacity to create a moving painting while also positioning Bowie as the central figure of gravitas. Bowie is not simply being filmed as a static object; he is commanding the camera, interacting with, and performing to it.

As a sequence, Rock's four 'promos' demonstrate not only his capacity for engaging in collaborative acts of representation, but also his remarkable insight into Bowie as a performance artist, a musician and a philosopher. A close examination of the four videos reveals a direct connection and collaborative trust. When combined with commentary about their relationship, it becomes clear that their collaboration was founded on a meeting of minds and a special ability to 'see' each other. In this respect, Rock's notion of 'bottling auras' is instructive. His photographs and videos depict an interiority and integrity that works in tension with the artifice that is also prominently featured. Somehow, Rock managed to express the inverse of that artifice at the very same time. In doing so, he was able to capture the authenticity of Bowie's energy in response to the attitude of the music. Most of all, it is Rock who should be credited for putting Bowie at ease in front of the camera, and for helping him to master the art of performing for music video. In fact, Bowie was ready to take this to another level.

4

Painting the Truth

I'm using myself as a canvas and trying to paint the truth of our time on it.

Bowie, 1976[1]

Bowie's artistic output of the late 1970s, often regarded as his 'Berlin period', is distinguished by experimentation, painting and performance.[2] Bowie was experimenting with sonic composition and developing what he described as a 'new musical language'.[3] This was also a period in which Bowie was deepening his knowledge of the visual arts and further developing his passion for painting. His sensibility towards the relations between audio and visual mediums was honed by an autodidacticism – an approach towards learning that enabled Bowie to explore the world of visual music. Aiming to generate new encounters between music and the visual arts, proponents of visual music strive to achieve a visual analogue to musical form, either by adapting musical elements and structures for composition via a visual medium, or vice-versa. An interest in the sensory affordances of audio-visual mediums is manifest through the exploration of analogies between colour, timbre, light, pitch, texture, rhythm, movement and spatial composition. Although rarely described as a visual music artist, Bowie conjured visual imagery through lyrics and sonic strategies, something that is apparent in his earliest songs and promotional films.

By 1977, his interest in experimenting with audio-visual relations was piqued by a mixture of circumstance and environment. Berlin was a petri-dish for Bowie to experiment with the relations between sonic and visual artforms. Integrating his passion for the visual and musical arts, Bowie strengthened his knowledge of

---

[1] Rook, 'Waiting for Bowie'.
[2] A YouTube playlist for chapter 4 is available at https://tinyurl.com/3u6r7pb4.
[3] David Bowie, Nacho Video, 'David Bowie. Interview. Hotel de L'Europe. Amsterdam, Holland. 14 October 1977', YouTube video, 00:31:08, 7 July 2019, https://tinyurl.com/yc7svnaa.

art history while developing his capacity to 'paint' music. Not only were his paintings informed by musical elements, but his music during this period also portrays a distinct visuality; one could describe these songs as composed with the hue, tone or brush strokes of a painter. These observations are not isolated to his paintings and songs, however. Bowie's late 1970s videos are distinctive for their dialogue between visual and sonic compositional elements. His experience of personal pain, purging and grounding produced a sense of rebirth and optimism which is also apparent in his videos from this period. These outcomes could only have happened as a result of Bowie's collaborations with particular artists who practiced the tenets of visual music.

With visual music and painting being the salient features of Bowie's artistic drive during the late 1970s, this chapter explores these influences upon the videos directed by Stanley Dorfman, Nick Ferguson and David Mallet between 1977 and 1979. These videos reveal the idiosyncratic aesthetic and distinct contribution that each director made to furthering music video as an artform. It is also important to consider the impact of Bowie's collaborations with Brian Eno and Tony Visconti, both of whom indirectly influenced the videos discussed in this chapter. Bowie's collaboration with Visconti spanned five decades, resulting in the production of numerous songs and albums. The characteristic sonic spatiality of songs such as "Low", "Heroes", "Moss Garden" and "Warszawa" can be attributed in part to Visconti and Eno's idiosyncratic approach to sonic production. As a practicing visual music artist,[4] Eno not only contributed a distinctive ambience to these songs, he also influenced Bowie's appreciation for sonic and visual analogues. Eno inspired Bowie to experiment with aleatory production methods, resulting in innovative musical compositions that evoke strong visual associations. In a 2001 interview for *Uncut*, Bowie recalled the collaborative spirit underpinning the Berlin 'triptych' – *Low* (1977), *Heroes* (1977) and *Lodger* (1979):

> For whatever reasons, for whatever confluence of circumstances, Tony, Brian and I created a powerful, anguished, sometimes euphoric language of sounds. In some ways, sadly, they really captured, unlike anything else in that time, a sense of yearning for a future that we all knew would never come to pass. It is some of the best work that the three of us have ever done. Nothing else sounded like those albums. Nothing else came close. If I never made another album, it really wouldn't matter now. My complete being is in those three. They are my DNA.[5]

---

[4] Christopher Scoates, *Brian Eno: Visual Music* (San Francisco: Chronicle Books, 2013).
[5] Rob Hughes and Stephen Dalton, 'David Bowie Remembers Berlin: I Can't Express the Feeling of Freedom I Felt There', *Uncut*, April 2001, https://tinyurl.com/yrr3n5z4.

While Bowie was evidently excited about this triumvirate of collaborative experimentation and its production of 'a euphoric language of sounds', his optimism for this new sonic language is tinged with sadness about yearning for a future that he sensed would not come to pass. As we shall see, Bowie would return to this sentiment time and again, especially when he felt he was reaching a creative pinnacle.

While Bowie's music of this period has been given much acclaim for its innovative production methods and avant-garde aesthetics, less attention has been given to the visual composition of the music videos accompanying these songs. This chapter addresses this gap by focusing on the ways in which Bowie's late 1970s videos respond visually to the new sonic language he was developing with Visconti and Eno. While Eno instigated new methods of aleatory composition (such as with his Oblique Strategies cards), Visconti developed innovative production methods to experiment with vocality and acoustic space. These significant collaborations form an important context for my examination of the music videos for 'Be My Wife' (1977), 'Heroes' (1977), 'Boys Keep Swinging' (1979), 'Look Back in Anger' (1979) and 'Space Oddity' (1979).

Bowie's Berlin period

To understand the creative energy behind these videos, it is important to consider the context in which Bowie was living and creating during his Berlin period. In a 1977 interview for *NME*, Bowie revealed his sense of the psychic quagmire that instigated his move to Berlin and his drive toward self-re-evaluation.

> [*Low*] was a reaction to having gone through ... that dull greenie-grey limelight of America ... and its repercussions; pulling myself out of it and getting to Europe and saying, For God's sake re-evaluate why you wanted to get into this in the first place? Did you really do it just to clown around in LA? Retire. What you need is to look at yourself a bit more accurately. Find some people you don't understand and a place you don't want to be and just put yourself into it. Force yourself to buy your own groceries.[6]

---

[6] Charles Shaar Murray, 'David Bowie: Who Was That (Un)masked Man?' *New Musical Express*, 12 November 1977, https://tinyurl.com/mrheyrye.

While this statement suggests a healthy dose of self-reflection and a desire to be grounded, Bowie's subsequent recollections of his time in Berlin indicate a tortured mental state that was neither healthy nor grounded:

> At that time, I was vacillating badly between euphoria and incredible depression. Berlin was at that time not the most beautiful city of the world, and my mental condition certainly matched it. I was abusing myself so badly. My subtext to the whole thing is that I'm so desperately unhappy, but I've got to pull through because I can't keep living like this. There's actually a real optimism about the music. In its poignancy there is, shining through under there somewhere, the feeling that it will be all right.[7]

Having been ravaged by drug and alcohol abuse during the mid-1970s, Bowie's relocations to Switzerland, Paris and Berlin became crucial to enabling a process of purging demons and facing up to realities. With the dissolution of his marriage, it was necessary to become grounded enough to fully embrace the responsibility of fatherhood. These were significant life changes that helped shape not only the lyrics and music, but Bowie's conceptual approach to the music videos and his performances for them. Along with his internal struggles, external factors played a role in shaping his creative outputs during the late 1970s. Bowie was experiencing the city and culture of Berlin in all its harsh realities, which provided the grounding he had been yearning for. In a 2001 interview for *UNCUT*, Bowie acknowledged that his drug-addled 'academic' interest in Hitler was met with a fatal dose of reality after moving to Germany. Being suddenly aware of meeting young people of his own age whose fathers had been members of the SS (*Schutzstaffel*), Bowie explained that it 'was a good way to be woken up out of that particular dilemma, and start to re-function in a more orderly fashion ... I came crashing down to earth when I got back to Europe'.[8] Picturing the impact of Berlin upon Bowie, David Buckley describes Berlin as possessing 'both an astonishing energy and a forceful darkness, weighted down by a blighted past, yet constantly receptive to new ideas'.[9] These observations echo Bowie's recollections of Berlin:

---

[7] Jon Pareles, 'David Bowie, 21st Century Entrepreneur', *The New York Times*, 9 June 2002, https://tinyurl.com/sxydrhx5.
[8] Hughes and Dalton, 'David Bowie Remembers Berlin'.
[9] David Buckley, 'Revisiting Bowie's Berlin', in Devereux, Dillane and Power (eds), *David Bowie: Critical Perspectives*, 222.

At that time, with the [Berlin] Wall still up, there was a feeling of terrific tension throughout the city. It was either very young or very old people. There were no family units in Berlin. It was a city of extremes. It vacillated between the absurd – the whole drag, transvestite nightclub type of thing – and real radical, Marxist political thought. And it seemed like this really was the focus of the new Europe. It was right here. For the first time, the tension was outside of me rather than within me. And it was a real interesting process, writing for me under those conditions.[10]

As suggested by these comments, it was the city of Berlin that aroused Bowie's awareness of external tensions rather than those cogitating within himself. On other occasions, Bowie had explained the environmental impact on his writing as an idiosyncrasy of his creative process. In 1977, he reflected on the fact that he was particularly 'vulnerable' to whatever environment he lived in, and that from a musical perspective his 'environment and circumstances affect[ed] [his] writing tremendously'.[11] In a similar vein, Tobias Rüther suggests that Bowie 'is in search of himself in the city. He sees himself in relation to it.'[12] This vulnerability to his environment is evident across Bowie's *oeuvre*. Just as the culture and geography of London are present in songs such as "London Boys" (1966) and "London Bye Ta Ta" (1968),[13] specific aspects of American culture are present in the songs he produced while touring and living there. The presence of Berlin in Bowie's work has been explored by a number of scholars, contributing astonishing observations about Berlin's impact upon his creative process.[14] While Berlin may not appear to be explicitly present in the music videos discussed in this chapter, an in-depth examination of the videos shows that Bowie's experience of Berlin is very much present.

Berlin was a petri-dish for experimentation, and Brian Eno was an ideal catalyst to trigger Bowie's experimental urge, providing him with a toolbox of aleatory compositional methods. Having held a long-term admiration for American culture, Bowie was now ready to reject many of the rock star conventions that were sacrosanct in the USA, and his discovery of avant-garde practices provided him with strategies to subvert these conventions. Having

---

[10] David Buckley, *David Bowie: The Music and the Changes* (New York: Omnibus Press, 2015), 222.
[11] Allan Jones, 'Goodbye To Ziggy And All That', *Melody Maker*, 29 October 1977, *Bowiegoldenyears.com*, https://tinyurl.com/4nprfxd4.
[12] Tobias Rüther, *Heroes: David Bowie and Berlin* (London: Reaktion Books, 2014), 98.
[13] O'Leary, 'London Bye Ta-Ta', *Pushing Ahead of the Dame*, 29 October 2009, https://tinyurl.com/4946en3u.
[14] See, for instance Buckley, 'Revisiting Bowie's Berlin', and Rüther, *Heroes*.

already implemented a version of Burrough's cut-up technique when composing songs for the *Diamond Dogs* album, Bowie and Eno were primed for further experimentation on the production of the 'Berlin triptych' albums.

In tandem with his embrace of avant-garde musical production methods, Bowie was regularly painting and deepening his knowledge of art history – activities that provided rich resources for conceptualizing his music videos and album cover art. Bowie's iconic pose on the *Heroes* (1977) album cover has come to signify the pinnacle of his conjunction of avant-garde aesthetics and popular music. His distinctive angular arm gesture intertextually references Eric Heckel's painting *Roquairol* (1917) and Egon Schiele's gestural paintings, including *Self Portrait with Raised Arms* (1914), *Self Portrait with Raised Right Hand* (1916) and *Self Portrait with Plaid Shirt* (1917). These references exemplify Bowie's penchant for migrating gestures across mediums, as does a rare clip on YouTube titled 'David Bowie – Sense of Doubt – Rare Video'.[15] This video includes repeated takes of Bowie miming gestures that bear a striking resemblance to those depicted in Heckel's and Schiele's paintings. While there is some debate about the initial purpose of this footage, its existence illustrates Bowie's determination to use gesture as an intermedial thread of continuity across painting, album cover art and promotional film.

This chapter examines further examples of gestural migration across mediums, cultures and time, while also exploring Bowie's interest in painting and his maturing approach to performance. While all of these aspects helped to shape the videos Bowie released during the late 1970s, these videos bear the distinctive signature of the music video directors he collaborated with. I begin with Stanley Dorfman, whose video for 'Be My Wife' (1977) was the first official video to be released after 'Life on Mars?' (1973).

Stanley Dorfman

He was a really good painter. We had that in common. He was a sweet man.

Stanley Dorfman, 2016[16]

---

[15] Joseph Holc, 'David Bowie – Sense of Doubt – Rare Video', YouTube video, 00:03:09, 18 February 2007, https://tinyurl.com/28bsynw8.

[16] Jordan Riefe, 'Music Video Pioneer Stanley Dorfman Recalls Bowie, Sinatra and Lennon', *The Hollywood Reporter*, 2 November 2016, https://tinyurl.com/mr4372vf.

Dorfman shared with Bowie a love of painting and an appreciation for the significance of light in visual art. Both artists had a penchant for working across media and for bridging the fine arts and popular culture. Despite only directing two official videos for Bowie, Dorfman made an important contribution to Bowie's *oeuvre* and to the art of music video. After studying art at Paris' *Ecole des Beaux Arts* and *Académie Julian* in the 1940s, Dorfman moved to the United Kingdom and became a member of the St. Ives School of Art, a small collective who considered themselves vanguards in modern and abstract painting. His art practice moved across the mediums of mosaic and sculpted wall constructions in architecture and included abstract paintings and music videos. Whatever the medium, his work is distinctive for his treatment of light as both a painting medium and a sculpting tool. This emphasis on light characterizes the videos he directed for Bowie and is also apparent in the 'Heart of Glass' video he directed for Blondie (1979). During his time in the UK, Dorfman worked as an art director and producer for the BBC *Top of the Pops*.[17] This role provided him with an entry point into making promotional films that exposed emerging pop stars to a broad audience. Since not all bands entering the 'top 10 chart' were physically available to give a televised studio performance for *Top of the Pops*, Dorfman would often film local youths dancing to the tracks. Alternatively, he would edit a collage of found footage to provide a visual accompaniment to the song. Dorfman's move to Los Angeles in 1974 opened the door to producing promotional content for several high-profile pop stars. He developed a personal and collaborative relationship with Yoko Ono and John Lennon, which led to the task of weeding through yards of video footage shot by Lennon. The outcome was a handful of unofficial music videos, one featuring slow motion footage edited to accompany the unreleased track "Grow Old With Me" (1983).[18] As we shall see, editing audio-visual material was a strength of Dorfman's, as was sculpting with light and composing within the cinematic frame – all strong features of the two videos Dorfman directed for Bowie in 1977 – 'Heroes' and 'Be My Wife'.

---

[17] See here for a YouTube playlist of videos directed by Stanley Dorfman: https://tinyurl.com/223nsn3j.
[18] Amy Haben, 'Stanley Dorfman: *Top of the Pops* and Beyond', *Please Kill Me: This is What's Cool*, 15 April 2019, https://tinyurl.com/mfr7vbbe.

"Be My Wife" – the song

Recorded in 1976 at the Château d'Hérouville in France, "Be My Wife" became the second single on *Low* (1977). While many critics considered the song too odd to become a *Billboard* success upon its initial release, it later gained popularity, particularly following Bowie's death in 2016. In his book *David Bowie's Low*, Hugo Wilcken suggests that the enigmatic lyrics are directly related to Bowie's failing marriage to Angie.[19] Bowie had commented that the lyrics were 'genuinely anguished . . . but I think it could have been about anybody'.[20] The way in which Bowie delivers the lyrics 'please be mine, share my life, stay with me, be my wife' is not quite the tone you'd expect from a sincere marriage proposal. As Wilcken put it, the lyric's 'dumb simplicity is something of a tease. Could this be anything but irony?'[21] Noting that Bowie's marriage was disintegrating around the time the lyrics were written, Wilcken adds '. . . so it was a rather strange refrain to be singing. And yet . . . the song isn't exactly ironic either. At least a part of the "sincerity" is sincere . . . the song ends poignantly with the first line of a verse that is never completed.'[22] Taking into account Bowie's traumatized mental state at the time, ending the song with 'sometimes you get so lonely' seems in hindsight to be a 'genuinely anguished' call for help.[23] However, the song's expression of loneliness was apparently generated by a desperate state that surpassed the loneliness of a marriage break-up. In 1989, Bowie described how his physical and emotional state at that time may have shaped the music on *Low*:

> You're up and down all the time, vacillating constantly. It's a very tough period to get through. So, my concern with *Low* was not about the music. The music was literally expressing my physical and emotional state . . . and that was my worry. So, the music was almost therapeutic. It was like, Oh yeah, we've made an album and it sounds like this. But it was a by-product of my life. It just sort of came out . . . I never talked to anybody about it. I just made this album . . . in a rehab state. A dreadful state really.[24]

Despite the anguish expressed by the lyrics and the tortured sounding guitar solo, the fundamental musical arrangement for "Be My Wife" is upbeat and

---

[19] Hugo Wilcken, *David Bowie's Low (33 1/3)* (New York: Bloomsbury, 2005), 97.
[20] Michael Watts, 'Confession of an Elitist', *Melody Maker*, 18 February 1978. https://tinyurl.com/2drrp988.
[21] Wilcken, *David Bowie's Low*, 97.
[22] Ibid.
[23] Ibid.
[24] Adrian Deevoy, 'David Bowie: Boys Keep Swinging', *Q Magazine*, June 1989.

catchy. With a repeated four-note motif, the piano provides the primary rhythmic drive of the song, while the guitar floats over the top, vying for – and at times achieving – instrumental prominence. This tension between the key instruments builds until the chorus, when the drum and bass become more prominent, providing musical accompaniment for Bowie's vocals. While the Cockney accent initially seems ill-fitting with the upper-class tone of the costume, Bowie's made-up face recalls his earlier fascination with Anthony Newley's accent and light entertainer theatrics. In combination, the accent and honky-tonk piano provide a suitable sonic foundation that grounds the ethereal, minimalist quality of the visual composition. Describing the video as 'a visual analogue to how Bowie sings "Be My Wife"', O'Leary explains that Bowie's vocal 'is trapped in a five-note range',[25] and that he uses this vocal minimalism as a strategy of rebellion against rock stardom:

> If *Low* is something of Bowie's rebellion (or act of petulance, RCA would have said) against being an American-approved rock star, then "Be My Wife" is a love song that questions the act of singing a love song. Its lyric is simple; its arrangement, with its crashing piano ... and guitar solos, is in the common language of 1970s pop. Yet you can never determine where Bowie stands; it's unclear whether he knows.[26]

Bowie's vocal performance in "Be My Wife" provides a perfect example of how the notorious ambivalence he performed in many aspects of his public life generated enigma. If he sounds ambivalent in the song, perhaps his performance in the video might clarify his stance? Listening to the song in isolation, Bowie is clearly using the common language of 1970s rock. For instance, the symbolic guitar solo might lead one to expect an impassioned Ziggy-type performance, but his vocal delivery is mysteriously lacking passion. Without a visual accompaniment, it is difficult to know where he 'stands'. As we shall see in the following section, the video provides some clues; Bowie's nonchalant attitude and ambiguous performance – his Buster Keaton-esque hairstyle, costume and makeup all work together to undermine the contemporary style, passionate stage performance and guitar playing glory associated with American rock stardom.

---

[25] O'Leary, 'Be My Wife', *Pushing Ahead of the Dame*, 17 February 2011, https://tinyurl.com/ytuz2y78.
[26] Ibid.

'Be My Wife' – the video

Initially intended to promote the release of *Low*, the video for 'Be My Wife' was directed by Dorfman and shot in Paris on 21 June 1977. The opening shot establishes what Michel Chion would describe as an 'anempathetic' audio-visual relationship, with the visual elements appearing to be mismatched with the tone of the song.[27] The first bars of a honky-tonk piano accompany a painterly image of Bowie's lowered head of hair, accented by the diagonal line of his guitar neck. Although his face is obscured in this opening shot, it is his face that turns out to be the most enchanting aspect of the video.

Just as Dorfman used this video as a canvas upon which to paint with light, Bowie used it as a canvas to experiment with masking and facial gesture. Donning the 'sad clown' mask of Pierrot, Bowie builds upon his long-standing engagement with this figure. Along with the versatile mask of Pierrot, he channels Keaton by raising his eyebrows, crinkling his brow and holding his mouth in a pert Keaton-esque manner (Figure 4.1). Bowie's deadpan facial expression is pronounced by his sustained direct address to the camera. His direct eye contact with the viewer is noted by Chris O'Leary, who describes how, after singing the lyrics 'share my life', Bowie:

> ...cocks his head and stares directly into the camera, as if noticing the viewer at last. There's no readable expression on his face – he could be suppressing a smile, he could be about to scream – and just before the image fades, the life drains from his face. It's unnerving to watch, as though a marionette is suddenly professing love to you, and worse, that the marionette may not really mean it.[28]

Associating Bowie's facial performance with a marionette is prophetic. The unnerving sensation O'Leary refers to here is in keeping with Bowie's strategic use of masking and puppetized performance in several of his subsequent videos.[29]

---

[27] 'Anempathetic sound' is a term coined by Michel Chion, to describe the use of sonic or musical elements that do not match what is happening visually at a specific point in a film or audio-visual text. For more on this, see Michel Chion, *Audio-Vision: Sound on Screen*, trans. Claudia Gorbman (New York: Columbia University Press, 1994).

[28] O'Leary, 'Be My Wife'.

[29] For more on this, see Perrott, *David Bowie and the Transformation of Music Video*.

Figure 4.1 Bowie channels Buster Keaton. 'Be My Wife' (Stanley Dorfman, 1977).

Figure 4.2 Bowie anthropomorphizes the guitar as an object of desire. 'Be My Wife' (Stanley Dorfman, 1977).

Guitar love

A ridiculously long electric guitar cable snakes across the white studio, leading the viewer's eye to the guitar and accentuating it as the second most salient feature of the video. Although Bowie's face is more prominent, it serves primarily to express his intimate relationship with the guitar. Employing facial and bodily gesture in synchronicity with the camera, Bowie acts out a relationship with his guitar that shifts along a scale from intimacy to irreverence. At times, he anthropomorphizes the guitar as an object of desire: gazing down upon the fretboard, he moves his head gently as though engrossed in the act of stroking its strings (Figure 4.2). This intense focus on the guitar develops into what might be perceived as a romantic encounter, as he runs his fingers gently up and down the length of the guitar-neck. The lens zooms in to emphasize this bizarre act of instrumental intimacy. In what follows, Bowie then shatters any illusion that he might be in love with his guitar. By the video's end he can't even be bothered pretending to play it, a stance that reinforces the fickleness of his earlier performance. The irony of this act is picked up by Momus (aka Nick Currie), who describes the video as:

> ... a mime sketch of a rock star making a rock video, yet too comically glum and sulky to go through the required hoops, and lacking the necessary gung-ho conviction.... The character ... makes to play his guitar and gives up halfway through the phrase. He just can't be bothered.[30]

Just as he had performed guitar-love with a nod to rock-star integrity, Bowie does an equally convincing job of acting the part of a character who can't be bothered playing his guitar, but having freed his hands, he doesn't know what to do with them. After a half-hearted attempt at pointing and sweeping his arm to gesticulate the lyric 'I've been all over the world', he awkwardly puts his hands in his pockets while the extradiegetic guitar continues to play. Once he has finished singing, he has another go at playing the guitar but then gives up, nonchalantly propping the guitar on his shoulder. Turning his back on the camera/audience midway through the guitar outro, Bowie deftly acts out the antithesis of the commitment expected of a rock musician (Figure 4.3). This subversive act is multifaceted, however: by drawing attention to the extradiegetic guitar that continues playing the outro, Bowie overtly breaks the conventional verisimilitude of synchronized instrumental play and parodies the music video code of illusory authentic performance. Furthermore, by rendering the guitar as

[30] Wilcken, *David Bowie's Low*, 98.

Figure 4.3 Bowie enacts the antithesis of the commitment expected of a rock musician. 'Be My Wife' (Stanley Dorfman, 1977).

a fetishized but otherwise useless prop, he parodies the heightened presence and feigned authenticity of guitar playing in rock videos of the 1970s and early 1980s. This deadpan thwarting of conventions creates a pastiche of the conventional relationship between a rock musician and their guitar. Bowie's treatment of the guitar in 'Be My Wife' may also be understood as forming one node in a thread of continuity across his music videos, in which the guitar is variously anthropomorphized, bastardized or treated as a subversive signifier. In this respect, his performance in 'Be My Wife' serves as an intertextual reference to his earlier awkward studio performance for 'Let Me Sleep Beside You' (1969), in which he pretends unconvincingly to play the guitar, and then treats it as a phallic prop, flamboyantly flinging it around with one hand. With the exception of the 1972 and 1979 videos for 'Space Oddity' and a few videos comprising live performance clips, Bowie is rarely depicted playing guitar in a music video. On those rare occasions, he usually treats it as a functional prop. For instance, in 'John, I'm Only Dancing' (1972) the guitar is a stylistic prop slung across Bowie's back to connote a punk attitude. And in the *Top Pop* video for 'Rebel Rebel'

(1974),³¹ Bowie treats the guitar as a toy he doesn't know what to do with, but it serves its function as a stylistic accessory to match his red jump-suit. In 'Let's Dance' (1983) Bowie's pretence at playing his guitar with gloves parodies the falsity of pop stardom, while in 'Valentine's Day' (2013) the guitar serves as an overt signifier of gun violence.³² These examples suggest that Bowie is again using the guitar as a complex signifier in 'Be My Wife'.

Painting with colour, sculpting with light

Set against a minimalist white background, the form of Bowie's face and guitar create a sense of visual simplicity that belies the cinematic thought behind the composition of each shot. Much consideration has been given to the scale and positioning of Bowie's figure within the frame. At times he appears as a small distant figure in the centre-rear of the frame. His scale shifts dramatically, however, as the shot transitions into a close-up of his face or a mid-shot of his torso, which forms a diagonal line within the frame. Along with Bowie's figure, Dorfman also makes use of camera angle and movement to create aesthetically interesting compositions. Alternating between high-angle and low-angle shots, the camera subtly roams around Bowie's body, offering the audience subjective camera views from behind him. For the most part, Bowie focuses on his guitar and does not look at the camera. On the odd occasion that he does look into its lens, his direct address and facial expressions are pronounced. As was the case in 'Life on Mars?' (1973), Bowie shifts between indirect and direct address, thus alternating his position as a subject or an object to be gazed upon. Just as Rock had done in 1973, Dorfman also responded to this positioning by framing Bowie in close-up to accentuate the moments of direct address. Like the overexposed effect of the film bleaching process that was used for 'Life on Mars?', these close-ups are further intensified by their juxtaposition with wide shots, which feature overexposed lighting and large areas of white space that expand the limits of the frame. Due to his background in fine arts and painting, Dorfman is acutely attentive to positive and negative space and to the arrangement of lines and shapes within the frame. In this sense, it is possible that Dorfman has taken

---

[31] TopPop, 'David Bowie – Rebel Rebel. TopPop', YouTube video, 00:04:21, 7 November 2015, https://tinyurl.com/4pz3s33w.

[32] For more on this, see Perrott, *David Bowie and the Transformation of Music Video*.

inspiration from the minimalist paintings of his muse Piet Mondrian, who translated body parts and objects into lines and shapes, sometimes creating the illusion of perspective. Just as the diagonal line formed by the electric guitar cable enhances the sense of perspective within the frame, Bowie's body also forms a diagonal line across the frame. Much like Mondrian might have done with his abstract paintings, Dorfman has arranged body parts and props to form positive (coloured) spaces that are aesthetically balanced with the negative space of the white studio background (Figure 4.4). These observations raise questions about the possibility that Dorfman was subconsciously remediating a Mondrian painting.

This Mondrian-like approach to composition is consistent with the distinctive ways in which Dorfman sculpts with light. The lighting of Bowie's hair and skin produces textural qualities similar to that of ceramic sculpture. High-key (overexposed) lighting throughout the video generates painterly qualities suggestive of translucent paint and textured brush strokes, which serve as abstract transitions between shots. Most of the transitions appear as cross-dissolves and

Figure 4.4 Dorfman composes body parts and props like an abstract painting. 'Be My Wife' (Stanley Dorfman, 1977).

many include moments where two semi-translucent images of Bowie are overlaid within the frame. These moments of transition involve a gradual shift in lighting exposure, opacity, colour saturation and contrast, all of which reinforces the Pierrot mask-like appearance of Bowie's face. In one such transition, a subjective shot from behind Bowie's back fades out just as a shot of his frontal view fades in and eventually dominates the frame. Breaking the 180-degree rule of continuity editing, this cross-dissolve simultaneously provides a view of Bowie from front and behind. Mutating levels of light exposure, opacity and colour saturation enhance the abstracted quality of the lines and shapes in the video. Depending on the level of saturation or the translucency of overlapping images, the resulting colour graduates between pastel hues of amber, pink and purple, with the texture resembling a chalk drawing. These painterly qualities are a result of the way in which Dorfman treats each frame of film as a canvas upon which to sculpt with light – a trait that is even more apparent in his direction of the video for 'Heroes' (1977).[33]

"Heroes" – the song

> The danger *did* create the sound.... When you record a group of musicians, you're not only recording the music, you're recording the *environment*. And Berlin was the perfect place.
>
> Tony Visconti, 2014[34]

Heroes was recorded in July and August of 1977 in Hansa Tonstudio, West Berlin, a studio that was situated very close to the Berlin Wall. According to Visconti, Bowie would gaze out the studio window to see the weaponized East German border guards on duty at their guard tower, diligently watching for anyone daring enough to cross the Wall.[35] 'The hall by the Wall' was the phrase Bowie used to refer to the studio, which had previously been used as a Nazi social club.[36] In Bowie's words, 'it was a Weimar ballroom ... utilised by the Gestapo in the thirties for their own little musical soirées'.[37] Thomas Seabrook explains how this position of the recording studio came to inflect *Heroes* with history:

---

[33] 'Heroes' was released on 23 September 1977 to promote the *Heroes* album.
[34] Citywire, 'Bowie's Berlin: Tony Visconti Returns to Heroes Studio', YouTube video, 00:04:03, 26 November 2014, https://youtu.be/V9ROgbefCKA.
[35] Ibid.
[36] Hughes and Dalton, 'David Bowie Remembers Berlin'.
[37] Ibid.

...and as such it is the album on which the culture, the history and the very essence of Berlin came to bear most fully on Bowie's work. The fact that he and his fellow musicians were working directly in the shadows of the Wall, surrounded not just by echoes of wars past, but by reminders of the contemporary conflicts between East and West, instilled a drive and seriousness into their work.[38]

Although this drive and seriousness is apparent in all the songs on *Heroes* the album, the shadow of the Wall has a particular presence in "Heroes" the song. While the Wall is overtly present in the lyrics, the sonic elements contribute an emotional complexity that escapes the limits of analysis. Emotionally, the song is enigmatic, conveying a strange combination of profound gravitas and ethereal optimism, tinged with sadness. This emotional complexity is largely a result of the musical arrangement, Bowie's vocal intonation and the particularities of the recording sessions, but the lyrics to 'Heroes' play a vital role in evoking visual imagery.

The song developed in stages, with the music being recorded before Bowie wrote the lyrics. It wasn't until the vocals were recorded and added to the mix that the full emotional impact of the song came to fruition. Without knowledge of the context in which Bowie was living and working when he wrote the lyrics, one might assume that Bowie was writing in an autobiographical mode; perhaps drawing upon experiences of unrequited love or a romantic relationship having existed against adversity. According to comments made by Bowie and Visconti, however, the lyrical and sonic construction of "Heroes" was generated through the synchronicity of place, people and circumstance. The song is not only a reflection of Bowie's response to Berlin, but also each musician's response – to Berlin, to the recording studio, and to the recording process. The unique energy of this process was summed up by Radio 1 broadcaster Mark Radcliffe, who said 'there was a sense that everybody was playing a different song at a different speed at the same time, and yet somehow creating something effortlessly glorious'.[39]

As is the case for several songs on *Heroes* and *Lodger*, the sonic construction of "Heroes" owes much to improvisation and chance occurrence, which is not surprising given Bowie's embrace of avant-garde creative processes during the late 1970s. For *Heroes*, the studio recording process involved composing layered

---

[38] Thomas Jerome Seabrook, *Bowie in Berlin: A New Career in a New Town* (London: Outline Press, 2008), 171.
[39] David Buckley, *Strange Fascination, David Bowie: the Definitive Story* (London: Virgin Books, 2005), 280.

tracks that would later inspire lyric and melody, much like building a frame before painting a picture. During this period, Bowie would sometimes use Eno's Oblique Strategies cards that, when randomly generated, provided creative dilemmas in the form of aphorisms.[40] When considered in relation to the existing compositional framework (including the studio space, collaborators and instrumental tools at hand), the aphorism offered by a particular card provided a potential direction for approaching the following steps in the creative process. This aleatory process is hilariously illustrated by Adam Buxton's animated cartoon, which spoofs the recording session for Bowie's song "Warszawa" (*Low*, 1977).[41] In addition to the cards, Bowie made use of a range of other experimental approaches that were intended to provide aleatory creative direction external from himself. He explains, 'Maybe I'd write out five or six chords ... then discipline myself to write something only with those five or six chords involved. So that particular dogma would dictate how the song is going to come out, rather than me and my sense of emotional self.'[42] These approaches toward chance composition and using only the limited materials at hand extended to the collaborative musical composition of "Heroes". A horn section that was intended for the second verse was improvised by a 'brass' sound on a Chamberlin electro-mechanical keyboard, and planned string sections were replaced with basslines by Carlos Alomar and George Murray.[43] Although Bowie had envisaged the distinct sound of a cowbell, he was happy to improvise with whatever random items were available in the studio. In the absence of a cowbell, Visconti recalls hitting an empty tape canister with 'either a fork or a drumstick.'[44] This improvisational manner carried over from the recording sessions into the way in which the song's lyrics were written.

It was only after the music was recorded that Bowie started writing the lyrics. Sitting alone in the studio, Bowie was immersed in the residual spirit of improvisation that lingered after weeks of recording. According to the "Heroes"

---

[40] Oblique Strategies cards were designed in 1975 by Brian Eno and painter Peter Schmidt. For more on this, see the interview with Brian Eno at Colin Marshall, 'Jump Start Your Creative Process with Brian Eno's Oblique Strategies Deck of Cards (1975)', *Open Culture*, 2 July 2013, https://tinyurl.com/mrje8chb.

[41] Adam Buxton, 'David Bowie, Brian Eno and Tony Visconti record Warszawa Adam Buxton', 00:03:30, YouTube video, 9 September 2014, https://www.youtube.com/watch?v=FODvjYoVEi8.

[42] Bill DeMain, 'The Story Behind the Song: Heroes by David Bowie', *Loudersound.com*, 4 February 2019, https://tinyurl.com/u4ukrbxa.

[43] O'Leary, 'Heroes', *Pushing Ahead of the Dame*, 11 May 2022, https://tinyurl.com/yc4w62vy.

[44] Tony Visconti, 'David Bowie's Heroes Producer Gets to the Heart of the Song', *BBC Arts*, 10 January 2020, https://tinyurl.com/483kmh4v.

legend (which Visconti has confirmed), while sitting there at the studio window writing lyrics, Bowie happened to glance out the window just long enough to catch a glimpse of Visconti and back-up singer Antonia Maass kissing next to the Berlin Wall. Much to Visconti's astonishment, this moment of happenstance gave birth to the lyric 'and we kissed, as though nothing could fall'. According to O'Leary, however, this chance occurrence only cemented an image of lovers by the Wall that was already partly drawn in Bowie's mind. After an earlier visit to Die Brücke Museum, Bowie had been inspired by the painting *Liebespaar Zwischen Gartenmauern* (Lovers Between Garden Walls), which Otto Mueller had painted at the end of the First World War. According to O'Leary, 'Bowie transplanted Mueller's image of two lovers embracing by a high stone wall, placing them before the Wall' that he had seen every day from Hansa's studio window.[45] 'At once he had found his lyric's resolution, a snapshot of love and bravery set against the concrete madness of governments, despite it being a shabby act, a man cheating on his wife.'[46] Referring to the fact that Visconti was married to Mary Hopkin at the time of his legendary kiss by the Wall, O'Leary observes an important point: when writing lyrics, Bowie's inspirations were not as obvious as legend might have us believe.[47] Consistent with his magpie-like foraging tendencies, he would often compose a single lyric from a combination of artistic inspirations, chance occurrences, including his subconscious response to the environment in which he was living at the time. O'Leary observes this combination of inspirations at work in the lyrics for several Bowie songs. Noting that "Heroes" is distinctive for words that are 'simple and precisely chosen',[48] he observes the following two European post-war sources:

> One was the short story *A Grave For A Dolphin* by the Italian aristocrat Alberto Denti di Pirajno, which details a doomed affair between an Italian soldier and a Somalian girl during the Second World War (it inspired the 'dolphins can swim' verse).... Bowie also nicked the occasional line from elsewhere: 'I will be king, you will be queen' is from the English folk song "Lavender's Blue", which Bowie would sing onstage sometimes as a prelude to "Heroes".[48]

In a 2021 YouTube video, Iman provides further context to O'Leary's tale of how the lyrics 'dolphins can swim' were inspired by *A Grave for a Dolphin*,[50] a story that had

---

[45] O'Leary, 'Heroes'.
[46] Ibid.
[47] Ibid.
[48] Ibid.
[49] Ibid.
[50] Alberto Denti di Pirajno, *A Grave for a Dolphin* (London: Andre Deutsch, 1956).

been adored by both he and Iman long before they met.[51] While the lyrical inspirations for "Heroes" included a short story, an English folk song, a painting and a chance observation of a kiss, the song can be boiled down to three precisely chosen words – 'I', 'you' and 'we'. Bowie used these words very deliberately to conjure an allegorical sense of separation and eventual unity – either between individuals or wider society. Ultimately, the lyrics express not only the anguish of separation but a yearning for what could be; the desire to transcend not only the physical, but the ideological barriers to human unity. The lyrics also conjure images related to Berlin's history of control ('and the guns, shot above our heads'), as well as imagery that resonates with a desire for liberation ('I, I wish you could swim, like the dolphins, like dolphins can swim'), connection ('and we kissed, as though nothing could fall'), and transcendence ('we can beat them, for ever and ever'). The profound notion of transcendence suggested by these lyrics is perhaps indicative of the sense of control and human polarity Bowie may have experienced while living in Berlin.

While the lyrics work to conjure visual imagery, the sense of authentic emotion is generated by moments of raw vocal intensity. In his analysis of "Heroes", Pegg observes how the recording of Bowie's vocal moves along a spectrum from 'calm and playful to a near-scream, a style he called "Bowie histrionics".'[52] He belts out the lyrics 'I, I will be King, and you, you will be Queen'. Portraying the emotion he had personally invested in the song, the power of Bowie's vocal performance is also partly due to a pragmatic need to open up the gates in the mics, which were situated several metres away from Bowie in the recording studio. Visconti described how he 'put an electronic gate on the middle microphone and the distant microphone and set them to a specific threshold',[53] so that if Bowie 'sings loud enough, he'll open the microphone. If he sings quiet, the microphone won't open and you'll just hear the sound in front of him.'[54] After Visconti told David Buckley about this gating technique, Buckley commented 'the image of Bowie standing in the Hansa studios with its cold decadence, blowing Visconti's mics to smithereens, was one of his finest moments'.[55] With the emotional power of Bowie's vocals, the improvisational nature of the recording sessions and the imagery-conjuring quality of the lyrics, the resulting song generates a visuality and sense of transcendence that would have been

[51] Vogue, 'Inside Iman and David Bowie's scenic home filled with wonderful objects', YouTube video, 00:09:03, 9 December 2021, accessed 4 July 2022, https://youtu.be/fk9cq3gRCP0.
[52] Pegg, *The Complete David Bowie*, 110.
[53] Visconti, 'David Bowie's Heroes Producer Tony Visconti Gets to the Heart of the Song'.
[54] Ibid.
[55] Buckley, *Strange Fascination*, 280.

difficult for any video director to match, but on 27 September 1977, directors Stanley Dorfman and Nick Ferguson knew exactly what was required.

'Heroes' – the video

Out of the darkness we see the silhouette of a dark figure engulfed by white haze. At first glance, the figure looks like an alien emerging from the smoke of a crashed spacecraft (Figure 4.5). This mysterious image resembles backlit shots of the alien in the 1977 film *Close Encounters of the Third Kind* (Figure 4.6), which was released three months after 'Heroes' was shot. Accentuating the intrigue of this opening image, we hear an ethereal guitar-synth which seems to confirm the possibility of a science fiction setting. Cautiously, the camera tracks forward. Closer framing and frontal light reveal this dark creature to be thirty-year-old Bowie, dressed in a white singlet, with a low-cut neckline revealing his chest and long neck. As he tilts his head very slightly, the shaft of light emerging from behind his head also tilts. There's an uncanny similarity between the puppet-like

Figure 4.5 Bowie's backlit pose is much like an alien emerging from haze. 'Heroes' (Stanley Dorfman and Nicholas Ferguson, 1977).

Figure 4.6 The alien in *Close Encounters of the Third Kind* (Steven Spielberg, 1977).

motion of Bowie's neck movements with those of the alien in *Close Encounters*. Dense with enigmatic haze and intertextual references, the first seventeen seconds of the video go some way to reinforcing Bowie's reputation as the divine alien who fell to Earth.

Shot only three months after 'Be My Wife',[56] the two videos are in many ways inversely related, yet they have enough in common to be placed within a sequence of minimalist Bowie videos that might begin with 'Life on Mars?'. All three videos are visually uncluttered, structurally simple and devoid of narrative, with the sole focus being Bowie's performance. Despite the similarities, there are some notable differences between the two Dorfman videos. The white studio setting and high-key lighting of 'Be My Wife' emphasizes a visibly definable area of white space, whereas in 'Heroes', the white light emerges from a seemingly limitless dark void. Bowie wears a black leather bomber jacket and tight black

[56] 'Heroes' was shot on 27 September 1977. 'Be My Wife' was shot on 28 June 1977.

pants, a proto-punk look that contrasts with Bowie's Dandyish style in 'Be My Wife'. While the former video is all about his face, arguably the most striking feature of 'Heroes' is Bowie's figure.

A statuesque figure of divinity

Emerging from shafts of 'Divine Light' shot through haze, Bowie's figure appears as a Jesus-like silhouette. In Judeo-Christian and some Eastern traditions, 'Divine Light' is the belief that light is the manifestation of divine presence. In art history, it has been considered by some artists and lighting designers to be an important means of communicating a divine or spiritual presence. This is evident in Byzantine art and architecture, including the mosaic and fresco ceilings, stained windows and sculptures of ancient churches in Rome, Greece and Paris.[57] The spiritual signification of a figure floating in space, framed by shafts of Divine Light, recalls paintings depicting The Divine Mercy (Figure 4.7), and shares similarities with the glowing halo surrounding the deity figures of Byzantine mosaics. These references are consistent with Dorfman's and Bowie's shared passion for fine art, and in particular, Dorfman's interest in light, mosaic, fresco and sculpted wall constructions in architecture.[58] Bowie had impressed upon Dorfman his strong appreciation for the paintings of Gustav Klimt during the month they spent together in Paris in 1977. There is an affinity between the golden backlit glow of Klimt paintings and the halo effect of the back-light framing Bowie's face, which has a slight golden hue. These associations which divinify light provide an appropriate accompaniment to the ethereal sounds of Brian Eno's synthesizer and his rendering of Robert Fripp's 'feedback ostinato'.[59] One might say that the light performs alongside the music to create an allusion of a divine alien hero emerging from the heavens.

The cold 'colour temperature' of the back light creates a bluish-white light. In contrast, the warm temperature of the front and side lights give Bowie's face a soft golden glow. Standing in the same spot and only moving his head and arms slightly, Bowie appears statuesque – an impression that is intensified by his form being outlined by light. The close-up frontal shots are lit with front and fill lights. When the camera moves to capture Bowie's face in profile, it becomes sculpted

---

[57] For more on this, see Slobodan Ćurčić, 'Divine Light: Constructing the Immaterial in Byzantine Art and Architecture', in Bonna D. Westcoat and Robert G. Ousterhout (eds), *Architecture of the Sacred: Space, Ritual and Experience from Classical Greece to Byzantium* (Cambridge: Cambridge University Press, 2012).
[58] Riefe, 'Music Video Pioneer Stanley Dorfman'.
[59] O'Leary, 'Heroes'.

Figure 4.7 'The Divine Mercy', painted after St Faustina's death. (Adolf Hyła, Kraków 1944).

with warm light from either side, creating a low-key effect with parts of his face momentarily in shadow. The dark and light contours of his face change from moment to moment, a transitory effect assisted by the gradual tracking and panning of the camera and accompanying light source. While Bowie stands still, for the most part maintaining the direction of his gaze, it is the camera and the lights that move, enabling the viewer to observe the form of his head from constantly changing perspectives. This combination of bodily stasis and camera movement closely resembles the filming of Liza Minnelli's song 'Maybe This Time',[60] which appears in the Berlin-based 1972 film *Cabaret*.[61] While

---

[60] Turner Classic Movies, '"Maybe This Time" – Full Song – Cabaret 1972 – Liza Minnelli', YouTube video, 00:03:33, 9 June 2018, https://youtu.be/yMpSQV1-bsA.

[61] Pegg, *The Complete David Bowie*, 111.

this example features some distinct differences to 'Heroes', some sequences feature remarkably similar combinations of light source, framing and camera movements. As is the case in 'Heroes', the statuesque pose of Minnelli is also shot with a moving camera, with use of back light and haze to cast shafts of Divine Light. Just as 'Heroes' draws to a conclusion, there is a distinct moment of divinity when a lens flare washes Bowie in a Byzantine-like golden glow; a result of the camera momentarily catching the warm back light entering the lens. As the camera continues to pan around Bowie's form, the golden flare is replaced by a cooler back light. Although inspiration may well have been drawn from the cinematic examples I have observed here, Dorfman's use of light as a sculpting tool is articulated in perfect harmony with the emotional trajectory of the song. As such, I would describe 'Heroes' as a masterpiece of Divine Light, akin to the paintings, sculptures and architecture of the Renaissance period.

Dorfman doesn't only use light as a sculpting tool; he also uses it as a transitioning aid in both of the videos he directed for Bowie. In 'Heroes' there are fewer transitions and they don't rely on high-key lighting as they do in 'Be My Wife'. The first transition doesn't occur until 00:01:20 minutes into 'Heroes', allowing the opening shot to create enigma, while the camera gradually tracks into an intimate close-up of Bowie's head and then retreats back to a long shot of his body. Cross-dissolves initially serve to transition between a long-shot and a close-up, which creates the momentary effect of seeing Bowie's full body nestled inside his head (Figure 4.8). The fourth and fifth transitions break the 180-degree rule, by overlapping images of Bowie's head shot from opposite angles, thus creating the impression of two Bowie's facing and singing to one another.

While 'Heroes' and 'Be My Wife' both include Dorfman's signature approach to lighting and editing, these videos differ markedly when it comes to Bowie's performance. For 'Heroes', Bowie does away with the guitar prop altogether, delivering an impassioned performance of controlled vehemence. He expresses genuine emotion through his voice, his face and his poised bodily gestures. His bodily stance is that of an immovable statue. The only discernible movement is a gentle tilt of his trunk forwards and backwards in a very controlled manner, with his arms resting by his sides, employed minimally only for the occasional expressive gesture. This poised bodily control is unnerving, much like watching a statue turn into a marionette and then surprise us with a highly sentient gesture. At one point, he raises his hand up and runs his fingers seductively through his hair – a self-touching gesture that maintains continuity with other instances of self-touching, such as the throat clasp and the head touching depicted in his photo shoot for the

Figure 4.8 A painterly cross-dissolve. 'Heroes' (Stanley Dorfman and Nicholas Ferguson, 1977).

Hunky Dory album cover. As with these earlier examples, in 'Heroes', Bowie again positions himself as an object of the gaze, which shows his actor's awareness of 'frontality', as explained in chapter three. While Bowie's disciplined frontality to camera ensures that his performance works in concert with subtle changes to lighting, framing and camera movement, Dorfman responds in kind. One very notable example is the shaft of back-light that emerges through the gap between Bowie's thighs with the slight movement of his body (Figure 4.9).

These examples show how Bowie, Dorfman and Ferguson worked together to achieve a dialogue between bodily movement, light, framing and music. By focusing tightly on the choreography of these elements, the directors achieved the visual minimalism necessary to accompany such a powerful song. In this respect, 'Heroes' is notable for the absence of any cut-away footage that might point toward the meanings in the lyrics. A more conventional music video treatment might include footage of the Wall or of the architecture and people of Berlin, or it might include visual signifiers of romance. Instead, all we see is Bowie wrapped in light, which works as a suitably minimalist accompaniment to

Figure 4.9 Divine light emanating from Bowie's 'thigh-gap'. 'Heroes' (Stanley Dorfman and Nicholas Ferguson, 1977).

the enigmatic lyrics and emotionally intense vocals. This judicious directorial approach allows the lyrical and sonic elements to generate visual imagery by themselves. Despite the strong artistic affinity he shared with Bowie, Dorfman did not direct another video for Bowie after 'Heroes'. This should not be interpreted as indicative of a souring collaborative relationship, for Bowie has explicitly stated his need to move on, especially when things were going well.[62] This often meant closing one collaborative door in order to open another.

David Mallet

By opening a new door, Bowie discovered David Mallet, a prolific music video director who would become a long-term collaborator and 'inextricable part of his creative process'.[63] During the late 1970s, Mallet was a prominent figure in the

---

[62] Bowie, *Inspirations*.
[63] Pegg, *The Complete David Bowie*, 49.

audio-visual entertainment industry in the UK. He worked as a music video director with MGMM,[64] an enormously successful enterprise founded by Scott Millaney, who was known in some circles as 'the Godfather of the music video'.[65] Having directed videos for Blondie and Queen during the 1970s, Mallet became one of the most prolific music video directors during the eighties. Described by Pegg as 'a restless pioneer of cutting-edge video technology',[66] Mallet developed a reputation for innovative production techniques and for capturing the essence of the performance. As a producer and director of a wide variety of television and video modes, he is noted for his work on television documentaries and shows specialising in popular music and comedy. He directed twenty-eight episodes of the *Kenny Everett Video Show* between 1978 and 1980, which is how he came to work with Bowie.

It all started with Bowie's televised performance of 'Boys Keep Swinging' on the *Kenny Everett Video Show* on 14 April 1979. After working with Mallet on the show, Bowie invited him to direct an official video for the song. A few days later, the video was shot in the same television studio in time to accompany the song's official release on 27 April.[67] Although standing out as a remarkable video, 'Boys Keep Swinging' is unlikely to be described as an artistic masterpiece. The cliché television studio background and standard studio lighting give the video a dated feel. Despite these banalities, the video is significant for its strategic cultural impact, and for displaying the playful magic of Bowie's conjunction of chance composition, performativity and popular culture. The subversive intent of the video is best understood with knowledge of the song's creative process.

"Boys Keep Swinging" – the song

By all accounts, the song itself had a difficult labour, though once the music was delivered, Bowie wrote the lyrics quickly. Frustrated by what he called a 'too professional sound' emerging from the initial takes of the rhythm track, Bowie took inspiration from an Oblique Strategies card suggesting he 'USE UNQUALIFIED PEOPLE'.[68] He responded by having the band members switch

---

[64] 'David Mallet', *Thinwhiteduke.net*, https://tinyurl.com/y4fsdfkb.
[65] MGMM Studios, 'Scott Millaney – Producer', *MGMM Bios*, http://mgmm.tv/bios.
[66] Pegg, *The Complete David Bowie*, 49.
[67] 'Boys Keep Swinging' was released on 27 April 1979, as a single on the *Lodger* album.
[68] O'Leary, 'Boys Keep Swinging', *Pushing Ahead of the Dame*, 27 July 2011, https://tinyurl.com/58em9s4f.

their usual instruments with each other. According to O'Leary, 'Alomar competently played drums and Dennis Davis not-so-competently played bass'.[69] While this meant Visconti had to redo the bassline during the mixing stage, he 'used the opportunity to play a hyperactive line that echoed his work on *The Man Who Sold the World*'.[70] As a result, Visconti's 'patch-up' bassline 'became one of the track's main hooks'.[71] The exuberance of the resulting musical arrangement suggests the musicians were having fun playing an instrument they weren't accustomed to playing. Alomar later described the result as 'the best-sounding horrible young teen punk sound you ever heard'.[72] Musicologist Leah Kardos explains that the 'roughly played arrangement' of the song is attributable to the switching of instruments, and that 'the song's structure and chord progression [are] a direct quotation of … "Fantastic Voyage"', a song that also features on the *Lodger* album.[73] Kardos observes how Bowie frequently played with various types of 'experimental self-quotation' where he reworked his own previously performed musical gestures.[74] Experimental self-quotation is a distinctive audio-visual and gestural characteristic of Bowie's later music videos, such as 'The Stars (Are Out Tonight)' (2013), 'Blackstar' (2015) and 'Lazarus' (2016).[75]

While aleatory process in the recording studio gave the music an underlying subversive edge, the lyrics and performance of the vocals add a layer of semantic enigma. Interpreting Bowie's tone as 'beyond detachment or parody', O'Leary suggests 'the lyric and performance could be an extra-terrestrial's baffled report on human gender roles. If you are a male of the species *you can wear a uniform! You can buy a home of your own!*'[76] These words are consistent with Bowie's use of allusion in many of his songs and music videos. Richard Fitch argues that Bowie 'is a master of allusion, and as a master his allusions allow for more potential connections'.[77] Noting that 'etymologically, allusion can be traced to the Latin *alludere*, which means "to play with"',[78] Fitch explains how allusion generates for fans the pleasure of gameplay and making connections:

[69] Ibid.
[70] Ibid.
[71] Ibid.
[72] Carlos Alomar, interview with David Buckley (1999), quoted in Devereux, Dillane and Power, *David Bowie: Critical Perspectives*, 222.
[73] Leah Kardos, 'I Don't Want to Leave, or Drift Away: The Transition from David Bowie's Lodger to Scary Monsters', *Academia.Edu*, https://tinyurl.com/2p8stf3a.
[74] Ibid.
[75] For more on this, see Perrott, *David Bowie and the Transformation of Music Video*.
[76] O'Leary, 'Boys Keep Swinging'.
[77] Richard Fitch, 'In This Age of Grand Allusion: Bowie, Nihilism and Meaning', in Devereux, Dillane and Power (eds), *David Bowie: Critical Perspectives*, 20.
[78] Ibid., 19.

> Allusion allows the curious to play countless games of fruitful interpretation with Bowie's songs and performances. The curious can play by making their own connections because, in the absence of direct reference, there is no way of determining, once and for all, what connections Bowie had in mind when he crafted his allusions.[79]

While the rich tapestry of allusive references in Bowie's sonic and visual works offer fans the pleasure of gameplay and 'drillability', many of his songs portray the world from the position of an outsider or alien who might find 'normal' behaviour baffling. In addition to this sense of alterity, several of his early songs portray an innocent naivety about social codes, which adds a further layer of enigma. O'Leary observes how "Boys Keep Swinging" calls back to the naivety expressed in Bowie's earlier songs. Paradoxically, he also positions the song in relation to other parodic songs about masculinity:

> 'Boys' isn't really that far apart from 'In the Navy', with its lustily-chanted chorus, its barely-hidden gay anthemic qualities, its goofy delight in the cartoon masculine. It calls back to Bowie's early 'childhood' songs in that the lyric's perspective seems like a boy's cracked idea of what manhood is, with lines suggesting adulthood is like joining a Scout troop: *Uncage the colours! Unfurl the flag!*[80]

As O'Leary observes here, "Boys Keep Swinging" shares some continuity with the ambiguity and tone of Bowie's early songs "Uncle Arthur" (1967), "The Laughing Gnome" (1967) and "When I'm Five" (1968), albeit with additional layers of cultural subversion and performativity. Talking about "Boys Keep Swinging" in 2000, Bowie told Iman, 'the glory in that song is ironic. I do not feel that there is anything remotely glorious about being either male or female. I was merely playing on the idea of the colonization of gender'.[81]

'Boys Keep Swinging' – the video

The video begins with Bowie singing and dancing. As a caricature of a hyper-masculine crooner, or perhaps channelling the sexualized swagger of Elvis Presley and the boyish energy of Mick Jagger, Bowie indulges in vigorous hip

---

[79] Ibid., 20.
[80] O'Leary, 'Boys Keep Swinging'.
[81] Iman Abdulmajid, 'Watch That Man: Interview by Iman', *Bust Magazine*, October 2000, 32–3, also available at Bowie Wonderworld, https://tinyurl.com/mvzjv6pr.

thrusts and expressive arm gestures. His exaggerated posturing is cross-cut with three parodically feminine characters, all performed by Bowie. Much like the hybrid citations comprising his album covers, Bowie achieved these drag performances by mimicking and melding recognizable gestural traits associated with the Hollywood starlets such as Elizabeth Taylor, Katherine Hepburn, Lauren Bacall, Bette Davis and Marlene Dietrich.[82] While YouTube commenters have associated the three female characters in the video with various actresses, one viewer attempts to settle the confusion, writing 'according to the man himself: Lauren Bacall is the glamour puss. The beehive female is based on a 1950s era tarty girl from the midlands of England, and the old dear is based on Marlene Dietrich in her final years'.[83] Adding further complexity to this claim, Camile Paglia describes the character in the middle of the threesome as a 'blowsy, blasé, gum-cracking Elizabeth Taylor in a tendrilous chignon wig and a big crinoline skirt topped with a violet cinch belt'.[84] Showing off her (and Bowie's) extensive knowledge of cinema, Paglia interprets the character on the right as:

> ...an icy Valkyrie in a svelte metallic gold sheath dress with fetishistically deformed sleeves – boxy Joan Crawford shoulder pads sprouting lateral wings like shark fins ... Her full, dark hair resembles that of the enigmatic Lauren Becall in *To Have and Have Not* as well as the stormy Bette Davis in *All About Eve*. The dress itself recalls the clinging metallic moth costume worn by Katherine Hepburn...in *Christopher Strong*, and also the spectacular skin-tight nude dress of beaded silk soufflé designed in 1953 by Jean Louis for Marlene Dietrich's cabaret concerts.[85]

In addition to these references, Paglia associates this second character with Jerry Hall's entrance in Bryan Ferry's music video for 'Let's Stick Together' (1976), then unequivocally interprets the third drag character as Marlene Dietrich, noting that Bowie had recently acted alongside her in *Just a Gigolo* (1978). The fact that so many 'stars' are associated with these three drag characters is an indication of Bowie's 'magpie' tendency to forage and synthesize multiple intertextual references, a process that, in this instance, creates a simultaneous sense of familiarity and estrangement for viewers.

---

[82] Camille Paglia, 'Theatre of Gender: David Bowie at the Climax of the Sexual Revolution', in Victoria Broackes and Geoffrey Marsh (eds), *David Bowie Is* (London: V&A Publishing, 2013), 80.
[83] Mangasky7, comment on David Bowie, 'David Bowie – Boys Keep Swinging (Official Video)', YouTube video, 00:03:17, 25 June 2018, https://youtu.be/2KcOs70dZAw.
[84] Paglia, 'Theatre of Gender', 80.
[85] Ibid.

While Paglia praised the video for its 'camp wit', she derided it for having 'shabby production values'.[86] On face value, there's nothing particularly imaginative about the cinematography, lighting, setting, and editing transitions. Shot in the style of the *Kenny Everett Show*, this approach would seem to be a step backward from the artistry of Bowie's preceding videos. However, it is likely that Bowie may have deliberately intended the video to parody the aesthetic banality of pop TV shows. By establishing a sense of bland normality, the low production values accentuate the impact of the drag performances when they suddenly appear as a strange 'arty' interjection to what might otherwise be just another popular television show performance. After fifty-two seconds of manly swagger, the sense of TV show familiarity is abruptly defamiliarized by the first shot of Bowie in drag, performing as three back-up singers (Figure 4.10). This composite drag queen shot is used several times as a repetitive cross-cutting device, having an almost subliminal effect each time it appears. With each of the drag shots flashing on screen for only a second, it took several takes for viewers to realise that it was Bowie performing

Figure 4.10 Bowie performing as three back-up singers. 'Boys Keep Swinging' (David Mallet, 1979).

[86] Ibid.

in drag. YouTube commenter Erik Stevens wrote, 'I first noticed Bowie singing backup in his own song when I saw his teeth and had to playback the video and started to freak because it was Bowie doing drag'.[87] The technique of cross-cutting between longer shots of a masculine Bowie and the composite drag shots has the effect of emphasizing the contrast between masculine and feminine codes. Bowie's modish hairdo, suave suit and confident posture signify a debonair masculinity that contrasts with the tacky glamour of the dresses, jewellery and hairstyles of the female characters. Repetitively cross-cut against each other, these shots juxtapose diametric gender codes. This editing technique – known as Soviet Montage,[88] produces a conglomerate image of Bowie as beautiful man *and* beautiful woman – a combined image that has been described by YouTube commenters as both attractive and perplexing.[89]

As we shall see, what follows is even more perplexing for the audience, as the drag characters take possession of both stage and screen. The 'TV show' set segues into a faux Berlin nightclub set, complete with an Austrian Scallop curtain and a runway stage adorned with upright globe lights. The curtain rises to reveal 'gum-cracking Elizabeth Taylor',[90] who fixes her dress before strutting across the stage with the attitude of a well-worn drag queen. In a striking dual act of gestural contempt, Bowie pulls off his wig, tosses it away, and then performs a provocative back-handed lipstick smear (Figure 4.11). This act is repeated a second time by the 'icy Valkyrie' who Bowie plays cannily well, announcing her entrance with a fabulous hair flick and owning the stage with shimmering poise. As the first two drag characters prance across the stage, Bowie's gestural subversion is propelled by Adrian Belew's eccentrically liberated guitar solo, which builds, screeches and plummets, only to ascend again, serving as a musical commentary to each of Bowie's outrageous drag performances. YouTube commenters quip that Belew's 'washing machine on overdrive guitar solo' also sounds like 'a broken television or a radio you buy at the Goodwill store'.[91] For the third reveal, Bowie emerges from the curtains as an elderly Marlene Dietrich with twinset cardigan and buttoned up collar-shirt. Hobbling across the stage with a walking stick, 'Dietrich' shoots a disdainful glare before blowing a kiss to the audience. With hindsight,

---

[87] Erik Stevens, comment on David Bowie, 'David Bowie – Boys Keep Swinging (Official Video)'.
[88] Soviet Montage is an editing technique developed by Lev Kuleshov and Sergei Eisenstein, which creates new meaning through the juxtaposition of imagery within a filmed sequence of shots. For more on this, see David Bordwell, 'The Idea of Montage in Soviet Art and Film', *Cinema Journal* 11, no. 2 (1972): 9–17.
[89] John L, comment on David Bowie, 'David Bowie – Boys Keep Swinging (Official Video)'.
[90] Paglia. 'Theatre of Gender', 80.
[91] Douglas Milton and Markus Antonio, comment on 'David Bowie – Boys Keep Swinging (Official Video)'.

Figure 4.11 Bowie performs a back-handed lipstick smear. 'Boys Keep Swinging' (David Mallet, 1979).

we can see how this gesture exemplifies the way Bowie uses absurdist humour to conclude other videos, such as 'The Next Day' (2013) and 'The Stars (Are Out Tonight)' (2013).[92] This bizarre drag act is accompanied by Belew's equally bizarre guitar solo, winding out at the video's end to leave the audience with a residual sense of discomfort. The anarchic sound of the guitar, along with the musical freedom unleashed by switching instruments, provides a perfect accompaniment to the liberating wig-toss and lipstick smear.

This jaw-dropping drag performance left many viewers utterly perplexed, as expressed by YouTube comments like 'this disturbed the living shit out of me',[93] 'WTF was he thinking?! This is weird sht! Now at thirty-two I'm like this sht is genius!!!'[94] and 'I LOVED THIS – it damn near gave my father a stroke when Bowie came on TV looking like this. You can't imagine the utter dreariness of 1970s Yorkshire. Bowie, Bolan, Mercury put some life into our world.'[95] Not only

---

[92] For an analysis of these videos, see Perrott, *David Bowie and the Transformation of Music Video*.
[93] John L, comment on 'David Bowie – Boys Keep Swinging (Official Video)'.
[94] Mt. Zod, comment on 'David Bowie – Boys Keep Swinging (Official Video)'.
[95] Lulu Saintly, comment on 'David Bowie – Boys Keep Swinging (Official Video)'.

do these comments exemplify the social and cultural impact of this video upon its initial release in 1977, they demonstrate its continuing impact more than four decades later.

While the origins and communicative functions of lipstick smearing are multiple and culturally specific, this particular combination of lipstick smearing – followed by removal and tossing of a wig – was a specific performative act that Bowie added to his repertoire after observing it at Romy Haag's Berlin nightclub. Years later, Bowie said it 'was a well-known drag act finale gesture which I appropriated'.[96] This was not simply a matter of appropriating a gesture and performing a direct copy, however. Bowie inflected this powerful gesture with anarchistic intent and cynical posture, a point he openly acknowledges: 'I really liked the idea of screwing up the makeup after all the meticulous work that had gone into it. It was a nice destructive thing to do, quite anarchistic.'[97] This combination of avant-garde pastiche with popular musical and visual references has led to multiple interpretations and numerous reiterations. As an act of gender transgression, the lipstick smear has a mimetic life of its own, which Bowie may have foreseen. A similar gesture resurfaces in 'China Girl' (1983),[98] another video directed by Mallet (Figure 6.8), and in 1993 Bowie again performed a back-handed lipstick smear in the video for 'Jump They Say' (Figure 4.12).[99]

Figure 4.12 'Jump They Say' (Mark Romanek, 1993).

[96] Pegg, *The Complete David Bowie*, 49.
[97] Ibid.
[98] David Bowie, 'David Bowie – China Girl (Official Video)', YouTube video, 00:04:05, 19 June 2018, https://youtu.be/_YC3sTbAPcU.
[99] David Bowie, 'David Bowie – Jump They Say (Official Video)', YouTube video, 00:04:02, 22 June 2018, https://youtu.be/xPZWgCLMsW8.

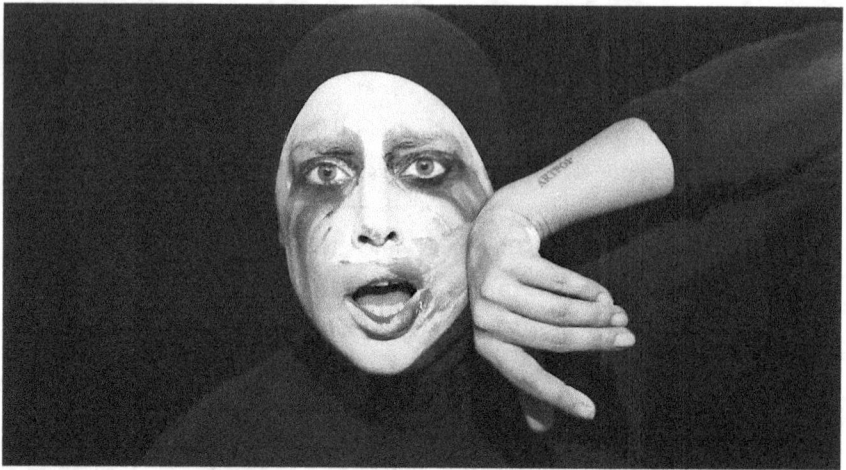

Figure 4.13 Lady Gaga re-enacts Bowie's lipstick smear. 'Applause' (Inez and Vinoodh, 2013).

However, in this context, the gesture appears as a cynical attitude towards corporate simulacra. In 2013, Lady Gaga performed a Bowie-esque smearing of her face paint in her video for 'Applause' (Figure 4.13).[100] And at the 2014 American Music Awards, Lorde ended her song by smearing her distinctively vampish lipstick across her face with the back of her hand (Figure 4.14). After Lorde's tribute to Bowie (with a nod to Dietrich) at the 2016 BRIT Awards, along with her Facebook post directly following Bowie's death,[101] her lipstick smearing gesture seems obviously indebted to Bowie.

'Boys Keep Swinging' – *Saturday Night Live* (1979)

One of the ways Bowie spread his work across mediums was by releasing several of his songs in conjunction with both official music videos and televised performances. With the passing of time and the advent of YouTube, the boundaries between these different forms have become blurred. While there is only one official music video for 'Boys Keep Swinging', the song was first released in the form of a live television performance on the *Kenny Everett Show*, which was

---

[100] Lady Gaga, 'Lady Gaga – Applause (Official Music Video)', YouTube video, 00:03:34, 20 August 2013, https://youtu.be/pco91kroVgQ.
[101] Lorde, Facebook post, 11 January 2016, https://tinyurl.com/4uz68u7x.

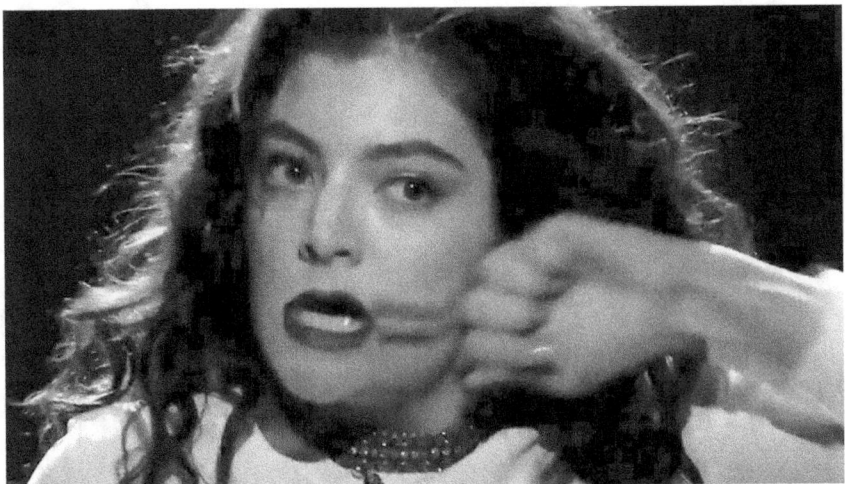

Figure 4.14 Lorde re-enacts Bowie's lipstick smear. 'Yellow Flicker Beat' (Live at the AMAs, 2014).

recorded on 23 April 1979. Since both were filmed in the same TV studio, the boundaries between the televised music show and the official music video are blurred. In addition to these two versions of the song, Bowie also performed 'Boys Keep Swinging' for the *Saturday Night Live (SNL)* television show, which was broadcast in the United States on 15 December 1979.[102] As Bowie explains, this performance was inspired by a trick he had seen in the fairgrounds in Germany:

> Standing in a kind of Punch and Judy booth, the performer, dressed in black, would attach a small body puppet (just trunk and limbs) below his chin. This gave the effect of a huge human headed marionette. He would then sing his oom-pah songs and everyone would drink and sing along. Very hearty. By using TV trickery we achieved the same effect while the puppet itself was seen to be of regular human height performing alongside the 'real' band.[103]

The 'TV trickery' Bowie refers to is a chroma-key video compositing technique which involved Bowie being filmed wearing a matching green outfit. An editor would then 'composite' footage of the dancing puppet in place of the green outfit. While it was an emerging technique in the late seventies, video compositing is now so commonly used that it would no longer be perceived as trickery. Bowie

---

[102] Gia, 'Bowie – TMWSTW, TVC15 & Boys Keep Swinging SNL 79', Vimeo video, 00:09:01, 2000, https://vimeo.com/348064534.
[103] Bowie, cited in Buckley, 'Revisiting Bowie's Berlin', 222.

Figure 4.15 Bowie performing with Klaus Nomi and Joey Arias. 'Boys Keep Swinging' (*Saturday Night Live*, 1979).

performed the song flanked by Klaus Nomi and Joey Arias, whose Dadaist costumes, face-paint and gestural performance added to the avant-garde sensibility (Figure 4.15). Adding artistic legitimacy to the strange image of Bowie as a floppy puppet, Nomi and Arias were an ideal support band. Bowie's puppetized body was to become a reiterated feature in his subsequent music videos, albeit using different techniques and with different strategic affects.[104] In the *SNL* performance, puppetry serves as a strategy of estrangement, particularly given the odd pairing of German trick puppetry with the popular American TV show format, and the limited audience awareness of the compositing technique in 1979. As he had done with the drag act in the official video, Bowie used this song again as a means to subvert the banality of television shows, but for *SNL*, he used a different approach to parody the glory of masculinity. Ironically, the show's censors blanked out the lyrics 'other boys check you out', but they failed to notice the puppet's giant phallus popping out from its clothing toward the end of the clip.[105] Both the *SNL* show and the official video for 'Boys Keep Swinging' demonstrate the idiosyncrasy of Bowie's absurdist humour, his penchant for parody and his cheeky subversion of normative culture and conventional media.

---

[104] For more on this, see Perrott, *David Bowie and the Transformation of Music Video*.
[105] 'David Bowie on *Saturday Night Live* in 1979', ThinWhiteDuke.net, https://tinyurl.com/369pzpj9.

Bowie's pop-up puppet phallus finale may have come as a shock to regular viewers of *SNL*. This finale came at the end of a three-song performance, which included Bowie dressed in a Bauhaus costume, followed by a dress and high heels accessorized by a pink poodle. Bowie was in the mood for subversion and Klaus Nomi was an ideal counterpart. It was the end of a decade and Bowie's work had reached a point of maturity, a point that seemed to lead further and further into parody. As Josh Jones observes, Bowie was entering a period of transition from one artistic phase to another, 'leaving behind his high concept work with Brian Eno on his Berlin trilogy … and entering another high pop phase. It was an abrupt, but natural, shift for Bowie; tapping into Nomi's art-pop affectations may have seemed a perfect way to bridge the two'.[106] In this sense, Bowie's television show and video outputs during the latter months of 1979 could be viewed as a means to segue from one creative phase into another.

'Look Back in Anger' – the video

During 1979 David Mallet also directed the videos for 'DJ' and 'Look Back in Anger', which were released in June and August of that year. While 'DJ' is aesthetically and thematically unremarkable, 'Look Back in Anger' is memorable for its gauche reinterpretation of the conclusion of Oscar Wilde's novel *The Picture of Dorian Gray* (1891).[107] Playing a Dorian-esque character, Bowie paints a self-portrait (Figure 4.16), and gazes upon it repeatedly, only to find that the painted likeness of himself becomes increasingly handsome while he himself physically degenerates. Bowie's physical decay is depicted through the addition of clay and paint to his face, a technique that lacks subtlety and is poorly executed. O'Leary aptly describes the video: 'Bowie, in an artist's loft, paints himself as an angel and then, reverse-*Dorian Gray* style, transforms into a grotesque with paint-and clay-encrusted skin'.[108] The video concludes with Bowie dragging himself up the stairs and crawling under a bed, which O'Leary interprets as an act of self-loathing: 'It's as though he's been made leprous by his art, and he's sickened by himself'.[109] Just as the story is played out in an overly dramatic and

---

[106] Josh Jones, 'David Bowie and Klaus Nomi's Hypnotic Performance on SNL (1979)', 5 September 2014, *Open Culture*, https://tinyurl.com/56e97cae.
[107] Oscar Wilde, *The Picture of Dorian Gray* (London: Ward, Lock and Company, 1891).
[108] O'Leary, 'Look Back in Anger', *Pushing Ahead of the Dame*, 22 July 2011, https://tinyurl.com/3v98dceb.
[109] Ibid.

Figure 4.16 Bowie with his self-portrait. 'Look Back in Anger' (David Mallet, 1979).

literal manner, the video also suffers from unimaginative editing, which is pronounced by the repetition of some of the mirror shots.

While the idea for the video may have been inspired by Bowie's passion for painting, it seems ironic that the video itself is far from a shining example of Bowie's artistry or Mallet's cinematic eye. There's further irony in the fact that RCA chose to promote the *Lodger* album with the video for 'Look Back in Anger' rather than 'Boys Keep Swinging', believing the former video would be a more palatable option for the US audience; an assumption that was not reflected in record sales.[110] Despite its drawbacks, the video is interesting for the role that Bowie plays: a painter (the flipside to his rock star personas), driven insane by the art he has created. This notion of being destroyed by one's artistic creation is a recurring theme in Bowie's *oeuvre*, recalling his acting role in the short film *The Image* (1969),[111] his film 'The Mask', and his last performance as Ziggy Stardust at London's Hammersmith Odeon (1973). As with these examples, Bowie used

---

[110] '1979 – "Lodger" – AUS/NZ', Bowiedownunder.com, http://www.bowiedownunder.com/lodger.html.
[111] Classic Multimedia, 'The Image (1969) Short Film Starring David Bowie', YouTube video, 00:13:19, 18 July 2021, https://tinyurl.com/3h9bva6a.

'Look Back in Anger' as a canvas to explore the links between creativity, destruction, and insanity. O'Leary alludes to these themes in relation to what he perceives as the song's function as a farewell to the past:

> If *Lodger* and *Scary Monsters* are Bowie finally considering the prospect of decline and tearing himself up, sampling and dispersing himself, 'Look Back in Anger' is at the heart of these records. It's a dry, weird farewell to a muse, decades before Bowie (apparently) stopped recording and performing.... So, on the far end of a decade that Bowie, in part, had authored was 'Anger', which sets the stage for the even grander renunciation of 'Ashes to Ashes'.[112]

As indicated by the examples above, Bowie had always needed to farewell his past, even if that meant performing a destructive act to put to death a decaying persona. With the decade drawing to a close, he used the video for 'Look Back in Anger' – much as he used his various performances on television shows – as a vehicle to bid farewell to the past and to bookend the decade, thus allowing him to move on to the next decade with a clean canvas. To achieve this, he needed to segue from 'Look Back in Anger' to his final television show videos of the decade; that segue was to be the theme of insanity, and the focal point of show was 'Space Oddity' (1979).

'Space Oddity' (1979) – the televised videos

In 1979, two new videos were shot for 'Space Oddity,' both released on television shows on New Year's Eve. The first was shot for Dick Clark's *Salute to the Seventies* tribute show, which was broadcast on US NBC on 31 December 1979.[113] In this video, Bowie is dressed in grey overalls cinched in at the waist with a wide belt and heavy buckle. The overall costume resembles a futuristic Soviet space suit, a look enhanced by Bowie's stern facial expressions and rigid militaristic poses. He folds his arms and places his fists on his hips in a masculine manner; the antithesis to Ziggy's feminized hand-on-hip pose. Perhaps a low budget attempt to create a façade of the imagined interior décor of a futuristic spacecraft, the set comprises minimalist curved structures, repetitively arranged so as to create the illusion of receding perspective. The uniformity of the set, subdued light and monochromatic

---

[112] O'Leary, 'Look Back in Anger'.
[113] A remastered version of this video is available on YouTube. While the televised video was initially broadcast with Bowie miming to the 1969 version of the song, YouTube user Mister Sussex has reedited this video to fit with the 1979 recording of the song. See Mister Sussex, 'David Bowie "Space Oddity" remastered 1979 vocal version', YouTube video, 00:04:49, 15 May 2016, https://youtu.be/yU2hRBdrYS8.

tone is consistent with stereotypical notions of Soviet space missions. The overall look of the video is so quintessentially Soviet that in some shots Bowie's guitar could easily be mistaken for a *balalaika*. It remains unclear what the rationale was for broadcasting a Soviet stylized video in the US at the height of the Cold War. Since the cultural palatability of US and UK audiences differed around this time, it's worth comparing this video with another version of "Space Oddity", which was broadcast on UK television on the same night. For the US show, Bowie mimed to the 1969 version of the song; for the UK show, he mimed to a freshly re-recorded 'acoustic' version, which bears some striking differences to the other recordings of "Space Oddity". Directed by Mallet and shot at Ewart Studios, Wandsworth on 18 September 1979, the video was broadcast on 31 December on the New Year's Eve special edition of the *Kenny Everett Show*.[114]

"Space Oddity" (1979) – the song

As discussed in chapter two, the popularity of the 1969 recording of "Space Oddity" did not wane; in fact, the song became iconic. So why did Bowie heavily revise such a popular song? Few popular musicians have undertaken such a severe revision of their own song. In 1980, Bowie explained that this new recording eventuated because Mallet wanted him to appear on his show and he wanted him to sing "Space Oddity":

> I agreed as long as I could do it again without all its trappings and do it strictly with three instruments. Having played it with just an acoustic guitar onstage early on, I was always surprised as how powerful it was just as a song, without all the strings and synthesizers. In fact, the video side of it was secondary; I really wanted to do it as a three-piece song.[115]

Given that it was the prospect of a new video that led to the song's re-recording, it's interesting that Bowie viewed the video as secondary. The upcoming video provided an opportunity for Bowie to conduct an experiment. His collaborations with Eno and Visconti had convinced him of the creative benefits of musical experimentation, and this gave him the confidence to experiment with one of his most iconic songs, by stripping it down to bare bones. The song was re-recorded

---

[114] 'Will Kenny Everett Make it to 1980?' *Kenny Everett Show*, broadcast on 31 December 1979. The video of the show was shot at Ewart Studios, Wandsworth, on 18 September 1979.
[115] Angus MacKinnon, 'The Future Isn't What It Used to Be', *New Musical Express*, 13 September 1980, https://tinyurl.com/3a79uwhc.

in September 1979 at Visconti's Good Earth Studios in Soho, London. With Visconti's production skills and three backing musicians, a radical new recording of this song was achieved, one that recontextualized the song's themes of alienation and outer space. According to Adrian Cepeda, the 1969 version:

> ...had this lifted exploration spirit that gave hope to a new generation.... A decade later, that hope had been extinguished with a dramatic sparse sound reflecting back to the paranoid alienation Bowie felt in the 1970s.... "Space Oddity" sounds more powerful grounded in this Lennon inspired stripped down primal arrangement.[116]

Apparently inspired by John Lennon's instrumentation for his 1970 album *Plastic Ono Band*,[117] Bowie's vocal and acoustic guitar are accompanied by only three instruments: bass by Zaine Griff, drums by Andy Duncan and piano by Hans Zimmer. Locked in unison, each of the instruments serve a specific purpose; the bass and drums provide a solid yet minimalist rhythmic bedrock and the piano adds emotional texture. These instruments are played with restraint so that acoustic space is provided and Bowie's harrowed vocal is enabled to soar. His vocal always seems to be floating above the instruments, perhaps aptly situated in outer space, while the raw sound of his acoustic guitar grounds the song on Earth. This arrangement is appropriate, given this is a song about Major Tom having fallen to Earth. The notion of 'falling to Earth' takes on a different connotation in this version of the song, however, so it is fitting that the electronic synthesizer sounds are absent and the lift-off sequence is replaced by twelve seconds of silence. The resulting song is remarkable for its sonic space, which propels Bowie's powerful vocal performance and enhances the sense of isolation evoked by the video. As O'Leary describes it, 'Bowie clarified "Oddity" down to the vocal melody, a harshly-strummed twelve-string guitar, a basic bass-drums rhythm section. Instead of a countdown, silence. Instead of the measured back-and-forth of Major Tom and Ground Control's interplay, a pained solitary vocal.'[118] This clarified version was the first step toward estranging a song that had become perhaps too familiar for Bowie. The next step was the video.[119]

---

[116] Onlylovecanleavesuchamark, 'Space Oddity [1979 Re-record]', *Don't Forget the Songs 365*, 12 August 2012, https://tinyurl.com/mr3as54p.
[117] Ibid.
[118] O'Leary, 'Ashes to Ashes', *Pushing Ahead of the Dame*, 13 September 2011, https://tinyurl.com/22c69vuv.
[119] Nacho Video, 'David Bowie • Space Oddity • Will Kenny Everett Make It To 1980? Show • 31 December 1979', YouTube video, 00:04:54, 1 January 2020, https://tinyurl.com/mrxhv7my.

'Space Oddity' (1979) – the Mallet video

> It's familiar, yet strange... like we're watching a transmission from a parallel past, that draws on our collective pop memories but renders them skewed, distorted. But the closer you look, the clearer things become. (Bauer Xcel, 2013)[120]

The video begins with the strum of an acoustic guitar and a white screen, which gradually reduces opacity to reveal Bowie's face in close-up. Deep in character, he stares intensely into the camera lens singing 'Ground control to Major Tom...' His eyes dart nervously away then quickly return with a strained fixity (Figure 4.17).

Bowie's performance appears fragile and on-edge, the antithesis of his mastery of the camera in previous videos. No longer is he seductively playing with being the object of the gaze; he appears disempowered, controlled, as though he is the object of surveillance. His paranoid disposition suggests that he is performing to

Figure 4.17 Bowie stares intensely into the camera lens. 'Space Oddity' (David Mallet, 1979).

---

[120] Bauer Xcel, 'David Bowie and Kenny Everett's "Space Oddity"', *Mojo*, 23 July 2013, https://tinyurl.com/38ecshee.

the camera under duress. As he stops singing and places his guitar beside his chair, his eyes remain glued to the camera. What happens next is a magnificent breach of both music video and television show conventions. During an uncomfortably long ten seconds of silence, Bowie leaves his seat and walks briskly across the studio with his arms folded and shoulders hunched over. Breaking the 'fourth wall', the camera tracks Bowie's exit, divulging lighting rigs, a monitor and other technical apparatus strewn across the 'off-screen' studio. Panning across the studio, the camera reveals that Bowie is being surveilled by a woman in a nurse's uniform at the helm of a camera (Figure 4.18). He turns his head, anxiously clocking the panoptical nurse, before entering an 'on-screen' set within the studio – a padded cell containing only a chair and a guitar. A high louvre window casts streaks of white light across the back wall. This stark set instantly signifies mental instability and institutional entrapment, just as the sustained silence builds tension and accentuates the sense of spatial isolation. Bowie picks up the guitar, sits on the chair and faces the camera ready to continue the song. Breaking the long stretch of silence, a drumbeat coincides with an abrupt cut to a black and white close-up shot of Bowie's face, surrounded by flexible tubes. Only lasting for the length of a single drumbeat, this image

Figure 4.18 Breaking the 'fourth wall' of the television studio. 'Space Oddity' (David Mallet, 1979).

subliminally suggests another reality before returning to a wide shot of Bowie alone in the padded cell. This time, when he sings 'This is Ground Control to Major Tom' the song sounds fuller with the inclusion of the accompanying instruments. While Bowie's voice appears to echo off the sides of the padded walls, in retrospect we know this studio set had no bearing on the construction of this eerie voice, contained in three-dimensional space. Coincidentally, Visconti generated this entrapped sense of acoustic space during the recording of the song before the video shoot. He would not have been aware of how well the recorded sound would match the visual sense of entrapment in the video.

Still in wide shot, Bowie sings, 'You've really made the grade, and the papers want to know whose shirts you wear.' The camera slowly tracks in closer, then cuts to a black and white wide shot as it tracks toward Bowie reading a newspaper and sitting in what looks like an astronaut's chair. Adorned with flexible tubes and flashing lights, the chair looks out-of-place in its domestic setting, which is furnished with 1970s kitchen décor and a nurse preparing something at the bench. The familiarity of the kitchen setting is estranged by the nurse, who appears incongruous in a kitchen, and operating a camera in a television studio. The nurse is prefaced in Kenny Everett's introduction to the video, where she is cleaning a wall of television screens with a giant clock to one side, as though priming the audience to take special note of these screens as intertextual references to Roeg's film *The Man Who Fell to Earth*, along with other potential clues, which might help explain the meanings generated by the video.

In addition to the sense of desperation and edginess of Bowie's performance, viewers are likely to feel perplexed by the angular lighting, the strange images and the analogical way in which these are edited. Bowie and the nurse appear unfazed by the exploding oven and rubbish bin. A potential kitchen catastrophe is averted by cutting back to the deeper tragedy of Bowie singing, alone in the padded cell. His intensely desperate stare into the camera lens is accentuated by a slow tracking shot that moves into an extreme close-up of his eyes. A cross-dissolve transitions into a wider shot of the padded cell (Figure 4.19). Singing 'The planet Earth is blue and there's nothing I can do', Bowie sits in darkness, lit only by a small spotlight, casting his shadow on the back wall. Here we see an excellent example of the film noir lighting that Bowie and Mallet used again in 1981 in 'Wild is the Wind' and 'The Drowned Girl', videos that were lit to diminish the presence of the studio set. In contrast, the noir lighting in 'Space Oddity' (1979) characterizes Bowie and the constructed set as psychologically unstable characters. An angular shaft of light stretches across the wall, creating a venetian

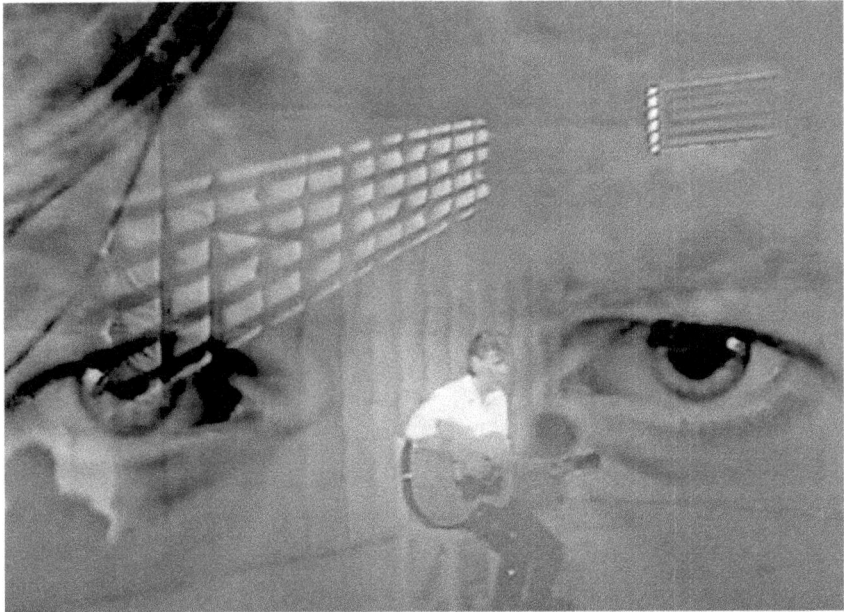

Figure 4.19 A cross-dissolve creates dramatic effect. 'Space Oddity' (David Mallet, 1979).

blind pattern across the wall and sharply pointing toward the shadow cast by the spotlight (Figure 4.20). Accentuated by wafts of haze, the low-key angular light creates an expressionistic feel, reinforced later in the video by a series of rapidly cut images that are shot from oblique angles. Building upon the sense of entrapment and psychological instability already created by the music and the set design, the expressionistic lighting and oblique camera angles conjure images from *The Cabinet of Dr Caligari* (1920),[121] a German Expressionist film that features imagery of an insane asylum. Specific images from *Dr Caligari* are also intertextually referenced by shots of Bowie's body against the padded wall in 'Space Oddity' (Figures 4.21 and 4.22). Along with the film *Metropolis* (1927),[122] *Dr Caligari* was a key inspiration for the preparatory drawings Bowie drew in 1974 for an unrealized film set in 'Hunger City', which further inspired the stage set designed by Mark Ravitz for the *Diamond Dogs* tour.[123] These examples show

---

[121] *The Cabinet of Dr Caligari*, directed by Robert Wiene (1920, Berlin: *Lixie-Atelier* film studio).
[122] *Metropolis*, directed by Fritz Lang (1927, Berlin: UFA studios).
[123] David Cantello, 'Diamond Dogs – An Unfinished Film', YouTube video, 00:02:49, 21 March 2021, https://tinyurl.com/y2rvhe98. See also, Broackes and Marsh (eds), *David Bowie Is*, 130–5.

Figure 4.20 Noir lighting references 1920s expressionistic film sets. 'Space Oddity' (David Mallet, 1979).

Figure 4.21 Expressionistic aesthetics in *The Cabinet of Dr Caligary* (Robert Wiene, 1920).

Figure 4.22 References to German Expressionist film. 'Space Oddity' (David Mallet, 1979).

how, on more than one occasion, Bowie drew on German Expressionist artistic strategies as a means of expressing the instability of psychological space through set design, camera angles, and light.

While earlier versions of 'Space Oddity' alluded to the alienation of outer space, Mallet's 1979 version alludes to the alienation of internal space via visual and sonic signifiers of psychological instability. In conjunction with Bowie's eerie vocal and nervous gestural performance, the padded cell, the nurse, and the kitchen setting work together to signify the entrapment of institutional space and the neurosis of domestic space. Building upon the sense of alienation conjured by these images, the sight of Bowie sitting in an astronaut's chair reading a newspaper intertextually calls up images from *The Man Who Fell to Earth*,[124] which includes shots of Bowie sitting in a similar chair within a domestic setting, while watching television. The television screens and astronaut's chair serve as travelling transmedial motifs that transport the theme of alienation across the past and future of Bowie's *oeuvre* (a point that is reinforced by the presence of such motifs in audio-visual productions created after Bowie's death, such as Tom Hingston's

[124] *The Man Who Fell to Earth*, directed by Nicolas Roeg (1976, UK: Cinema 5).

posthumous video for Bowie's song 'No Plan' (2017)[125] and the 2022 television series *The Man Who Fell to Earth*).[126] As discussed in the following chapter, Bowie is seated in a reduced version of this time travelling chair in his next video, 'Ashes to Ashes' (1980), which also includes shots that were filmed in 'Space Oddity's' padded cell and kitchen sets. These explicit threads of continuity between the two videos reinforces the fact that 'Ashes to Ashes' was intended as a sequel to 'Space Oddity'. As we shall see, Bowie wove further threads of continuity beyond these two videos, thus extending the story of Major Tom to the videos released just before, and beyond, his death. Bowie built a surreal storyworld for 'Space Oddity', inhabiting it with enigmatic characters and worldbuilding components. The universal theme of alienation has enabled the song to endure ongoing reconfiguration across mediums, time, and space.

Denouement

This chapter began by exploring Bowie's collaborations with Visconti, Eno, Dorfman and Mallet. While Bowie's collaborations with Visconti and Eno had a longevity that lasted until his death, his working relationships with music video directors were often short lived. Despite the brilliance and obvious artistic compatibility of the directors discussed in this chapter, Bowie was a strong believer in the creative renewal of working with new people, and he would restlessly move on to further collaborators. However, with Mallet, he was starting to appreciate the continuity and reliability of a longer-term collaboration, which is explored in the following chapter. Through his collaborations, Bowie learnt the art of aleatory composition, which left its mark on much of his creative work, but particularly on his songs and videos of the late seventies.

Bowie's videos of this period portray a maturity, a seriousness and a parodic wit not evident in his earlier videos. His performance to camera is more nuanced than in previous videos, something that is particularly evident in the videos for 'Be My Wife', 'Heroes' and 'Space Oddity' (1979). These three videos are remarkable for their lighting, composition within the frame, and for their references to key moments and movements in art history.

---

[125] Bowie, 'David Bowie – No Plan (Video)', YouTube video, 00:04:02, 8 January 2017, https://tinyurl.com/354wcnwb. See Perrott, *David Bowie and the Transformation of Music Video*.
[126] *The Man Who Fell to Earth*, created by Jenny Lumet and Alex Kurtzman (2022, CBS Studios, Secret Hideout, Timberman-Beverly Productions).

While the videos discussed in this chapter provide a window into Bowie's passion for art, they are also artworks in their own right. Bowie treated each of these videos, not only as an extension of himself, but as a canvas, upon which paint could be applied. In this respect, Bowie was deeply affected by the history, culture, and cities of Eastern Europe, and especially Berlin. Each of these videos is shaped in some way by those experiences, whether that be working in a studio under the shadow of the Wall, experiencing drag acts in a Berlin nightclub, frequenting art museums, enjoying puppetry tricks, or watching early German films.

Bowie's passion for painting, visual art and cinema is expressed in these videos via lighting, transitions, set design and performance. Not only do these videos reference paintings, films and film stars, they are significant for establishing the capacity for music videos to function as works of art in their own right. The videos discussed in this chapter are fascinating resources for anyone studying the links between music video, art history, and cinema. The next chapter will extend and deepen our understanding of the remediation of music video.

5

Future Nostalgia

An old man searching for driftwood on the beach was asked to move away from the set. When Mallet pointed at Bowie and asked the old man if he knew who he was, the old man replied, 'Of course I do. It's some c*** in a clown suit.' Bowie later said, 'That was a huge moment for me. It put me back in my place and made me realize, 'Yes, I'm just a c*** in a clown suit.'

Bowie 1993[1]

Retold here by Michael Dignum,[2] Bowie's 'clown suit' anecdote became the basis for a humorous animated skit directed and narrated by Adam Buxton.[3] While mythologizing the production process for 'Ashes to Ashes' (1980), the skit has provided a fan-made extension to the storyworld elaborated by the video. For many fans, 'Ashes to Ashes' is now associated with the comic tone of Buxton's portrayal of Bowie's voice, along with hilarious caricatures of his personas, and a 2D cartoon aesthetic (Figure 5.1). When working as a production assistant on the video shoot for 'Miracle Goodnight' (1993), Dignum asked Bowie about his favourite moment in his career. According to a post Dignum shared on Facebook,[4] Bowie responded with the above anecdote, before describing it as a life-changing moment during the production of 'Ashes to Ashes' – a timely reminder not to take himself too seriously.

Despite the frivolity of Bowie's anecdote, the clown suit was not meant as a caricature, and it was not new. As discussed in chapter two, Bowie had been

---

[1] Jason Heller, 'How Ashes to Ashes Put the First Act of David Bowie's Career to Rest', *NPR*, 6 October 2017, https://tinyurl.com/2whjrj5n.
[2] A YouTube playlist for chapter 5 is available, at https://tinyurl.com/2dcxyptn.
[3] Adam Buxton, 'David Bowie – 'Ashes to Ashes' Clown Suit Story   Adam Buxton', YouTube video, 00:02:19, 9 January 2021, https://tinyurl.com/yj8ar296.
[4] Michael Dignum, Facebook post, 12 January 2016, https://tinyurl.com/bde9343e.

Figure 5.1 'Ashes to Ashes Clown Suit Story' (Adam Buxton, 2021).

fascinated with Pierrot as early as 1968, when he began articulating this figure across stage, television, and promotional film. In 1976, Bowie proclaimed that he *was* Pierrot:

> I'm Pierrot. I'm Everyman. What I'm doing is theatre, and only theatre.... What you see on stage isn't sinister. It's pure clown.... The white face, the baggy pants – they're Pierrot, the eternal clown putting over the great sadness of 1976.
>
> Bowie[5]

While demonstrating the continuity of Pierrot across Bowie's *oeuvre*, this comment also provides some clues for those who are perplexed by his music videos. By 1980, Bowie's long-standing relationship with the figure was not only a mnemonic for 'playing the clown', Pierrot had become a persona that would be indelibly imprinted in myths and legends. To comprehend the significance of the figure in relation Bowie's remediation of music video, this chapter explores the use of Pierrot as an artistic strategy in theatre and music. While I refer to the Mallet videos discussed in chapter four, this chapter examines three further videos directed by Mallet – 'Ashes to Ashes', 'Wild is the Wind' and 'The Drowned Girl'. These videos were selected because of their contribution to the artistry of music video. To comprehend the context in which these videos were produced, it is first necessary to consider Bowie's creative and collaborative situation in 1980.

---

[5] Rook, 'Waiting for Bowie'.

A new Art Decade

Having extracted himself from the psychic vortex that had come to a head during his time in Berlin, Bowie was entering a new decade and a new creative phase. Propelled by a growing urge to explore the artistic possibilities of music video, Bowie realized he needed to have more control over the artistic direction of his videos. Mallet was an ideal collaborator since he did not view himself as an auteur director of music video. He perceived his role as enabling the musician to achieve their artistic vision, rather than being the instigator or controller of that vision. Not only did Mallet's stance enable Bowie to achieve his vision in a directorial sense, it also enabled him to learn the specific steps of crafting a music video, such as concept design, storyboarding and casting. This urge to engage in the craft of music video characterized a new phase for Bowie, which happened to coincide with the ascendance of MTV. Although Bowie collaborated with an array of video and film directors across the MTV period, this chapter focuses primarily on his collaboration with Mallet. While Bowie's artistic vision is revealed by statements he made during media interviews published during the early 1980s, Mallet discussed his contribution to these videos during an interview with me in February 2021. This combination of interview material shows Bowie's intensifying directorial vision along with Mallet's innovation. This chapter also traces continuities and divergences portrayed across the videos released by Bowie between 1979 and 1982, showing how he used his videos as vehicles for the extension of storyworlds, while also using them as a means of emotional purging.

Scary Monsters

1980 heralded a new phase for Bowie. Not only was it a time in which he had decided to become more involved in the creative vision for his videos, it was also the year he had embraced a major Broadway acting role alongside recording a new album that introduced a new sound and attitude. The intermedial dialogue between these projects inflected the sonic, lyrical and visual flavour of the songs and videos that Bowie produced during this period. The *Scary Monsters* album was recorded in sessions at the Power Station in New York during February 1980, and subsequently at Good Earth studio in London during April

---

[6] Bowie's last performance as Merrick in *The Elephant Man* was on 3 January 1981. Later that month, Bowie relocated from New York to Switzerland.

1980. That year, Bowie spent several months in New York while he was acting in the Broadway production of *The Elephant Man*, a role that significantly impacted his psychic state.[6] In a 1980 interview, Bowie described the intermedial flow of ideas emerging from this experience:

> The play's in the evenings, I do my writing during the day and I can paint when I come home from the theatre. I'm a bit harassed because this play thing is hard on, daily, to sort of ... I find it hard to kick the part, daily. And it's very intense during the days of the week. It's not the physical thing either, it's the emotional chronology of what happens to him [Joseph Merrick's character] during the course of the play – sticks with you during the day sort of like, as though you're sort of covered with apple sauce or something, and you've washed it off but it's still sticky.[7]

Likening the experience of immersing himself in Merrick's emotional chronology to being covered with sticky apple sauce, Bowie is conscious of an emotional stickiness infiltrating his work across other mediums. He also put this stickiness down to synchronicity, unsurprising when considering his interest in the philosophies of Carl Jung. When an interviewer asked Bowie if he drew influence from his role in *The Elephant Man* when creating the music for *Scary Monsters*, he replied:

> Synchronicity! ... It's quite likely that the idea of *Elephant Man* did stay with me, as a title, but I know, just in my memory reference that it actually came from a Kellog's Cornflakes packet. On the back they were giving away, it said 'buy your packet of Kellog's Cornflakes, and inside you will find scary monsters and super heroes', so presumably [you] found supermen and Nosferatu's in your mouth, and as I was writing a New York album it seemed the perfect sort of collective title for the bits and pieces I was writing on.[8]

Further exemplifying his penchant for taking inspiration from chance occurrences, this comment signals how the emotional stickiness of Bowie's role in *The Elephant Man* may have coincided with all that he found to be scary and monstrous about New York City during his stay there in 1980. In another interview he remarked that, after spending longer than a month living in New York, 'the influx of the general paranoia, high jet-set fashion and abject poverty, all had an awful lot to do with the input that went into *Scary Monsters*',[9] likening his emotionally demanding acting role to 'sort of being thrown in the deep end

---

[7] David Bowie, interview by Andy Peebles on 7 December 1980, quoted in Nacho Video, 'David Bowie in New York 1980. The Elephant Man, Scary Monsters & Other Strange People', YouTube video, 00:37:48, 5 December 2020, https://youtu.be/F1fTtwGqdQw.

[8] Bowie, interviewed by Andy Peebles.

[9] Ibid.

to come back to New York with all its terrors and delights'.[10] These comments provide a sense of why Bowie felt the need to purge himself of discomforting feelings through the process of recording the album:

> *Scary Monsters* for me has always been some kind of purge. It was me eradicating the feelings within myself that I was uncomfortable with.... You have to accommodate your pasts within your persona. You have to understand why you went through them. That's the major thing. You cannot just ignore them or put them out of your mind or pretend they didn't happen or just say, 'Oh I was different then'.[11]

These comments are instructive when considering the emotional and psychic context penetrating the songs on *Scary Monsters* and the music video for 'Ashes to Ashes', which Bowie identified as the one song in particular that he used to purge himself of the 1970s. He described the song as 'long overdue – the end of something',[12] later explaining, 'I was wrapping up the seventies really for myself, and ["Ashes to Ashes"] seemed a good enough epitaph for it'.[13] This purging process, along with Bowie's engagement with persona, is evident when examining the lyrical, sonic, and visual composition of the video. A good place to start is to consider the potential meanings generated by the song's lyrics.

"Ashes to Ashes" – the song

Serving as a sequel to "Space Oddity", "Ashes to Ashes" extends upon the storyworld initiated in 1969, when Bowie first sung of Major Tom's alienation with his Earth-based counterpart, Ground Control. From his inception, Major Tom possessed a shape-shifting capacity to reappear at different times across Bowie's *oeuvre*. "Ashes to Ashes" provided an opportunity to reignite the decade-old storyworld of "Space Oddity" and to contemporize the plight of Major Tom.

During the decade following the initial release of "Space Oddity", Bowie had adopted a string of personas. He had also experienced psychic challenges, drug addiction and a marriage break-up, all of which provided material for character development, as exemplified by troubled character Major Tom. Having been left adrift in outer space for eleven years, Major Tom fell to Earth in a paranoid and

---

[10] Ibid.
[11] Chris O'Leary, 'Ashes to Ashes', *Pushing Ahead of the Dame*, 13 September 2011, https://tinyurl.com/22c69vuv.
[12] Pegg, *The Complete David Bowie*, 29.
[13] Ibid.

drug-addled state; strung out in heaven's high, hitting an all-time low'.[14] Beyond the dual functions of purging his troubled past and extending a storyworld, the song fulfilled a nostalgic desire for Bowie to engage with the purity of childhood emotions. In an interview in 1980, Bowie quipped that the song 'really is an ode to childhood, if you like, a popular nursery rhyme. It's about spacemen becoming junkies'.[15] He reiterated this idea in a 2003 interview, reflecting that "Ashes to Ashes" was partially inspired by the song "Inchworm," sung by Danny Kaye in the 1952 film *Hans Christian Andersen*:

> I loved it as a kid and it's stayed with me forever. I keep going back to it ... "Ashes to Ashes" wouldn't have happened if it hadn't have been for "Inchworm". There's a child's nursery rhyme element in it, and there's something so sad and mournful and poignant about it. It kept bringing me back to the feelings of those pure thoughts of sadness that you have as a child, and how they're so identifiable even when you're an adult. There's a connection that can be made between being a somewhat lost five-year-old and feeling a little abandoned, and having the same feeling when you're in your twenties. And it was that song that did that for me.[16]

This childhood sense of bereft abandonment became enmeshed into the emotional fabric of "Ashes to Ashes". The lyrics evoke imagery of abandonment, whether that be an image of an astronaut lost in space or a junkie plummeting from 'heaven's high'. Most salient in the chorus and concluding sections of the song, the nursery rhyme-like phonic pattern serves as a nostalgic mnemonic: 'My mama said, to get things done, you better not mess with Major Tom ...' is a direct riff off the British rhyme 'my mother said, you never should, play with the gypsies in the woods'.[17] As such, this lyric carries direct associations with those nursery rhyme mythologies of abduction, which were employed to generate fear of anyone who appeared as 'other'. When discussing the nursery rhyme element of the song in 1980, Bowie indicated his awareness of this literary form as a means of conjuring such associations, saying:

> It's very much a 1980s nursery rhyme [...] and I think that 1980s nursery rhymes will have a lot to do with the 1880s, 1890s nursery rhymes which were all rather horrid and had little boys with their ears being cut off.
>
> Bowie, 1980[18]

---

[14] Heller, 'How "How Ashes to Ashes Put the First Act of David Bowie's Career to Rest"&3x200A;'.
[15] MacKinnon, 'The Future Isn't What It Used to Be'.
[16] Bill DeMain, 'The Sound and Vision of David Bowie', *Performing Songwriter*, Issue 72, September/October 2003, https://tinyurl.com/44xs8dkv.
[17] Richard O'Neil, 'The Gypsy Exception', *The Guardian*, 14 November 2007, https://tinyurl.com/bdhzejhn.
[18] Bowie, TeenageWildlife, 'David Bowie – Scary Monsters Interview'.

This comment is indicative of Bowie's engagement with the collective unconscious, as philosophised by Carl Jung.[19] From a Jungian perspective, nursery rhymes are symbolically rich mythologies located in the collective unconscious. This somewhat amorphous 'medium' enables them to be transmitted orally and visually across communities and generations, thus providing a resilient mnemonic device for triggering emotions, anxieties and imagined scenarios. When combined with the visual imagery of a sad clown and a funeral procession in an otherworldly setting, the nursery rhyme elements of this song conjure a strange mixture of anxiety and a bereft sense of nostalgia related to an otherworldly future. Reinforcing this discomforting sense of dystopia and loss, Bowie uses vocal techniques that induce a sense of sadness. O'Leary explains how, in crucial parts of the song, Bowie's vocals are delivered as a sequence of octave drops, where the vocal octave starts high and then drops toward the end of the lyric line.[20] According to Devereux *et al.*, this technique of representing mood and emotion through melodic contour is a convention of various types of dramatic music performance. Furthermore, the song's repeated descending phrases are interpreted as 'musically representing the fall of the protagonist',[21] thus sharing similarities with the techniques used by Arnold Schoenberg:

> ...the melodic materials are repeated three times before the end of the phrase runs into a kind of speech-song articulation, the conversational 'Oh no, don't say it's true' and 'Oh no, not again', light allusion to, perhaps, the dramatic *Sprechstimme* technique used by Arnold Schoenberg ... the tone is overwrought and exaggerated, gossipy even, just like how the clown would muse conspiratorially in a show ... or how one might represent ... an interior exchange between two sides of one person, struggling perhaps, under the influence of drugs.[22]

A cross between singing and speaking, the *sprechstimme* technique produces a tonal quality in which the pitch is heightened and lowered along melodic contours. Just as Schoenberg used *sprechstimme* as a dramatic device to create tension, Bowie experimented with arrangements that combine singing, speaking, murmuring, and even guttural shouting, all of which are evident in songs on the *Scary Monsters* album.[23] Bowie also used innovative pitch-shifting techniques to achieve variations of *sprechstimme* and harmonic counterpoint in several songs,

---

[19] Carl Jung, *The Archetypes and the Collective Unconscious* (Princeton: Princeton University Press, 1969).
[20] O'Leary, 'Ashes to Ashes'.
[21] Devereux, Dillane and Power, *David Bowie: Critical Perspectives*, 49.
[22] Ibid.
[23] These techniques are evident in 'It's No Game', 'Scream Like a Baby' and 'Ashes to Ashes', songs released in 1980 on the album *Scary Monsters (and Super Creeps)*.

including "The Laughing Gnome", "Fame" and "Scream Like a Baby".[24] When recalling the production of the latter song, Visconti describes how he used EFX to enhance the mood of the lyrics, resulting in Bowie's voice going 'up and down in pitch contrarily on opposite sides' of stereo channels.[25]

'Ashes to Ashes' – the video

Considered the most expensive music video made up until that time,[26] 'Ashes to Ashes' was released on 1 August 1980, one year before MTV first went to air. Described by Victoria Broackes as a 'pioneering' music video,[27] 'Ashes to Ashes' was a source of inspiration for video directors, musicians, and subcultures. This video is distinctive for Bowie's visualization of surrealist and expressionist imagery, which is materialised through a combination of collaborative innovation and chance occurrence. When interviewed in 1981, Bowie described his approach to the production of the video:

> I always try and work out a storyline which is not going to just illustrate the story word for word. So, I try and develop a counter storyline that has the same kind of weight as the story as portrayed in the song, but usually deals with different images and different character situations. So, I had the idea as the clown as an everyman, the clown as a latter-day kind of astronaut. And I just followed that line in a series of images, incorporating those shady characters that crop up. And I did a storyboard for it, and I worked with pictures illustrating each of the situations and also a rough editing plan, and I got together with David Mallet ... and we started working out a technical plan.[28]

As primary director, this was possibly the first time Bowie was able to exert complete control over his artistic vision for a video, and this enabled him to develop the skills required to work across mediums. As director, he was 'open to

---

[24] 'The Laughing Gnome' was first released as a single in 1967; 'Fame' was released in 1980 on the album *Scary Monsters (and Super Creeps)*.
[25] Tony Visconti, interviewed in April 2017, quoted in *A New Career in a New Town (1977–1982)*, book accompanying the release of the box set of the same title. 2017, Rhino/Parlophone: USA.
[26] 'Ashes to Ashes' cost £35,000 to make, 'rendering it the most expensive rock music video for its time', as cited in Devereux, Dillane and Power, *David Bowie: Critical Perspectives*, 42. This information is based on an interview between Eoin Devereux and David Mallet on 16 April 2014.
[27] Victoria Broackes, 'Ashes to Ashes' in Broackes and Marsh (eds), *David Bowie Is*, 136.
[28] David Bowie, interviewed by Karen Mecklenburg, 'Television Week', *The New York Times*, 13 December 1981, YouTube video by Richard's David Bowie Channel, 15 February 2020, https://youtu.be/d7aJWFAu0Fo.

improvise with any ideas and materials presented to him'.²⁹ In practice, this meant that Bowie and Mallet engaged in a productive dialogue that enabled each of them to contribute particular ideas toward a co-authored audio-visual assemblage. Gleaned from his interview with Mallet in 2014, Eoin Devereux divulged who was responsible for specific aspects of the video:³⁰

> The cards (mini-screens) held by Pierrot and others which facilitate the transition between individual scenes, for example, came from Bowie. The umbilical cord through which the spaceman (Major Tom) is connected to the Cosmos at the video's conclusion came from Mallet who was inspired by the 1958–59 BBC science fiction series *Quatermass and the Pit*.³¹

This description fits with Bowie's approach towards collaborative assemblage and chance composition. Although Bowie was interested in the unexpected outcomes of collaboratively generated ideas, by positioning himself as director, he could be responsible for the concept and styling of the video. This gave him the opportunity to develop his skills as a storyboard artist, producing an eclectic collection of hand-drawn images, vibrantly coloured with felt-tip pens (Figure 5.2). Arranged in a non-linear manner, the images depict a surreal world with expressionist lighting and oblique camera angles. As seen in the *David Bowie Is* exhibition and book,³² Bowie's storyboard sketches portray his vibrant imagination and show how closely the final video achieved his initial vision.

While the interior settings were shot at Ewart Studios in Wandsworth, the outdoor location scenes were shot during May 1980, on video at Beachy Head and Hastings, on the East Sussex coast. Along with its incidental props, this bleak location provided naturalistic elements that could be estranged with unnatural lighting scenarios and technicolors, thus providing an ideal canvas for the surrealist imagery depicted by Bowie's storyboards. According to Bowie's anecdote at the start of this chapter, this beach turned out to be the perfect location for Bowie to be figuratively 'brought down to Earth' by a local passer-by. Comic anecdotes aside, as co-director, Mallet played an important role in enabling Bowie to achieve his vision using the benefits of videotape technology. In an interview for the documentary series *Music Video Exposed* (2010), Mallet explained what it was like to work with Bowie on 'Ashes to Ashes':

---

[29] Devereux, Dillane and Power, *David Bowie: Critical Perspectives*, 42.
[30] David Mallet, interview by Eoin Devereux, 16 April 2014.
[31] Devereux, Dillane and Power, *David Bowie: Critical Perspectives*, 42.
[32] Bowie's original storyboards appear as figures 90 and 93 in Broackes and Marsh (eds), *David Bowie Is*, 138–9.

With Bowie, it's a genuine creation because he knows exactly what he wants. The discussion was 'I wanna be a clown, I wanna be on the beach, and I want some modern Romantics with me.' Then I say, 'Well wouldn't it be great if the sky was black', and he would say, 'Yes and we can have a burning brazier', and then I would say, 'Yes, and then we can do the scene from *Quatermass* where you're plugged into a spaceship'. And he would say, 'Great, and I can hang like this', and I said, 'Yes great, we'll extend your veins out to the space ship'. From an initial concept of his, within probably an hour we had something fleshed out. And then, thank you very much Mr Bowie, then you've got to work out how to do it. Which would be relatively easy *now*, but *then* – wasn't easy.[33]

Figure 5.2 Storyboard image for 'Ashes to Ashes' (David Bowie, 1980).

---

[33] David Mallet, *The Music Video Exposed* (2010, US), 'David Bowie, "Ashes to Ashes" Director David Mallet', posted by Steve Lamb, YouTube video, 00:02:43, 13 July 2010, https://tinyurl.com/4x2czeyf.

Mallet conjures an image of two boys playing make-believe, the way children come up with imaginary game-play scenarios. Despite Bowie's desire to have more directorial control in his videos, Mallet was in charge of the treatments used and he played an active role in fleshing out Bowie's vision for the video. When I interviewed Mallet in 2021, he reiterated this aspect of the video's production process, adding that he viewed his directorial role as that of an enabler of the artist's vision. Rather than singularly driving the creative insight for a video as an auteur director might do, he believed his role was to collaboratively support the vision of the musician or band he was working with. His approach to collaboration may have suited Bowie during a time in which he wanted to have more directorial control over his videos, and this may have clinched their long and productive relationship, with Mallet directing more videos than any other director Bowie worked with.

Raking over the 'Ashes'

A wobbly Wurlitzer-like sound accompanies an abstracted aerial shot depicting an orange beach landscape flanked by a murky black sky.[34] While the musical sounds associated with the Wurlitzer serve to underscore the songs 'carnivalesque aspect',[35] the sounds of this instrument also call up memories of its accompaniment for 1920s silent films.[36] Strengthening this sonic association with early cinema, the otherworldly beach scene conjures my own memories of the seaside scene in the surrealist film *Un Chien Andalou* (Luis Buñuel, 1929).[37] Further reinforcing these references to art history, the camera zooms in to reveal Bowie – as Pierrot – sitting beside a brazier on a desolate beach. The image gradually fades into a close-up of Bowie's exquisitely painted face (Figure 5.3); a base of white *kabuki* foundation is adorned with full red lipstick, Pierrot's distinctive forehead mark and a beauty spot reminiscent of Marlene Dietrich. Bowie's immaculately painted face, along with the layered Pierrot costume designed by Natasha Korniloff, work together to achieve a teleportation of the centuries-old figure of Pierrot, jaunting him into the 1980s.

[34] Bowie initially intended to use a Wurlitzer organ when recording the song. O'Leary outlines the process undertaken by Visconti to achieve a Wurlitzer-like sound. See O'Leary, 'The Shore at Pett Level', *Pushing Ahead of the Dame*, 11 June 2020, https://tinyurl.com/5nadh8v2.
[35] Devereux, Dillane and Power, *David Bowie: Critical Perspectives*, 37.
[36] Mark K. Miller, 'It's a Wurlitzer', *Smithsonian Magazine*, April 2002, https://tinyurl.com/4vxmnzv7.
[37] *Un Chien Andalou*, directed by Luis Buñuel (1929, France: La Havre).

Figure 5.3 Bowie performing as Pierrot. 'Ashes to Ashes' (David Mallet, 1980).

Inviting us to call up earlier instances of Major Tom, Bowie turns to look into the camera lens with furrowed brow and sad clown eyes, singing, 'Do you remember a guy that's been, In such an early song? I've heard a rumour from Ground Control / Oh no, don't say it's true.' While these lyrics allude to a character from the past, their accompaniment with strange visual imagery generates enigma. What is this beautiful sad clown doing sitting alone on a dystopian beach? And why is he then seen partly submerged in a black sea? (Figure 5.4). The beach is usually a familiar setting, usually associated with nature, open space, blue sky and lightness of mood. 'Ashes to Ashes' defamiliarizes this setting with the intrusion of a sad clown, a priest, a bulldozer and a funeral procession comprising strangely familiar figures, such as key members of London's New Romantic subculture. The naturalistic qualities of this outdoor beach setting are also estranged by unnatural colours and illogical lighting; the light source seems inverted, as though the video was shot on an alien planet that produces and emits its own light, rather than absorbing and reflecting light from the sun. Against the black sky, Bowie's bright pink skin emits an iridescent glow.

Figure 5.4 Bowie performing as Pierrot. 'Ashes to Ashes' (David Mallet, 1980).

The process behind this strange imagery has been a mystery. If this video had been shot on film, one might wonder if each frame had been painted with black inks and brightly coloured paints, much like the processes Len Lye used to colourize his films *A Colour Box* (1935) and *Rainbow Dance* (1936). As precursors to the music video form, Lye's abstract films share similarities with 'Ashes to Ashes', such as the estranged colours, the solarized look of the beach scenes, the iridescent glow emitted from the human characters, and the juxtaposition of movement and stasis within shots.[38] While Lye's films were the result of deliberate artisanal hand painting on strips of film, the colourization of 'Ashes to Ashes' was brought about by a happy accident with the video camera settings. Mallet explains:

> Well, the hard bit with 'Ashes to Ashes' was to get the sky to go black without ruining everybody's faces because there was no such thing as post-production colours in those days. What went in the can is what you had. I'd previously

[38] *Rainbow Dance*, directed by Len Lye (1936, UK: GPO Film Unit).

discovered how to do that by accident. Every single effect on 'Ashes to Ashes' was done live in the camera, there was nothing done afterwards – simply because you couldn't do anything afterwards.[39]

While described here as 'the hard bit', finding an innovative technique to achieve a black sky effect turned out not to be so difficult after all. Aiming to discover the process by which Mallet achieved the surreal colour effects in 'Ashes to Ashes', I asked him to comment on journalist Jason Heller's claim that 'Mallet used the new computer graphics workstation Paintbox to radically alter the colour palette of the short film, rendering the sky black and the ocean pink'.[40] Refuting this claim, Mallet pointed out that 'Ashes to Ashes' was released the year before the release of the Paintbox technology in 1981. When I asked him to explain how the effect was achieved using only a video camera, he replied:

> I was on the beach with an outside broadcast company ... which in those days was a huge van ... and I just happened, out of the corner of my eye, to see ... while this engineer was setting up this camera, I suddenly saw the bones of this effect, I said 'Stop stop stop! How the hell did you do that?' And he said, 'I don't know'. So, there's two people who haven't got a clue how we did it. And I said, 'Whatever you did, don't touch anything, because you've just made the video'. And it was a complete accident. ... I don't know what he did. It was just something with lining it up.[41]

Mallet clarified that he was referring to an accident that had occurred on a previous video shoot, and that a similar type of outside broadcast van was required for the 'Ashes to Ashes' shoot. This time, he was working with 'the cleverest engineer ever, Collin Reynolds', who 'figured out how it was done, and could recreate it with a different van'.[42] While Mallet was unable to recollect the specific camera settings, his description of what happened alludes to the confluence of chance occurrence:

> It was something to do with lining the camera up. ... I just happened to see it. ... I think it was the sky, the first thing that happened. And then it vaguely made those weird colours ... the picture is not solarized at all. It's just some weird thing that happened to all the colours where they all went out of line. And this guy Collin Reynolds figured out how I'd done it and managed to recreate it and that

[39] David Mallet, 'David Bowie, "Ashes to Ashes" Director David Mallet'.
[40] Heller, 'How Ashes to Ashes Put the First Act of David Bowie's Career to Rest'.
[41] David Mallet, interview by Lisa Perrott, 17 February 2021.
[42] Ibid.

was 'Ashes to Ashes'. We altered the effect for every shot. It wasn't just an effect that ran through the [video]. Let's say, to put it crudely, there was like a knob that made it more or less or different. And for every single shot we altered that.[43]

It seems fitting that the estranged colours in the video resulted from the deliberate re-use of a earlier accident that Mallet just happened to witness, and that Reynolds just happened to recreate by tweaking a knob. Particularly apt, when considering the ways in which chance occurrences and collage-like assemblage were at play in the song's lyrical and musical construction. Due to Bowie's propensity to re-appropriate all manner of literary, sonic, and visual paraphernalia, he has often been described as a musical and cultural magpie. His song lyrics often made use of random words that he happened to stumble across. For example, his close childhood friend George Underwood was particularly amused when he discovered the message he'd left on Bowie's answerphone – 'I'm happy, hope you're happy too' – had found its way into the lyrics for "Ashes to Ashes".[44] The song's musical arrangement also involved a 'magpie' approach, where sonic forms were gathered from a range of disparate influences and treated much like visual collage. O'Leary observes that '"Ashes to Ashes" seems composted from old records, stitched together out of discarded rhythm tracks and random overdubs', adding that the song 'came together in pieces, Bowie and Visconti relying (as usual, by this point) on a series of happy accidents'.[45] Comparing the song to "Space Oddity", O'Leary surmises that:

> By contrast, "Ashes" is vertical, organic, a deliberate mess. There's a density to the mix; it's like a black hole absorbing whatever sounds approach – the percussion mixed in the left channel (often a shaker, but a stick hit off-beat appears briefly in the verses), Carlos Alomar's ska guitar, George Murray's popped bass, a synthesizer choir, a synthesized guitar solo, Davis' intricate hi-hat work, the muttered backing vocals, and the little noises that you only hear once or twice (a sprinkle of piano notes, Bowie's groans during an instrumental break, a few piercing guitar chords).[46]

This 'composted' arrangement of the song underscores the collage-like, seemingly illogical arrangement of the visual imagery and sets up the audio-visual relations

---

[43] Ibid.
[44] Svetlana Sukhanova, '"Don't Ask Me How David's Mind Worked": George Underwood and Steve Schapiro about David Bowie', *Birdinflight.com*, 25 January 2019, https://tinyurl.com/3m4z3t7y.
[45] O'Leary, 'Ashes to Ashes'.
[46] Ibid.

of the video. Devereux *et al.* expand upon O'Leary's assessment of the song, adding that it is a 'tightly structured composition, full of deliberate historical and structural allusions and crafted with technical sophistication',[47] a description that could equally apply to the visual composition of the video. While both the song and the video were crafted with a deliberate intent to allude to historical artforms, both have a distinctly organic feel, due in part to Bowie's 'magpie' approach toward assemblage, and also due to collaborative processes involving chance composition and collage. While these processes contribute to the overall surreal quality of the video, this quality is also a result of the audio-visual composition and the use of innovative visual transitions that traverse time and space. The extensive use of the dissolve editing technique creates bizarre relationships between shots. For instance, towards the end of the video, an elderly woman walks along the shoreline in deep conversation with Pierrot; a scene that prompted rumours that Bowie had cast his mother in the video.[48] As they walk, a cyborgian image of Major Tom emerges and then increases saturation until it fills the space left by the black sky, thus creating a strange connection between Pierrot, Major Tom and the elderly character alluding to Bowie's real life (Figure 5.5). This next shot becomes the dominant image, while the previous shot fades out. Although dissolves were conventional in music videos during the late 1970s and early 1980s, 'Ashes to Ashes' extended this convention by using dissolves to create analogical continuity between scenes and previous videos, rather than relying on narrative logic or linear editing conventions. In addition to non-linear editing and the use of dissolves, a sense of visual and temporal dissonance emerges from the juxtaposition of movement and stasis within the frame. This sense of disjuncture is intensified by the fact that Bowie's vocals are visually lip-synced by several different characters. Singing, 'I heard a rumour from Ground Control', Bowie (as Pierrot) introduces the second of his three characters, Major Tom, by holding up a postcard in the form of a static video-insert (Figure 5.6). Having introduced this new character, and despite being in mid song, Pierrot becomes a freeze-frame. He is rendered static in order to pass on his life force to Major Tom, who sings the next line. With this innovative intra-diegetic device, movement emerges from stasis and one character gives life to another.

---

[47] Devereux, Dillane and Power, *David Bowie: Critical Perspectives*, 45.
[48] 'ANCIANT Video Focus: Ashes to Ashes', *DavidBowie.com*, 27 September 2017, https://tinyurl.com/43pkdjv9.

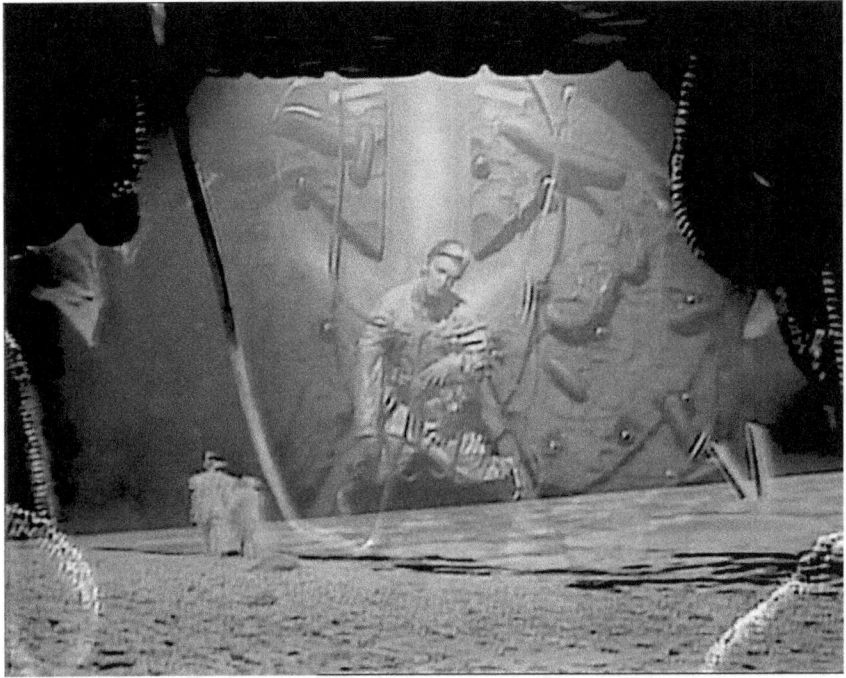

Figure 5.5 Dissolve editing creates bizarre relationships. 'Ashes to Ashes' (David Mallet, 1980).

As with Bowie's storyboards, the video is edited to achieve a non-linear narrative, held together by 'three interconnecting characters', a narrative strategy that was used in 'Space Oddity' (1979). The continuity between these two videos is also achieved by adopting a similar approach to cinematography, such as the use of close-ups to emphasize Bowie's intense address to camera, stark lighting and cross-fades between scenes. 'Ashes to Ashes' also includes flashbacks to scenes that were shot during the filming of 'Space Oddity' (1979). Scenes such as Major Tom seated in the kitchen, provide a direct conduit between the different storyworlds in which the two videos are set. Despite this, the worlds depicted by these two videos are qualitatively different. In terms of their resonance with art traditions, 'Space Oddity' depicts a world following the distorted angular 'logic' of German expressionism, while 'Ashes to Ashes' portrays an illogical world that looks and feels more like a surrealist short film. As mentioned, this logic-defying world is established by the blackness of the sky, the illogical light-source, the strange colours, and by the inversion of motion and stasis.

Figure 5.6 Pierrot becomes a freeze-frame, giving life to Major Tom. 'Ashes to Ashes' (David Mallet, 1980).

Intertextual references

In addition to the sense of an illogical world, 'Ashes to Ashes' shares other similarities to the surrealist film *Un Chien Andalou* (1929). This is perhaps not surprising given that Bowie's admiration for the film led to it being screened as a precursor to his 1972 Rainbow show and his 1976 Isolar shows.[49] While both *Andalou* and 'Ashes to Ashes' use surrealist compositional strategies that challenge our expectations of narrative coherence, they also share a similar dream-like quality, and the video includes several intertextual references to this surrealist film. The metaphorical 'shooting scene' when Pierrot is 'shot' by the photographer is followed by a close-up of his 'injured' hand. This recalls a

---

[49] For more on this, see 'David Bowie Performs "Lady Stardust" Live in 1972', thinwhiteduke.net, https://tinyurl.com/ytxpv7mf. See also, Paul Morley, 'Dali, Duchamp and Dr. Caligari: The Surrealism that Inspired David Bowie', *The Guardian*, 22 July 2016, https://tinyurl.com/26ts6vdc.

sequence in *Andalou* in which an actor retorts at being 'shot' by the camera, followed by a close-up of an armpit, which dissolves into a close-up of a *kina* (sea-egg) within the palm of a hand. In both *Andalou* and 'Ashes', the slow dissolves not only serve as transitions between incongruous settings, they also generate new meaning by merging one visual signifier with another, much like the technique of Soviet montage.[50] The internal settings of the padded cell and domestic kitchen area are cross-cut with external settings depicting a dystopian beach, not unlike the uninviting beach setting in *Andalou*. As mentioned, in the penultimate scene of 'Ashes to Ashes', we see Pierrot walking down the beach beside an elderly woman who is chatting and gesticulating (Figure 5.7). The scene is reminiscent of the concluding scene in *Andalou*, where a man and woman are walking down a beach arm-in-arm (Figure 5.8). Interestingly, in 1969 Bowie had depicted this scenario in his rough drawings for the *Space Oddity* album cover. His sketch of Pierrot and an elderly woman arm-in-arm as

Figure 5.7 Pierrot walks beside an elderly woman. 'Ashes to Ashes' (David Mallet, 1980).

---

[50] For more on this, see David Bordwell, 'The Idea of Montage in Soviet Art and Film', 9–17.

Figure 5.8 Image from *Un Chien Andalou* (Luis Buñuel and Salvador Dalí, 1929).

they walk along the beach is also featured in George Underwood's artwork for the back cover of *Space Oddity* (1969).[51]

The priest-like white circular collar worn by the cyclist in *Andaloou* is echoed in the ecclesiastic costumes worn by key members of London's New Romantic scene (known as the Blitz Kids), who flank Pierrot as they walk in funereal procession in front of a bulldozer (Figures 5.9 and 5.10). These actors include Judith Frankland, Darla Jane Gilroy and Steve Strange (from the band Visage). While it looks like they are performing a ceremonial bowing gesture, Strange confirmed that this repeated movement was merely a graceful solution to prevent their robes being dragged under the encroaching bulldozer.[52] As suggested by O'Leary, Bowie's casting of the 'Blitz Kids' as 'emissaries of the future', was an astute move by Bowie, one that exemplifies his prescient tendency to play a formative part in the development of new subcultures.[53] On one hand, it helped to situate his new music and persona as emblematic of the emergent New

---

[51] See Underwood's cover art, and Bowie's preliminary sketch for this in figures 94 and 96 of Broackes and Marsh (eds), *David Bowie Is*, 142–3.

[52] Steve Strange, Culture Club History, 'The Blitz Kids – Whatever Happened to the Gender Bender's 2005', YouTube video, 00:31:45, 17 December 2020, https://www.youtube.com/watch?v=zaIkKdWhlNg.

[53] O'Leary, 'Ashes to Ashes'.

Figure 5.9 The New Romantics flank Pierrot. 'Ashes to Ashes' (David Mallet, 1980).

Figure 5.10 Image from *Un Chien Andalou* (Luis Buñuel and Salvador Dalí, 1929).

Romantic subculture. On the other, it contributed to its aesthetic and avant-garde sensibility, popularizing the subculture, and leading bands such as Visage to adopt imagery directly inspired by the video's portrayal of characters such as Pierrot and Major Tom.

Apart from these references to the New Romantics and *Andalou*, there are other intertextual references worth mentioning. As indicated by Mallet,[54] the concluding shot of Bowie plugged into a spaceship took inspiration from a scene in the *Quatermass* series (Figure 5.4).[55] This image of Bowie connected to a spaceship by a series of 'veins' also taps into an emerging fascination (at that time) with cyborgs in cinema and popular culture, as depicted in the film *Alien* (1979) and the *manga* and cinema versions of *Ghost in the Shell* (Masamune Shirow, 1989; Mamoru Oshii, 1995). By appropriating such imagery at the very onset of its popularity, Bowie exemplifies his prescient engagement with popular culture.

Major Tom – the shape-shifter

> I suppose that Major Tom was a sort of a, there's a comfortable feeling with him, being such a sort of an old figure of mine, I mean he goes back to '68, '69. . . . I guess that … people still have some kind of empathy with him. Because he became a little sort of bouncy hero. I just wanted to sort of bring him up to date a little bit, and put him in a Victorian nursery rhyme kind of atmosphere, even though it's not Victorian, it has that queasiness of some of those 'ring-a-ring-a-rosy' – this is about the plague and we're all going to drop down dead – kind of thing about it, which is what I did with the piece.
>
> Bowie 1980[56]

As Bowie indicated in this interview, the song was intended to contemporize Major Tom, while at the same time, situate him within the timelessness of an age-old nursery rhyme. In this way, Major Tom became a time-travelling character, connecting us with the past and future. Major Tom is represented in two different guises – first, as a psychiatric patient in a padded cell, and then as an astronaut wearing a tube around his neck and seated in a space-traveller's

---

[54] Mallet, 'David Bowie, "Ashes to Ashes" Director David Mallet'.
[55] Mallet, *The Music Video Exposed* (2010, US).
[56] Bowie, interviewed by Tim Rice for BBC's *Friday Night, Saturday Morning*, 10 October 1980, posted by vidzaya, YouTube video, 00:17:47, 9 March 2022, https://tinyurl.com/2wbvpre2.

chair in a domestic kitchen setting. The incongruity of this arrangement is compounded by the presence of exploding kitchen appliances and a maid (or nurse) cleaning in the background. This image of an alienated domestic astronaut conjures associations from the film *The Man Who Fell to Earth* (1976), where Bowie, playing the alien Thomas Jerome Newton, sits in a similar chair in a domestic setting. This intertextual dialogue between characters and storyworld components articulates the changing characterization of Major Tom; once an astronaut falling through space, Major Tom has transformed into a drug-addled character, falling from a great high to a state of alienated psychosis. In an interview with RCA Records, Bowie explained how he reshaped Major Tom for 'Ashes to Ashes':

> I was thinking of how I was going to place ... Major Tom in ... what would be the complete disillusion with the ... great dream that was being propounded when they shot him into space ... and we left him there and now we come to him ten years later on we find the whole thing has soured because there was no reason for putting him up there ... so the most disastrous thing I could think of is that he finds solace in some kind of heroin type drug. ... Cosmic space itself was feeding him with an addiction and he wants now to return to the womb from whence he came.[57]

This explanation reveals how Bowie treated Major Tom as a persistent character undergoing transformation in response to an imagined backstory; a story in which the setting segues from outer space to cosmic space, from a space shuttle to a padded cell, and from references to drug addiction to the metaphorical image of a cyborgian womb. As we shall see, these scenes in 'Space Oddity' and 'Ashes to Ashes' form only part of the evolving saga of Major Tom, which unfolds across Bowie's *oeuvre*. While it is Bowie who has narrated Major Tom's transmutations across several decades, his on-screen narrator in 'Ashes to Ashes' is Pierrot.

Pierrot – the time traveller

As a stock character with historical longevity and cultural capital, Pierrot was the consummate 'rockstar' of each era in which this character found himself.[58]

---

[57] Bowie, *Scary Monsters and Supercreeps Interview disc*.
[58] Devereux, Dillane and Power (eds), *David Bowie: Critical Perspectives*, 40.

As alluded to here by Devereux et al., Bowie played his part in ensuring that Pierrot maintained his position as a consummate rock star, extending this to the MTV era and beyond. Cast alongside the elusive shape-shifting Major Tom, Pierrot is the central character of 'Ashes to Ashes'. He is both narrator and convener of the dialogue between himself and the other characters played by Bowie. Beyond his central role in the video, Bowie adopted Pierrot as a persona that characterized the cover art and other musical paratexts associated with *Scary Monsters*, thus providing branding and continuity across mediums. Pierrot can be understood, firstly by examining him as a time-travelling archetype, and secondly by considering the purpose with which Bowie used Pierrot as an 'eternal clown' and 'figure of continuity' throughout his *oeuvre*.[59]

By the early twentieth century, a darker, psychologically deeper Pierrot began to feature, as portrayed in Arnold Schoenberg's (1874–1951) expressionist theatrical performance *Pierrot Lunaire* (1912).[60] Having become prevalent in the expressionist work of avant-garde literary, musical and visual artists, it is this darker Pierrot that shares a similar expressionistic world and psychological depth to Bowie's Pierrot, and the storyworld he inhabits in 'Ashes to Ashes'. In this logic-defying world, psychological alienation and a sense of entrapment are evoked by expressionistic lighting and a black sky that threatens to engulf the frame.

Just as particular traits emerged that distinguished these different versions of Pierrot, continuity can be seen in the way the archetype of Pierrot persists across centuries, as a vessel to represent several different characters within one, or to depict interiority through the suggestion of an inner dialogue occurring within the one character. In contrast to other *Commedia* characters (many of whom wore removable black or coloured masks), the white powdered mask of Pierrot tended to denote an indelible fusion between the character and the actor, and audiences came to view the actor *as* Pierrot. As Robert Storey explains, with Pierrot, 'actor and type are still one, and part of the great attraction [of Pierrot] ... can perhaps be explained by this unity (we might even say sincerity) of conception and interpretation'.[61] For example, 'Harlequin seems, always ready to pull off his mask and put his role aside to chat amiably with the Columbines ... but Pierrot's pathetic white face cannot be unmasked: creator and role are fused into a single

---

[59] Ibid., 36.
[60] Carpenter, '"Give a Man a Mask and He'll Tell the Truth"', 5–24.
[61] Robert Storey, *Pierrot: A Critical History of a Mask* (Princeton: Princeton University Press, 1978), 30.

character."[62] While Storey is writing in 1978 about previous Pierrots and performers, his observation is pertinent when considering the fusion of Bowie and Pierrot. Alexander Carpenter observes how both Schoenberg and Bowie became so enmeshed with the persona that they behaved as though they had become Pierrot.[63] This point is also instructive in terms of the fusion between Bowie and the other personas he adopted, such as Ziggy Stardust and the Thin White Duke, and the characters he acted, such as Joseph Merrick and Thomas Newton. By pronouncing to the public 'I'm Pierrot, I'm everyman', Bowie alluded to his deliberate fusion with the persona; although clarifying that this was an artistic strategy, for he was not only using himself as a canvas, he was using the artifice of the mask as an artistic strategy to paint 'the truth of our time'.[64] This notion of masking as a tool for communicating the truth is elaborated by Carpenter, who claimed that by wearing the mask of Pierrot, Bowie and Schoenberg were 'able to explore and express profound truths about art and self'.[65]

While this strategy of masking is at the heart of Bowie's fusion with Pierrot, his magnetic attraction to the figure was also related to his affinity with alternative configurations of identity. Despite his characteristic naivety as a *Commedia* stock character, Pierrot was historically represented as a dandiacal object of unique and stylized beauty, qualities that collectively establish the character along the lines of Otherness and alienation from society. Having cut his theatrical teeth on pantomime, and given his persistent engagement with representations of alterity, it is not surprising that Bowie was insistently drawn to the figure of the Pierrot. Embracing its longevity, the archetype became a *leitmotif* woven across Bowie's *oeuvre* in dialogue with his reiterated use of the mask and the puppet. As with Schoenberg's Pierrot, Bowie's Pierrot served as a medium for channelling experiences of alienation and psychic disturbance, a point that is articulated by Devereux et al., who describe Pierrot as an archetypal character 'who channels universal trials and tribulations, triumphs and defeats, and that specific modernist Pierrot who takes us into dangerous places in our psyche'.[66] Against this backdrop, they propose that Bowie was considerably influenced by Schoenberg's musical theatre *Pierrot Lunaire*, 'not least because of the character's depraved, moonstruck delirium and his complex psyche, all supremely controlled

---

[62] Ibid., 30–1.
[63] Carpenter, '"Give a Man a Mask and He'll Tell the Truth"'.
[64] Rook, 'Waiting for Bowie'.
[65] Carpenter, '"Give a Man a Mask and He'll Tell the Truth"', 22.
[66] Devereux, Dillane and Power (eds), *David Bowie: Critical Perspectives*, 44.

in this tightly woven, avant-garde musical form'.[67] As evidence for this proposition, they refer to the 'dramatic and textured ensemble' of *Lunaire*, noting how its 'varied vocal techniques explored new depths in the psyche, deploying parody and ironic detachment to marshal excessive expressionistic tendencies'.[68] To this list of representational strategies, they add further evidence of Schoenberg's influence, noting *Lunaire's* 'taut and dramatic soundscape, song and speech blur', where 'male roles are sung by a woman and the subject position vacillates between first and third person, all tricks familiar to the Bowie *oeuvre*'.[69] Such tricks are evident in the sonic arrangement of "Ashes to Ashes", which is distinctive for its textured ensemble, vocal techniques such as speech blur and the mnemonic cadence of nursery rhyme. Beyond purely sonic forms, Schoenberg's influence upon Bowie is evident in the audio-visual composition of 'Ashes to Ashes'. For instance, the vocal allusion to the *sprechstimme* technique provides an expressionistic character that fits with the out-of-kilter soundscape and surreal world in which Bowie's Pierrot dwells.

Just as Schoenberg's Pierrot portrays an ambiguous multiplicity of voices, in which vocal authenticity and subject position remains uncertain, 'Ashes to Ashes' is distinct for its polyphonic layering of voices. Layered arrangement and alternating pitch produce the impression of a number of different voices within oneself, sometimes engaging in gossipy or conspiratorial conversation with one another. Carpenter describes this vocal multiplicity in "Ashes to Ashes" as a sonic representation of Bowie's multiple personas that presupposes a type of 'schizophrenia', whereby 'the voice of Bowie the singer is often doubled or echoed by Bowie's muted speaking voice in the background'.[70] This sense of different interior voices in dialogue with each other is also suggested visually, with Bowie appearing as three distinct characters, each potentially representing a distinct dimension of his psyche. Lyrically, sonically and visually, subject positions vacillate between first and third person. It is not entirely clear which character has agency over the vocal delivery, and whether they are actually discrete characters or a menagerie of internal voices in dialogue within one character. This assemblage of sonic and visual 'voices' produces a polyphonous audio-visual alignment, possibly alluding to a mental disorder or drug-induced psychosis, or maybe even an allusion to Jung's theory of the multiplicity of

[67] Ibid, 39.
[68] Ibid.
[69] Ibid.
[70] Carpenter, '"Give a Man a Mask and He'll Tell the Truth"', 18–19.

personality within oneself. While all of these possibilities are in keeping with themes appearing across Bowie's *oeuvre*, the latter interpretation is consistent with Bowie's engagement with Jung's ideas, as Tanja Stark has observed at play in his song lyrics and music videos.[71] This is particularly apparent in 'The Stars (Are Out Tonight)' (2013) and 'Love is Lost' (2013), videos that portray complex psychodramas, played out by Bowie's inner selves and previous personas.[72]

Carpenter points to further similarities between Schoenberg's *Lunaire* and Bowie's 'Ashes to Ashes'. Observing that both works exhibit expressionist formal characteristics and portray autobiographical elements dealing with interior psychic states, he notes that both denote significant turning points in the artistic direction of their creators. Both artists used these works as a way of purging the past, thus enabling themselves to move forward into a new phase of artistic expression. Schoenberg is not the only historical reference point for 'Ashes to Ashes', however. The sonic and visual techniques used in this video refer to older forms of musical theatre and avant-garde performance traditions. By merging these historical techniques and traditions with the technical apparatus, video tape materiality and cultural concerns of 1980, Bowie created an exemplar of the process of remediation. The video also provides a prototype for how the music video form might use intertextuality as an artistic strategy. While referencing earlier artforms and traditions, Bowie uses the video to refer to his own earlier songs and videos, and to revise the projected story arc of Major Tom. In doing so, 'Ashes to Ashes' shows how music video can engage with the past, while simultaneously pivoting toward the future.

Future nostalgia

While Pierrot is at the centre of the video as the primary character, 'narrator and disciplining figure',[73] Major Tom appears as a secondary character, embodying the melancholic sadness and alienation of Schoenberg's Pierrot. The two characters are locked in dialogue, yet the tropes of Pierrot seem to be inflected in Major Tom. Devereux *et al.* propose that, in his role as narrator, 'Pierrot recasts

---

[71] For more on this, see Tanja Stark, 'Crashing Out With Sylvian: David Bowie, Carl Jung and the Unconscious', in Devereux, Dillane, Power (eds), *David Bowie: Critical Perspectives* (London: Routledge, 2015), 82–110.

[72] For more on this, see Perrott, *David Bowie and the Transformation of Music Video*.

[73] Devereux, Dillane and Power (eds), *David Bowie: Critical Perspectives*, 41.

Major Tom and other Bowie characters in a particular way, but also points to the future through a compelling musical and visual statement that speaks to the timelessness of art and to the universalism of human nature in flights of fantasy and of the subconscious.'[74] In other words, Pierrot serves not only as a narrator to revise past characters and storyworlds, but also as a vessel to represent what Bowie describes as 'future nostalgia'.[75] When interviewed in 1980 about the creation of *Scary Monsters*, Bowie mused:

> I lapse into this sort of future nostalgia thing, often ... the evidence by looking at almost any album I've made. And that particular piece of music, it does reflect that. It's writing, taking a past look at something that hasn't actually happened yet. One kind of sees that Orwellian thing.
>
> Bowie 1980[76]

As discussed in chapters one and two, Bowie's references to future nostalgia can best be understood in relation to the concept of hauntology, which has been used to examine how mediatized cultural forms might trigger a sense of temporal disjuncture. Mark Fisher demonstrated how music and screen media can produce a nostalgic engagement with the past along with an eerie sense of dyschronia. Theorizing two opposing directions of hauntology, Fisher explains that the first refers back to what is 'no longer' actually present from the past 'but which remains effective as a virtuality', and that 'the second sense of hauntology refers to that which has not yet happened, but which is already effective in the virtual'.[77] Forever negotiating this dual sense of hauntology, many of Bowie's sonic and visual outputs refer to what is 'no longer' present from the past, and/or to what has 'not yet' happened in an imagined future.[78] This sense of yearning for a lost future is reiterated throughout Bowie's *oeuvre*, as discussed by Shelton Waldrep, Leah Kardos and myself.[79] Waldrep describes 'future nostalgia' as 'the distinctive way in which Bowie seems always presciently to forecast the future [which] is often tinged with a sense of futures that never were, or alternative timelines'.[80] As we shall see, this statement applies to many of Bowie's songs and videos. In the case of 'Ashes to Ashes', the material result of a mistake with the

---

[74] Ibid.
[75] Bowie, 'David Bowie – Scary Monsters Interview, PART 1 (12" Promo 1980)'.
[76] Ibid.
[77] Fisher, *Ghosts of My Life*, 24.
[78] Perrott, 'Time is Out of Joint'.
[79] Ibid; Waldrep, *Future Nostalgia*; Kardos, *Blackstar Theory*.
[80] Waldrep, *Future Nostalgia*, 5.

camera recalls the materiality of videotape, while also producing the sense of an apocalyptical future.

A distinctive aspect of Fisher's concept of hauntology is his theorization of the ways in which the affordances of particular sonic and audio-visual mediums conjure a sense of temporal disjuncture, which he describes as the sense that 'time is out of joint' – a phrase that Jacques Derrida borrowed from Hamlet to characterize his theory of hauntology.[81] Fisher explained how these forms can generate a sense of disjuncture by simultaneously referencing the past and the future. One example of this in "Ashes to Ashes" is the reiterated riff accompanying the nursery rhyme elements. As mentioned, this riff portrays a Wurlitzer-like sound that alludes to this instrument's earlier use in early cinema, carnival and street theatre. Not having a Wurlitzer instrument on hand during the song's production, Visconti has described how this unique sound was produced by feeding a grand piano through an Eventide Instant Flanger and a stereo EMT plate printed to tape, until he 'got a decent stereo image to emulate a Wurlitzer'.[82] This DIY process produced a sound that conjures a past instrument, while simultaneously alluding to the futuristic sounds of synthesizers and the soundscapes of science fiction films. As observed by Devereux *et al.*, this distinctive sound reappears thirty-three years later in Murphy's mix of 'Love is Lost' (2013), 'which accompanied Bowie's homemade video featuring Pierrot. That clown and this riff are inextricably linked'.[83] As he has done for centuries, Pierrot serves as a time-travelling vessel transporting us to the past and to the future.

There are several other ways in which the video produces a sense of future nostalgia. As already mentioned, a sense of nostalgia and loss is conjured by Bowie's vocal delivery, in which the lyrics follow a pattern of dropping pitch at the end of sentences. Temporal disjuncture is also evoked as a vague sensory response to the video's assemblage of sonic and visual elements, including the materiality of videotape, garish colours, the affordances of specific sonic, musical, vocal and lyrical elements, and the defamiliarization of signifying objects that appear incongruous to their settings. The beach and funeral procession scenes depict a dystopian view of the future, a painterly depiction of

---

[81] Derrida, *Specters of Marx*, 20.
[82] Tony Visconti, quoted in O'Leary, 'Ashes to Ashes'; see Visconti's explanation of this production method at Eventide Audio, 'Tony Visconti on the Making of David Bowie's "Ashes to Ashes"', YouTube video, 00:05:32, 19 May 2021, https://youtu.be/S4FjX2gKC7c.
[83] Devereux, Dillane and Power, *David Bowie: Critical Perspectives*, 48.

how the natural environment might look following a nuclear war or environmental disaster. Against this dystopian backdrop, the incongruously placed characters carry associations with the past and the future. Major Tom is a time-travelling character associated with outer space, science fiction and alienation. As suggested by the lyrics for "Space Oddity" (1969), Major Tom initially resided in a storyworld buoyed by a sense of optimism for a future that was bound up in the American dream. However, Major Tom is re-cast in 'Ashes to Ashes' as a metaphor for the death of such optimism. While Fisher has discussed this phenomenon in relation to hauntology, capitalism, neoliberalism and depression,[84] Bowie has described his felt need to revise Major Tom's character in response to 'the complete disillusion with the ... great dream that was being propounded when they shot him into space'.[85]

While Major Tom travelled through outer space and psychic space, Pierrot travelled from the past as an archetype and harbinger of the future. Ushering in the birth of MTV, Pierrot turned up on television screens of the early 1980s, seemingly with prescient warnings of the potential for nuclear holocaust, a dying planet and psychic alienation. Not only does Pierrot signal the emergence of a new music video platform and a once-imagined future that will not come to pass, but his references to the future also occur simultaneously alongside allusions to past mediums, styles and subcultures. Bearing the gifts of improvised theatre, pantomime, masking, Romantic aesthetics and dandyism, Pierrot inspired the aesthetic direction of an emergent subculture. As illustrated by Visage's video 'Fade to Grey' (1980), the New Romantics adopted dandified clothing and hairstyles, along with Pierrot-esque face paint and head attire (Figure 5.11). The direct influence of Bowie's Pierrot is obvious, especially considering the presence of Visage's lead singer Steve Strange alongside Pierrot in 'Ashes to Ashes'.

Characters and signifiers

Secondary to Pierrot and Major Tom, 'Ashes to Ashes' is populated by enigmatic characters, such as the ecclesiastical Blitz Kids and the loquacious elderly woman. Major Tom appears to have a caregiver or nurse who busies herself in the kitchen;

---

[84] Fisher, *Ghosts of My Life*; Fisher, *Capitalist Realism: Is There No Alternative?* (New Alresford: John Hunt Publishing, 2013).
[85] Bowie, *Scary Monsters and Supercreeps Interview disc.*

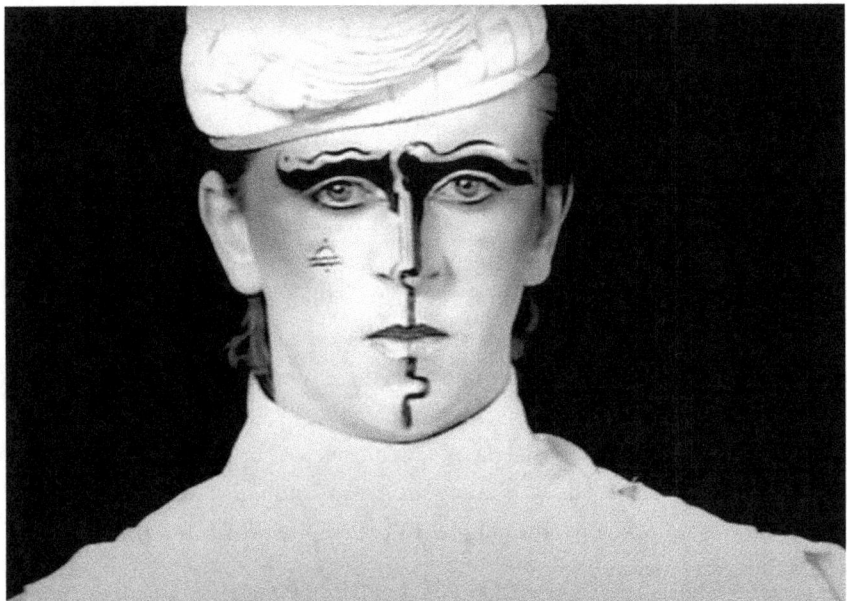

Figure 5.11 Image from Visage's video 'Fade To Grey' (Godley & Creme, 1980).

the same nurse who was seen operating a camera in 'Space Oddity' (1979). A press photographer stands on the rocks and takes a flash photo of Pierrot, apparently shooting him in the arm with his camera flash. Each of these characters are incongruously placed in these settings and their actions contribute to an overall sense of enigma, which is accentuated by the incongruously placed objects that operate as signifiers. When coming across a bulldozer on the beach during the shoot, Bowie had proposed incorporating it into the video, suggesting that it could symbolize 'oncoming violence'.[86] Over four decades later, a YouTube commenter marvelled at the video, describing the slowly driving bulldozer as an 'excellent idea', suggesting it represented 'inevitable, rolling doom'.[87] In their analysis of the video, Devereux et al. suggest potential interpretations for specific objects, such as the bulldozer:

> The powerful bulldozer, the funeral pyre, the unleashing of the dove all point to a ritual cleansing. ... In setting the dove free, Pierrot is conceding that Columbine is in love with Harlequin. The bonfire represents a funeral pyre being readied to

---

[86] Devereux, Dillane and Power (eds), *David Bowie: Critical Perspectives*, 44.
[87] Thomas Colb, YouTube comment, 'David Bowie – Ashes to Ashes (Official Video)', 7 August 2015, https://tinyurl.com/28u2bhtp.

dispose of a corpse (or corpses). Taken together, these specific images may be understood as a sweeping away of the past.... Pierrot's white face can be read as having the pallor of the dead. Serving as Bowie's alter ego, Pierrot is used to exorcise old ghosts, to bury the dead and to pave the way to a new future.[88]

The particular interpretations suggested here may or may not have been consciously intended by Bowie and Mallet. Individually or collectively, the objects in this video may potentially trigger associations of violence, danger, death, liberation and a ritual exorcism of the past. While the objects may have been selected for their semiotic affordances, they are placed into assemblages that defamiliarize their common-sense meaning, thereby estranging rational thought. It's also possible that certain objects and images were selected for their capacity to evoke a sense of 'future nostalgia'. When interviewed by Angus MacKinnon in 1980, Bowie referred to the way 'things' in 'Ashes' could be perceived as 'clichéd' when viewed in isolation, and pointed to the way in which his assemblage of those things removed cliché:

> There's an awful lot of clichéd things in the video, but I think I put them together in such a way that the whole thing isn't clichéd. The general drive of the sensibility that comes over is some feeling of nostalgia for the future. I've always been hung up on that; it creeps into everything I do ... and that's obviously what I'm all about as an artist.
>
> Bowie 1980[89]

So, although the video is rich with the signifying potential of objects and images, it would be a disservice to read too much into what individual objects may typically signify, without considering their analogical placement within the overall assemblage of other sonic and visual signifiers. We cannot determine the meaning of a work of art simply by attributing meaning only to the intentions of the artist, but it certainly helps to consider the points of continuity or obsessions that drive the artist. Bowie was interested in evoking meanings and emotions by way of analogy and allusion.[90] This respect for analogy is also indicative of his thoughts about the collective unconscious as a repository for symbolic transmitters of myth and archetype. These approaches to meaning are a reminder that there are limitations to a purely semiotic analysis, and to consider the capacity for sonic and visual materials to trigger affective responses.

---

[88] Devereux, Dillane and Power (eds), *David Bowie: Critical Perspectives*, 44.
[89] MacKinnon, 'The Future Isn't What It Used to Be'.
[90] For more on this, see Fitch, 'In This Age of Grand Allusion', 19–34.

If 'Ashes to Ashes' could be summarized as portraying Bowie's need to purge the past as well as his sense of disillusion about the future, one might say that the video was funereal in the sense that it was an epitaph to characters and personas that needed to be buried in order for Bowie to move on. The video served to bookend the previous decade, thus enabling Bowie a clean slate to undergo a remarkable process of metamorphosis.

Metamorphosis I: entering the cocoon

Following the release of 'Ashes to Ashes' in August and 'Fashion' in October 1980, Bowie was performing in *The Elephant Man* when personal circumstances precipitated his decision to leave New York in January 1981, and move to Switzerland to retreat from public life. At that point in his life, he needed to retreat from the 'scary monsters' and 'super creeps' he'd encountered over the past year or two. Having laid the past to rest with the help of Pierrot, Bowie had spent months immersed in the sticky emotional residue of performing as a disfigured outcast, only to be confronted with the horror of his friend's murder.

John Lennon was killed on 8 December 1980, the night before he was due to watch Bowie perform on Broadway as Joseph Merrick. Not only did Bowie have to process the death of his friend and creative muse, he also had to come to terms with having narrowly escaped the same fate, since he'd learnt he was second on the gunman's list. Lennon's killer, Mark Chapman had a front row ticket for *The Elephant Man* for the night after the murder. Aware that John and Yoko also had front row tickets, Bowie recalled how 'the night after John was killed there were three empty seats in the front row. I can't tell you how difficult that was to go on. I almost didn't make it through the performance.'[91] As was the case for many people, this tragedy caused Bowie to reconsider the world, and his place within it, through new eyes. In a 1983 interview for *Rolling Stone*, Bowie explained the personal impact of Lennon's death:

> A whole piece of my life seemed to have been taken away; a whole reason for being a singer and songwriter seemed to be removed from me. It was almost like a warning. I was saying: we've got to do something about our situation on Earth.[92]

---

[91] David Bowie, interviewed by Andy Peebles on 7 December 1980, quoted in Nacho Video, 'David Bowie in New York 1980. The Elephant Man, Scary Monsters & Other Strange People'.
[92] Kurt Loder, 'David Bowie: Straight Time', *Rolling Stone*, 12 May 1983, https://tinyurl.com/39y97b67.

While Bowie talks here about the sense of having lost so much through this event, at the same time he reveals having gained something quite significant. It's as though something of Lennon's sense of purpose and humanitarian spirit had been passed on to Bowie. This sense of purpose, of wanting to use his art 'to do something about our situation on Earth' would become evident in Bowie's videos from this point onwards, but before this could happen, he needed to use the process of creating music video as an outlet for his grief. This is one way to understand the emotional intensity exuded by two videos that were shot in 1981, only months after Bowie had started to retreat into his metaphorical cocoon.

A music video couplet

Both reinterpretations of pre-existing songs, the videos for 'Wild is the Wind' and 'The Drowned Girl' stand out as musically and aesthetically distinctive from Bowie's entire music video *oeuvre*. Viewed together, both videos evoke an unusual sense of gravitas, and they mark a time in Bowie's life of retreating, revising and resetting. These videos are unique for the stark dramatic quality of the lighting and the intensity of Bowie's performance. Watching them directly after his previous videos, it appears as though Bowie has temporarily removed his mask, enabling a flicker of authenticity to emerge.

Directed by Mallet and shot in the same Berlin recording studio, 'Wild is the Wind' and 'The Drowned Girl' appear as two inverted songs performed within a music video couplet. Both were shot on monochromatic film stock to perfectly capture the dramatic qualities of *chiaroscuro* lighting; stark angular shafts of light provide a dramatic contrast against the dark background, while casting sinister shadows across Bowie's angular facial contours (Figure 5.12). Although this approach to lighting is often associated with film noir, *chiaroscuro* first emerged as a painting technique during the Renaissance, where it was used to create tension between the light and dark elements in portraits and still life paintings. Caravaggio employed light and dark contrasts to create drama, and this use for the technique became prominent in theatrical stage lighting during the nineteenth century. Despite this use of the technique in painting and theatre, Bowie had his mind on a more specific use of the technique in a contemporary medium, recalling 'what we were trying to do when we were filming this was to keep in mind the style of the fifties jazz programmes that were on American television at the time'.⁹³ In 2014, Bowie returned to *chiaroscuro* lighting with a similar purpose in mind, for the video Tom Hingston directed for 'Sue (Or In A Season Of Crime)'. Whether collaborating with Mallet or Hingston, Bowie showed a good sense of how the instrumentation associated with jazz music can be symbiotically paired with the dramatic tension produced by *chiaroscuro*.⁹⁴ Mallet explained that, although 'Boys Keep Swinging' and 'Ashes to Ashes' were shot on video, the 1981 music video couplet was shot on 'black and white film stock and then afterwards cranked, to make them much more like the old forties Hollywood film noir. . . . I had this dream of making it very high contrast'.⁹⁵

'Wild is the Wind'

Written by Domitri Tiomkin and Ned Washington, 'Wild is the Wind' was first performed by Johnny Mathis in 1957, when it was released to accompany the film of the same name. While cover versions have been recorded by many artists, the most idiosyncratic interpretations of the song are those recorded by Nina Simone in 1966 and Bowie in 1976.⁹⁶ When listening to his recorded track in 1976, Bowie hinted at his fascination with future nostalgia, saying 'this has a good European sound . . . it feels like a bridge to the future'.⁹⁷ This may seem an unusual comment to make about a song that first appeared in 1957, particularly given that Bowie's interpretation took direct inspiration from Nina Simone's version of the song. However, this comment emphasizes Bowie's long-term fascination with future nostalgia. Noting that Bowie had later described his lead vocal on this recording as 'one of his finest vocal performances', O'Leary provides a particularly vivid analysis of Bowie's vocal interpretation:

> Bowie seems determined to outdo Simone's renovations to the vocal: there's a three-bar tortuous *'you – ooo – oooh – ooh kiss me,'* he hollows out vowels and elongates consonants into trills of sound ('willlllllllld is the winnnnnnnnnd'), there's the dramatic plunge into the depths on another 'you kiss me', and Bowie's

---

[93] 'David Bowie – 'Wild is the Wind' Promo Video', thethinwhiteduke.net, 23 November 1981, https://tinyurl.com/yc26t4wk.
[94] The lighting in these videos is similar to the expressionist aesthetic of Bowie's 1976 *Isolar* tour.
[95] Mallet, interviewed by author.
[96] This recording was released on Bowie's album *Station to Station* in 1976 and re-released in November 1981 with Mallet's video.
[97] O'Leary, 'Wild Is the Wind', *Pushing Ahead of the Dame*, 9 December 2010, https://tinyurl.com/bdew2edm.

final, increasingly manic, repetitions of the title line, the last ending with a sustained high B eventually subsiding to A. The vocal is on such a grandiose scale that no actual human being seems deserving of its efforts – it's a monumental performance seemingly intended for a monument itself.[98]

While this statement might seem over-the-top, O'Leary's analysis is no exaggeration, and neither is his concluding statement: 'magnificent stuff – the best cover Bowie recorded in his life'.[99] If this recording of the song is to be considered monumental and grandiose, the video on the other hand is unpretentious, small, and contained. As such, the video serves as a perfect accompaniment to a song that is grandiose and emotionally powerful. While the video does not compete with the song, it wraps the song with light and shadow, producing a sophisticated audio-visual performance that stands apart from most popular music videos. One quality that makes this recording idiosyncratically Bowie's is the raw emotional intensity of his vocal delivery, which is equally matched by his visual performance. When asking Mallet to comment on Bowie's performance in this video, he quipped, 'I think he got off on being with really good studio musicians, and Tony Visconti . . . was there as well. And it was in a recording studio, so I think he felt very at home, and very unexposed'.[100] Appearing to be completely consumed by the meaning and intent of the lyrics, Bowie's facial expressions convey a depth of feeling that is difficult to put into words (Figure 5.12). At moments of intensity, he closes his eyes, grimaces and grips his thighs. It is even possible to see his throat trembling as he belts out the most powerful vocals. All of this has an obvious affect upon audience members. One YouTube commenter wrote, 'Bowie sings from his soul here – I think this is his best performance and song ever; such depth of passion and need – it moves me to tears'.[101] Another viewer commented, 'I'm shivering, goosebumps up and down [my] spine, and tears coming into my eyes. Flushing emotions while listening to David.'[102] To comprehend how such emotions were triggered by the video, it is useful to look closely at how it was constructed.

With Bowie using his back to block light from entering the camera lens, the video starts with Bowie's head and shoulder silhouette emerging from a black

---

[98] Ibid.
[99] Ibid.
[100] Mallet, interviewed by author.
[101] Brian Scates, comment on David Bowie, 'David Bowie – Wild is the Wind (Official Video)', YouTube video, 00:03:33, 17 July 2018, https://youtu.be/YsqlXkkEKxI.
[102] Nothinglikethesun, comment on David Bowie, 'David Bowie – Wild is the Wind (Official Video)'.

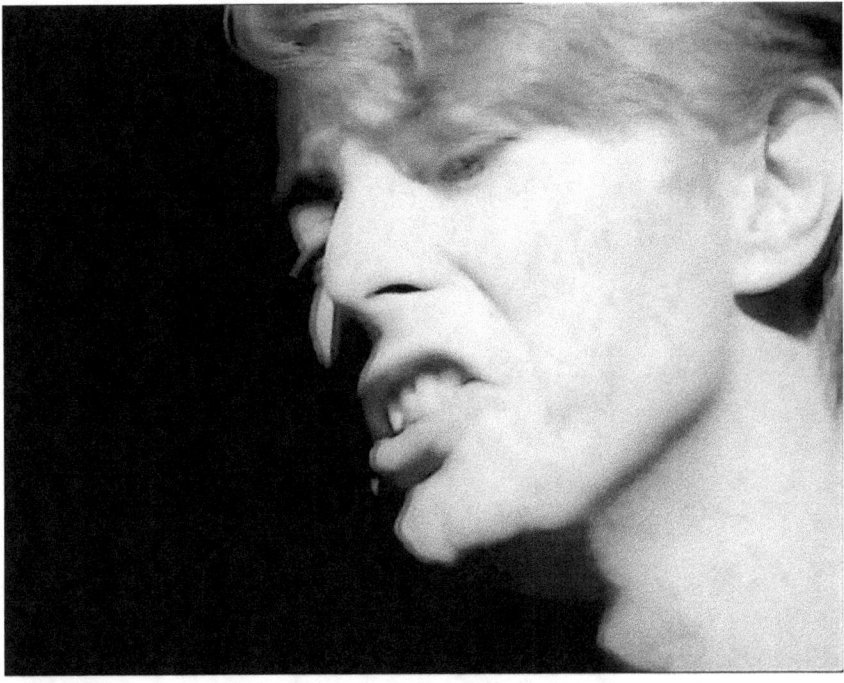

Figure 5.12 Bowie's emotional performance in 'Wild is the Wind' (David Mallet, 1981).

screen. As he walks towards the centre of the shot, a halo of light emerges around his torso, and then gradually illuminates his band, showing them playing in an intimate circular huddle. As Bowie sits upon a stool, the camera tracks closer, just in time to catch a close-up of his opening vocals, 'Love me love me love me, say you do'. The shallow Depth of Field and angular lighting work together to create a sense of Bowie's face as a white mask, floating in black space (Figure 5.12). Central to the entire video, close-ups of Bowie's head and torso are intercut with a series of transitions that dissolve subtly into mid-shots of the band, who mime playing their instruments. With Tony Visconti on double bass, Coco Schwab on guitar, Mel Gaynor on drums and Andy Hamilton on saxophone, all of these 'actors' contribute a sense of an intimate jazz band. Their gentle bodily movement contrasts appropriately with Bowie's solid stance as the central figure at the podium. What results is an expressionist play of light, shadows and forms, moving in and out of focal zones (5.13), which dance gracefully with the rhythmic sonic bedrock undergirding the soaring melodic contours of the vocals. Bowie's 'monumental' vocal performance is suitably matched by his

Figure 5.13 An expressionist play of light. 'Wild is the Wind' (David Mallet, 1981).

intense visual performance, as well as by the sophisticated composition of light, cinematography, and editing achieved by Mallet.

'The Drowned Girl'

A similar intensity of performance and expressionist compositional techniques are also apparent in 'The Drowned Girl', which although filmed in the same session, was not released until 1982 to accompany the release of the *Baal* EP. The EP was released to coincide with Bowie's performance in the BBC production of Bertolt Brecht's play *Baal*, which included Brecht's version of 'The Drowned Girl'. The song has a fascinating history, beginning with a poem titled *About the Drowned Girl*, written by Brecht in 1920.[103] Originally titled *On the Girl Beaten to*

---

[103] Tr.fowpe sharma, 'Rosa Luxemburg in the Works of Brecht', *Revolutionary Democracy* 15, no. 1–2 (April–September 2009), https://tinyurl.com/5n7vkmbx.

Death, the poem was inspired by the murder of Marxist revolutionary Rosa Luxemburg, whose beaten body had been thrown into the Landwehr Canal by Freikorps soldiers in 1919.[104] Brecht's poem is a beautifully macabre description of what happens to Luxemburg's decomposing body as it floats along the river, only to be dragged down by the weight of seaweed, algae, and flesh-eating fish. Her body lay rotting in the water, becoming 'carrion of which the rivers have a lot'.[105] Brecht performed the poem as a song titled "Ballad of the Drowned Girl" before recycling the song for his play *Baal* in 1923. Kurt Weill set the song to music in 1928 for '*Berliner Requiem*, a *cantata* for chorus and orchestra'.[106] By the time Bowie performed as Baal for BBC's *Baal* in 1982, the song had accrued new meaning. Baal, a debauched and murderous poet, sings "Drowned Girl" in reference to the suicide of Johanna, his former lover. This accrued meaning for the song provides an important context for interpreting Bowie's performance in the music video. The overall tone of the video is airy, yet there's a discomforting beauty in Bowie's morbid description of a decomposing body floating down a river.

Dominic Muldowney provided new musical settings for Bowie's *Baal* EP, although for "The Drowned Girl", he instead retained Weill's music. O'Leary describes "The Drowned Girl" as 'one of Bowie's finest vocals of the era', noting that Muldowney was 'struck with Bowie's nearly improvised yet masterful technique'.[107] Praising Bowie's version of "Drowned Girl" as the standout track on the *Baal* EP, Muldowney described it as:

> ...like an Ophelia song, where she dies in the river. He's singing about 'Her slow descent' below the water, right down in the bass baritone. Then halfway through he jumps up the octave ... When he sings up to the word 'smoke' it's got smoke all around it, it's cloudy. Then we get to the 'k' of smoke and you can see again. It's an absolute tutorial in how to paint a text. The only other person I know can do that is Frank Sinatra.[108]

Painting a text through vocal performance is a crucial skill employed within the various forms of musical theatre that Bowie engaged with. He often used his voice and lyrics to conjure visual imagery, a point that O'Leary has demonstrated

---

[104] O'Leary, 'The Drowned Girl', *Pushing Ahead of the Dame*, 11 October 2011, https://tinyurl.com/2xbhmw64.
[105] Tr.fowpe sharma, 'Rosa Luxemburg'.
[106] O'Leary, 'The Drowned Girl'.
[107] Ibid.
[108] Paul Trynka, *Starman* (London: Sphere, 2011), 307.

in his analysis of Bowie's songs.[109] This point raises an interesting question: if the vocal performance alone can conjure strong visual imagery, what role does the accompanying video play in the painting of a text? If we consider this question in relation to 'The Drowned Girl,' we can observe how the visual elements play an important role in painting the text. Contributing visual texture, emotive tone and dimension to the overall text, they provide a visual platform for the song, without competing with, or detracting from, the vocal conjuring of imagery. It is the simplicity and thought given to these audio-visual relations that shows Mallet's superb directorial skill.

On the surface, it would appear that 'The Drowned Girl' follows exactly the same cinematic treatment as its companion video. However, a few subtle differences show a deliberate point of difference in the way the two videos are lit, shot and edited. The first shot of 'Wild is the Wind' dissolves gradually from a completely black screen to a monochromatic image. Inversely, 'The Drowned Girl' opens with a white screen, which gradually dissolves into a POV shot of Bowie seated amongst his band (Figure 5.14). The band members are lit just

Figure 5.14 Bowie is central in the frame. 'The Drowned Girl' (David Mallet, 1981).

---

[109] As evident in his analysis of Bowie songs, O'Leary observes many instances in which Bowie uses vocal emphasis, pitch modulation, and enunciation of consonants and vowels, in ways that conjure visual imagery, memory, and emotion. See *Pushing Ahead of the Dame*.

enough to see their faces, with the back view of Bowie's silhouetted body rimmed by the light pointed towards him. The lighting setup for both videos follows a similar plan: there is one key light on Bowie, positioned at a 45-degree angle and pointing down just enough to cast angular shadows across from his nose and cheekbones. The band members and their instruments are lit with fill lights, which sweep across them rather than being focused on one of them. This lighting setup, together with the shallow Depth of Field, creates separation between Bowie and his band, emphasizing Bowie as the primary performer (Figure 5.14). When shot from the front, Bowie is lit brightly and starkly; his face and eyes are in sharp focus, while his band are often shot outside of the zone of sharp focus, and with subdued lighting. In one transition, an extreme close-up of Bowie's mouth gradually dissolves into a wide shot of the band, creating a haptic layering, which fuses sensory organs with the triangular arrangement of the instruments (Figure 5.15).

These are all simple yet sophisticated cinematic means of painting with light and focal depth to create mood and texture, while also establishing relationships between the performers. As noted, there are subtle differences in the crafting of each of the videos. There is comparatively more light on the band in 'Wild is

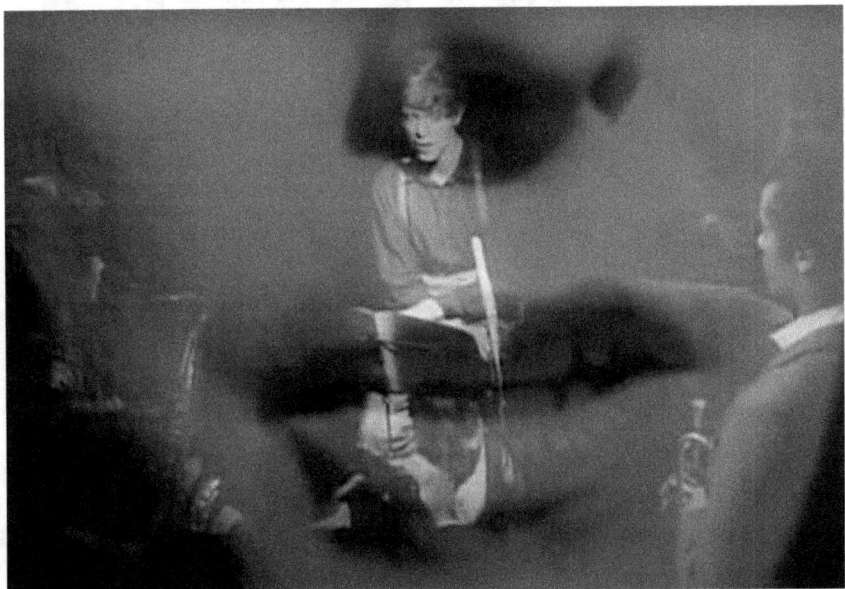

Figure 5.15 A haptic fusion of sensory organs and instruments. 'The Drowned Girl' (David Mallet, 1981).

the Wind', which seems fitting with the vocal-musical relations and the tone of the song. For 'Drowned Girl', the lighting on the band is more subdued, which emphasizes the stark lighting on Bowie's face. Again, this lighting arrangement reflects the vocal-musical arrangement of the song, along with its morbid tone.

As shown here, when conceiving this music video couplet, Bowie and Mallet had given much thought to crafting audio-visual relationships that would not detract from the power of the songs. On one side of the couplet, we have an intensely beautiful love song, and on the other, we have a morbidly beautiful death song. Unified by the intensity of Bowie's vocal performance and its capacity for painting a text, these videos are not only distinctive within Bowie's *oeuvre*; they stand apart from all other popular music videos because of their artistic conception, painterly lighting and cinematic form.

Although having released two exquisite music videos during 1981 and 1982, during this time Bowie had withdrawn from public life, wrapped in a metaphorical cocoon. This process of metamorphosis enabled him to complete his purge of the previous decade by shedding his Pierrot feathers, melancholic white mask and iridescent glow. Having spent several weeks of 1982 in balmy Rarotonga acting in the film *Merry Christmas Mr Lawrence*, Bowie emerged in 1983 with a tanned glow, a relaxed demeanour and a revitalized sense of purpose.

Metamorphosis II: leaving the cocoon

Released within a three-year window, the music videos examined in this chapter show continuities and divergences in Bowie's approach to the art of music video. While all the videos portray his increased agency in the collaborative roles of conceptualization, pre-visualization and direction, each video shows Bowie exercising this creative agency in a different way.

In 'Ashes to Ashes', Bowie used the figure of Pierrot along with avant-garde aesthetics and strategies such as masking to extend the storyworld surrounding 'Space Oddity' and Major Tom. Firmly establishing music video as an artform, 'Ashes to Ashes' inspired numerous future artists and catalysed the cultural emergence of the New Romantics. Along with these legacies to art and culture, the song and video functioned as a psychic purge for Bowie, enabling him to put a full stop on the trauma of the past decade. 'Ashes to Ashes' marks the end of one period and the start of a new phase in which Bowie was beginning to use his art to make a statement – one that was initially entangled with the concept of 'future nostalgia'. Although Bowie would not describe himself as a political person, lyrics from the songs on *Scary Monsters* indicate his intention to use his artistic outputs as vehicles for decrying the inhumanities associated with war, displacement, racism and fascism.

Following the death of Lennon, Bowie's withdrawal from public life coincided with the release of two videos that provide an aesthetic representation of his internal anguish. Created as a music video 'couplet', 'Wild is the Wind' and 'The Drowned Girl' are distinct for their exquisite *chiaroscuro* lighting, refined cinematography and editing, which work together to allow the raw integrity of Bowie's vocal performance to soar. While remarkable for their virtuosity, these music videos portray Bowie performing to camera during a profound watershed moment. They provide a rare insight into the capacity of music video to function as a vehicle for emotional purging, enabling Bowie to pivot toward a new sense of purpose.

6

Eclosion

A lot of things I've done, though I wouldn't deny them, have been pretty much in a direction of singularity and isolationist, and quite cold. I just felt that having been two years since I've been away from a recording studio ... that I wanted to do something with the kind of warmth that I feel missing from music generally – and from society. . . . I guess there'll always be something spiky about my stuff, but it's a wanting to integrate back in society that comes through. . . . I've just felt a lot more balanced about my personal life, musically . . . the outlook is positive. If I was going to even bother writing anything anymore, I would really want to contribute something optimistic and positive.

Bowie 1983[1]

With bleach-blond *bouffant* and a charming smile,[2] Bowie stunned an MTV News interviewer with his newly found optimism.[3] Similarly, *Rolling Stone's* Kurt Loder exclaimed how 'In Australia David Bowie was a man without masks. Open, jokey, very ... *warm*, is the only word.'[4] Yes, the 1983 Bowie was warm in disposition, but many misinterpreted this iteration of Bowie as real and maskless, a crucial point to keep in mind when interpreting the videos he released in 1983. While the Bowie of 1983 was certainly not maskless, his warmth and optimism were undeniably real. Many of his public comments during this time reveal a person with a new artistic approach and a new mantra. Talking to Loder in 1983 about his new passion for simplicity and directness, Bowie said, 'John Lennon

---

[1] David Bowie, 'David Bowie on Making Let's Dance & Black Artists MTV Full 1983 Interview', *MTV NEWS*, YouTube video, 00:17:07, 11 January 2017, https://youtu.be/L3i53rjh-PA.
[2] 'Eclosion' refers to the emergence of an adult butterfly from its pupal case, where it was in the form of a chrysalis.
[3] A YouTube playlist for Chapter 6 is available at https://tinyurl.com/24vbyx44.
[4] Loder, 'David Bowie: Straight Time'.

once said to me, "Look, it's very simple – say what you mean, make it rhyme and put a backbeat to it." And he was right: "Instant karma's gonna get you," *boom*. I keep coming back to that these days. He was right, man. There is no more than that. There is *no more*.'[5] Adding that with *Let's Dance* he had only touched the edge of what he really wanted to do, he said he wanted to go much further with his following album, maybe 'a protest album, I suppose'.[6] While that didn't eventuate, a Lennon-inspired protest spirit was generating a sea change of sorts.

Some fans found it difficult to comprehend why Bowie was suddenly interested in creating simpler, popular songs that would appeal to a much broader audience, but undergirding his seemingly new interest in the popular lay a less obvious motive. His desire to reach a mass audience was also a strategy to widely disseminate messages about the oppression associated with racism and colonialism. It was by no means new for Bowie to use subversive artistic methods to challenge his audience, particularly around issues related to identity and representation. However, circumstances had lit a fire in Bowie's belly. By 1983, his new mission was 'to do something about our situation on Earth'.[7] Connected to this mantra, he had acquired a newfound sense of agency and a new strategy for reaching people; the combination of historical consciousness, artistic strategy and mega-pop star status placed him in a prime position to serve as a catalyst for change. Bowie's new sense of purpose became publicly evident in 1983, when he initiated a canny role reversal while being interviewed by an MTV News reporter. After charming the interviewer with his conviviality and infectious humour, he became the first 'white' pop star to call out MTV on representational issues. Armed with an endearing smile and a twinkle in his eye, Bowie asked, 'It occurred to me, having watched MTV over the last few months, that it's a solid enterprise and it's got a lot going for it. I'm just floored by the fact that there's so few black artists featured on it. Why is that?'[8] Not being satisfied with the interviewer's attempt to minimize the problem, Bowie pressed further – 'It does seem to be rampant through American media. Should it not be a challenge to try and make the media far more integrated, especially if anything, in musical terms?'[9] He had successfully reversed roles with the interviewer, leaving the MTV reporter apologizing for MTV's representational failures. This astute

[5] Ibid.
[6] Ibid.
[7] Ibid.
[8] Bowie, 'David Bowie on Making Let's Dance'.
[9] Ibid.

calling out of MTV heralded a new phase in which Bowie set about using his rock star status, his music and his videos to make direct statements that would reach a large audience. He expressed his intentions about this in a 1983 interview for *Rolling Stone*:

> It occurred to me that one doesn't have much *time* on the planet, you know? And that I could do something more useful in terms of ... I know this is very *cliché*, but I feel that now that I'm thirty-six years old, and I've got a certain position, I want to start utilizing that position to the benefit of my ... brotherhood and sisterhood.... I think you can't keep on being an artist without actually saying anything more than, 'Well, this is an interesting way of looking at things.' There is also a *right* way of looking at things: there's a lot of injustice. So let's, you know, *say* something about it. However naff it comes off.[10]

To do this, Bowie realized that he'd need to reconsider his strategies for communicating his message. As O'Leary put it, 'Bowie wanted a public again, so he set about writing public songs – exhortations, common causes – keeping his lines (relatively) simple, writing words meant to be sung back at him.'[11] He began this process by writing the song "Let's Dance" (1983).

"Let's Dance" – the song

> Say what you mean, make it rhyme and put it to a backbeat – no fuckin' about!
>
> Bowie, 1983[12]

"Let's Dance" was Bowie's attempt to exchange 'mystery for mass connection', says O'Leary; the song is about 'Bowie trying to be communal: it seems intended to be shared, with its lyric's emphasis on the plural (even 'they' are playing music on the radio), how its chorus is like a pep cheer. It's open, expansive, a song meant to be flung out to a crowd.'[13] Also describing it as 'a mutant hybrid of a pop song, one built to conquer',[14] O'Leary observes how "Let's Dance" celebrates its own power to reliably call people onto the dance floor. Despite its popular appeal as a dance floor number, 'it's still weird, in a Bowie way: it's not quite comfortable

---

[10] Ibid.
[11] O'Leary, 'Let's Dance', *Pushing Ahead of the Dame*, 20 October 2011, https://tinyurl.com/4xm3h9a7.
[12] Loder, 'David Bowie: Straight Time'.
[13] Ibid.
[14] Ibid.

as an emcee'.¹⁵ Stripped of the critical significance imparted by the video, dancing to the song at a wedding reception or party can be a somewhat wooden and uncomfortable experience, but there's also something about the musical arrangement and the vocal delivery that contributes to this sense of discomfort. O'Leary's expert musicological analysis helps to explain my subconscious response to the song:

> The refrain chorus vocals sound hectoring; Bowie croaks out the second verse like he's still in character from his vampire movie *The Hunger*; there are odd phrases in the lyric that read like poor translations ('serious moonlight', 'for fear your grace should fall'); the mainly 'acoustic' instruments sound like synthesizers. There's a severity to "Let's Dance," from the imperative mood of the refrain (a set of commands from one lover to another) to how the instruments are recorded (sharply, massively) and mixed: often separated, kept in their own worlds, each threatening to dominate the track. Listening to the final mix is like spinning past row after row of iron sculptures.¹⁶

Despite the severity of its musical arrangement, "Let's Dance" is one of Bowie's most popular songs, having reached number 1 in several national pop music charts.¹⁷ The popularity of the song is often attributed to the input of its producer Nile Rodgers, who had produced several commercially successful hybrid-pop and post-disco songs. Rodgers has emphasized his own role in the commercial success of "Let's Dance"; he enjoys sharing the story of the morning he woke in Montreux to see Bowie peering over him with an acoustic guitar, saying 'Nile darling, I think this is a HIT!'¹⁸ Rodgers recalled that Bowie's initial version of "Let's Dance" was 'very reminiscent of a folky kind of song.... I thought it was really bizarre, but he was convinced it could be a hit, and I just kept working on it.'¹⁹ Upon the posthumous release of a demo version of "Let's Dance" in 2018, Rodgers again emphasized his role in the production of the song, boasting 'I took his "folk song" and arranged it into something that the entire world would soon be dancing to and seemingly has not stopped dancing to for the last thirty-five years! It became the blue-print not only for "Let's Dance" the song but for the entire album as well.'²⁰ Having substantial input into the song's arrangement,

---

[15] Ibid.
[16] Ibid.
[17] Pegg, *The Complete David Bowie*.
[18] Peter Helman, 'Hear David Bowie's Previously Unreleased 1982 "Let's Dance" Demo Featuring Nile Rodgers', *Billboard*, 1 August 2018, https://tinyurl.com/df3h478z.
[19] Pegg, *The Complete David Bowie*, 158.
[20] Helman, 'Hear David Bowie's'.

Rodgers branded it with his own pop signature. He was responsible for the song's beckoning intro, which involved appropriating the rising vocal sequence from The Beatles "Twist and Shout" (1963). Despite Rodgers' efforts to transform the song into an upbeat post-disco number, O'Leary views "Let's Dance" as 'a folk ballad, a Byrds-like piece', adding 'when stripped down to its melody and chords, "Let's Dance" is a sombre song, one tinged with melancholy.... Pried out of the metallic casing that Rodgers devised for it, "Let's Dance" can seem fragile, prematurely regretful.'[21] O'Leary's interpretation provides a useful insight into the melancholic impact Bowie may have initially intended for the song. He shows how quite a different interpretation can result from listening to a song as an isolated form, without taking into account the visual signification imparted by an accompanying video, or the enigma conjured by the lyrics.

As with many Bowie songs, there remains uncertainty about the source and meaning of the song's enigmatic phrases. Rodgers believed the phrase 'serious moonlight' was a reference to his own tendency to overuse the word 'serious'.[22] Pegg points to a more plausible source, noting that 'among the erotic poetry of Bowie's long time muse Aleister Crowley is a 1923 composition called "lyric of love to Leah"'.[23] Crowley's poem includes the words 'come my darling, let us dance / to the moon that beckons us ... let us dance beneath the palm / moving in the moonlight ... come my love and let us dance / To the moon and *Sirius*.'[24] Since Bowie was an avid reader of Crowley, it's possible that the lyrics to "Let's Dance" were partially inspired by this poem. As the brightest star in the solar system, Sirius (also known as the Dog Star), may well have held special significance to Bowie, particularly given the extent to which stars feature in his song titles and lyrics. The Crowley source is also in keeping with Bowie's 'magpie' tendency to forage from a variety of sources, which often included esoteric literature and cosmological references.

'Let's Dance' – the video

'Let's Dance' was shot during the first two weeks of March 1983 at various Australian locations including Sydney,[25] the Warrumbungle National Park and a

---

[21] O'Leary, 'Let's Dance'.
[22] Pegg, *The Complete David Bowie*, 158.
[23] Ibid.
[24] Ibid.
[25] 'Let's Dance' was released on 14 March 1983.

remote sheep-farming town named Carinda. Featuring prominently in the video, the Carinda Hotel celebrates its legacy by hosting the annual David Bowie Let's Dance Festival.[26] These locations provide a rugged backdrop to the narrative of a young Aboriginal couple who, while on holiday in Sydney, experience consumerist indulgences that are inaccessible to them as indigenous people. The couple are played by Joelene King and Terry Roberts, who were students of Sydney's Aboriginal and Torres Strait Islander Dance Theatre. Joelene and Terry are depicted in opposing scenarios that draw attention to the extremes of material wealth and poverty, ironic juxtapositions which allude to the colonialist oppression of the Aboriginal population.

The Carinda Hotel provided the focal point for the key performance shots, where Bowie sings alongside a double bass player with bemused locals looking on, smirking and mock-dancing. Years later, location manager Peter Lawless recalled that the shoot inside the hotel 'was so alien for both sides, Bowie, and the locals'. The locals 'didn't believe who he was. It was so off the wall. It was kind of weird.'[27] Similarly, Mallet's recollection of the shoot paints a picture of his discomfort:

> We shot in a bar in the morning and it was one hundred degrees outside. The people in the bar hated us, absolutely hated us. We were faggots from somewhere, and they were horrified that we had a young, attractive Aborigine girl in there, because they thought Aborigines were lower than dirt. She was dancing, and in order to show their hatred they started imitating her. I said, 'Quick, film them.' It looked as if they were enjoying themselves. Actually, it was a dance of pure hatred.[28]

By inviting the local residents to take part in the video shoot in the bar, Bowie and Mallet managed to inflect an otherwise staged performance with a *verité* quality. By merging the codes and conventions of music video and *cinéma vérité*, 'Let's Dance' opens a window onto the raw cultural idiosyncrasies and racism they saw in the Australian outback. But what was Bowie aiming to communicate with this discomforting semi-*verité* music video? A comment he made during a 1983 interview for *Rolling Stone* hints at his new approach toward music video:

---

[26] For more about this, see Dave Turner, 'David Bowie Let's Dance Festival Carinda', YouTube video, 00:02:41, 7 October 2018, https://youtu.be/aapW2DyIlLw.
[27] Ibid.
[28] Craig Marks and Rob Tanenbaum, *I Want My MTV: The Uncensored Story of the Music Video Revolution* (London: Penguin Group, 2011).

Let's try to use the video format as a platform for some kind of social observation, and not just waste it on trotting out and trying to enhance the public image of the singer involved. I mean, these *are* little movies, and some movies can have a point, so why not try to *make* some point. This stuff goes out all over the world; it's played on all kinds of programs. I mean – you get *free point time!*²⁹

Here, we see Bowie thinking in a fresh way (for the time) about the potential of music videos to comment on social and cultural issues and to catalyse change. He was considering his role as an active agent in this process – about his capacity to use artistic strategies to make his point to a broad audience. When asked specifically about the point he was making in 'Let's Dance' and 'China Girl', he elaborated, 'as much as I love this country [Australia] ... it's probably one of the most racially intolerant in the world, well in line with South Africa'.³⁰ He added that these videos are 'very simple, very direct. They're almost like Russian social realism, very naïve, and the message that they have is very simple – it's wrong to be racist. But I see no reason to fuck about with that message.'³¹ Six months later, in an interview for Australian television, Bowie explained that his aim for 'Let's Dance' was:

> to present *an* indigenous people in *a* capitalist, ... mainly white society, and the problems of the interrelationships between the two. It was taken at that symbolist level, that was the context of the thing. Obviously here [in Australia] it's going to be taken in a more personalised manner because the countryside is recognisable, and the particular peoples are recognizable ... overseas generally it was taken, in terms of representation of any given society, whether it be South Africa, America or Australia, or whatever, it was taken in a generalist manner.³²

This comment suggests that Bowie's intention was to use symbolism as a means to communicate allegorical messages that would be universally legible. While media commentators picked up on the references to capitalism and consumerism in 'Let's Dance', however, few examined the video's critique of colonialism and its enduring impact upon the Aboriginal population. Although this critical aspect of the video may be less obvious for those unfamiliar with the historical references, specific images in 'Let's Dance' were intended to impart a direct

---

²⁹ Loder, 'David Bowie: Straight Time'.
³⁰ Ibid.
³¹ Ibid.
³² Bowie, interview by Molly Meldrum on 6 November 1983, posted by James DeWeaver, 'David Bowie '83 the "Let's Dance" Interview on Countdown w/ Molly Meldrum', YouTube video, 00:06:39, 27 January 2016, https://tinyurl.com/uv8dmmu8.

statement about Australia's history of colonialist oppression. Images of Terry hauling a huge machine down the road and Joelene cleaning the road provide explicit references to the domestic slavery and oppressive plight of the 'Stolen Generation' – the Aboriginal children who were removed from their families between 1910 and 1970, through Government policy.[33] Another historical reference occurs when Joelene, Terry and their family look across their Aboriginal land to see a nuclear explosion in the mountains (Figure 6.1). For those in the know, this is a reference to the nuclear weapons tests undertaken by the British government in Maralinga, South Australia, between 1956 and 1963.[34] The Maralinga site is spiritually significant to the Pitjantjatjara and Yankunytjatjara people, and the use of their land for testing nuclear weapons was experienced by them as an act of violence.

Figure 6.1 The mountains lit by a nuclear explosion. 'Let's Dance' (David Mallet, 1983).

[33] For more on this, see 'Track the History Timeline: The Stolen Generations', *Australian Human Rights Commission*, https://humanrights.gov.au/our-work/education/track-history-timeline-stolen-generations.
[34] Mike Ladd, 'The Lesser Known History of the Maralinga Nuclear Tests – And What it's Like to Stand at Ground Zero', *ABC News*, 24 March 2020, https://tinyurl.com/499j49js.

As indicated by these interview extracts, in 1983 Bowie expressed a genuine intention to use music video as a means of calling attention to issues of racism, colonialism and capitalism. Rather than doing so in a didactic manner, he addressed these issues using the strategies of metaphor, symbolism, irony and juxtaposition. As he suggests, he was 'playing around' with strategies to draw in an audience, in the hope that they might then be confronted (or repulsed) by certain imagery:

> One thing I'd been toying around with was the repellent and attractive qualities of the other side of the world, be it the Middle East or the Far East ... how we're both drawn and repulsed by what happens and who they are, and the fact that we're all one. That basic idea came through on 'Let's Dance' with the Aborigines and Colonial English, and then in 'China Girl' and finally in 'Loving the Alien'.[35]

It is instructive that Bowie mentions these three videos in relation to the use of repellent and attractive qualities to provoke critical engagement. Each of these videos has provoked critical commentary and dialogue related to racism and representation, and they have also triggered a sense of discomfort from viewers of various identities. As we shall see, not everyone believes that Bowie's strategic critique of racism has been successfully received by audiences. Perhaps it is the case that his strategies are not always received in the critical manner for which they were intended. Discussing the use of symbolism in 'Let's Dance', Matthew Trammel suggests, 'at first glance, the video seems to mock the empty symbols of conspicuous consumption (expensive watches, fine wine).... But, like much of Bowie's work, an even more sinister layer hides in plain sight.'[36] Possibly explaining the tendency for reviewers to interpret the video primarily as a critique of consumerism, the sinister layer Trammel refers to is not so much hidden as it is lurking beneath the surface of what appears to be an otherwise upbeat love story. To make this masked sinister layer accessible to a broader audience, Bowie communicates his critique of racism and colonialism through salient symbols, such as red shoes and white gloves.

---

[35] Pegg, *The Complete David Bowie*, 158.
[36] Matthew Trammel, 'David Bowie and the Return of the Music Video', *The New Yorker*, 12 January 2016, https://tinyurl.com/msc548u5.

Red shoes and white gloves

Red shoes reappear throughout the video as a prominent signifier that could be interpreted in various ways. According to Mallet,[37] Bowie took inspiration from *The Red Shoes*,[38] a 1948 film adaptation of the Danish fairy tale of the same name, written by Hans Christian Andersen in 1845.[39] Since fairy tales were a rich source of inspiration for Bowie, it's likely that Andersen's *Red Shoes* inspired the use of this symbol as well as the lyrics 'Let's dance, for fear your grace should fall'.[40] Anderson's fairy tale tells the story of a little girl who was vainly compelled to wear red shoes to church despite being cautioned about their perceived improper connotation. Having ignored the warning, the girl falls from God's grace, and is cursed with shoes that won't stop dancing, even when she has her feet amputated.[41] Apart from this lyrical association with Andersen's sinister fairy tale, Bowie's explanation of the red shoes is in keeping with Jung's theory of the 'collective unconscious' as a shared repository for archetypes and symbols.[42] As Bowie explained, 'the red shoes are a found symbol. . . . They are the simplicity of the capitalist society. . . . Also, they're a sort of striving for success – black music is all about "Put on your red shoes, baby". Those two qualities were right for the song and the video.'[43] Unpacking this comment, Pegg argues that 'by choosing a symbol of capitalism which simultaneously references his beloved black music, Bowie confesses his own collusion in the process of cultural imperialism'.[44] Interpreting Bowie's appearance in the video as a corporate manager as suggesting 'an implicit anxiety about his own role as a global rock star, the ultimate cultural colonist',[45] Pegg casts light on an aspect of the video that is often taken for granted – Bowie's use of 'himself' as an icon and metacultural symbol. Within and beyond the video, Bowie strategically uses his new persona as a signifier of cultural imperialism. As mentioned earlier, Bowie's 1983 public image was perceived by some commentators as 'unmasked'.[46] Few have examined the strategic masking involved with the presentation of this new persona, as

---

[37] Mallet, quoted in Marks and Tanenbaum, 87.
[38] *The Red Shoes* directed by Michael Powell and Emeric Pressburger (1948, UK: The Archers).
[39] Hans Christian Andersen, 'The Red Shoes'. *New Fairytales* 1, no. 3. (Copenhagen: C.A Reitzel, 1845).
[40] Bowie, 'Let's Dance' (1983).
[41] 'The Red Shoes: Fairy-tale by Hans Christian Andersen', *Visit Andersen*, https://tinyurl.com/2p8ce3sw.
[42] Jung, *The Archetypes and the Collective Unconscious*.
[43] Bowie, quoted in Pegg, *The Complete David Bowie*, 159.
[44] Ibid.
[45] Ibid.
[46] Loder, 'David Bowie: Straight Time'.

operating within and beyond the diegesis of the video. While the strange mask of Pierrot signified Otherness, the mask of the rock star as cultural colonist is an attractive yet banal signifier. Adorned with designer suits, dangling neckties, and white gloves, his new persona appears as a hyperbole of a white rock star riding the wave of MTV. Noting that Bowie's 'Let's Dance' persona had been described as 'an avatar of pure fame',[47] O'Leary observes how, through this avatar, Bowie was 'becoming an international trademark of his own music, like the Apple logo or the Nike swish. The Man Who Sold Himself to the World, which bought him.'[48] Introducing this new avatar to the world, 'Let's Dance' exaggerates Bowie's impending fame in order to make it *so* – a strategy he'd achieved previously by constructing Ziggy Stardust as a messiah rock-god 'with god given ass', 'well hung' with an androgynous 'snow-white tan'.[49] Similarly, Bowie's 1983 persona (with a masculine bronze tan) promulgated his rising status as a mega rock star, while simultaneously performing a meta-critique of this very phenomenon. To succeed as a critique, however, 'Let's Dance' relied upon strategies such as irony, metaphor and allusion, along with the use of complex cultural signifiers.

The signification afforded by red shoes and white gloves appeared mysterious to some, yet blatantly obvious for fans willing to 'drill' through the semantic layers of this video. Red shoes have functioned variously as a symbol of power, control, seduction, dancing and sacrilege; the latter association being reinforced by the lyrics 'let's dance, for fear your grace should fall'. Red shoes reappear throughout the video; they're worn by the corporate woman who looks down upon Joelene as she scrubs the road on hands and knees. While Joelene and Terry look with fearful desire at red shoes in a shop window (Figure 6.2), Joelene is later seen dancing in ill-fitting red shoes on a hill overlooking her Aboriginal homeland, the same location where she destroys them by stomping on them, symbolically liberating herself from colonial oppression (Figure 6.3).

Although less explicit, white gloves connect logically with red shoes to form a symbolic coupling. While red shoes operate in this context to signify control over indigenous women, white gloves signify the power and control exerted by colonisers. White gloves are loaded with signification that varies across time and place. In Europe, white gloves were once symbolic of wealth, land ownership, status and high fashion. Traditionally worn by high-ranking clergy of the

---

[47] O'Leary cites 'a commentator of Tom Ewing' as having described this persona as 'an avatar of pure fame'. See O'Leary, 'Let's Dance'.
[48] O'Leary, 'Let's Dance'.
[49] David Bowie, 'Ziggy Stardust' (1972).

Figure 6.2 Joelene and Terry look at red shoes. 'Let's Dance' (David Mallet, 1983).

Christian faith, by the Freemasons and by royalty, this tradition has endured. In America, white gloves have a complex history related to slavery, racism and the control of women. In response to the gendered and racist control signified by the wearing of white gloves, a liberation movement initiated by the Southern Association of Women Historians coined the phrase 'taking off the white gloves'.[50] The white gloves worn by cartoon characters such as Micky Mouse and Felix the Cat indicate how early American cartoons were inextricably linked with blackface minstrelsy and vaudeville performance,[51] a historical trajectory that is *détourned* in Jay-Z's music video 'The Story of OJ' (2017).[52] White gloves are also a complex signifier in Japan, being associated with purity, authority, corporate attire and with various Western cultural influences. Numerous films set in Japan

---

[50] Michelle Gillespie and Catherine Clinton (eds), *Taking off the White Gloves: Southern Women and Women Histories* (Missouri: University of Missouri Press, 1998), 1.
[51] Nicholas Sammond, *Birth of an Industry: Blackface Minstrelsy and the Rise of American Animation* (Durham: Duke University Press, 2015); Estelle Caswell, 'Why Cartoon Characters Wear Gloves', *Vox*, 2 February 2017, https://tinyurl.com/2k5622rw.
[52] JAY-Z, 'The Story of OJ', 6 July 2017, https://youtu.be/RM7lw0Ovzq0.

Figure 6.3 Joelene liberates herself from colonialism. 'Let's Dance' (David Mallet, 1983).

feature white gloves worn by policemen, taxi drivers and military personnel.[53] In 1982, Bowie acted alongside white glove-wearing militia in the film *Merry Christmas Mr Lawrence* (1983). The white gloves may have been another one of Bowie's found symbols, foraged and recontextualized in a similar manner to the red shoes, the lightning bolt icon, the lipstick smear and numerous other symbols and gestures.

Although not likely to be a source of inspiration for Bowie, another contemporary association can be found in the cult white-glove-wearing phenomenon initiated by Michael Jackson when fans across the globe first saw him wearing a single white glove during his televised performance of 'Billie Jean' on Motown's twenty-fifth anniversary TV special.[54] Filmed on 25 March and broadcast on 16 May 1983, this performance followed the release of 'Let's Dance' on 14 March, so could not have been a source of inspiration for this video. Given the timing of these events, it's

---

[53] Daisuke Miyao, 'Cinema and the Haptic in Modern Japan', *Screen Bodies* 3, no. 1 (2018): 23–36.
[54] Le BigMac, 'Michael Jackson – Billie Jean (live 1983 first time moonwalk)', YouTube video, 00:05:38, 23 January 2017, https://youtu.be/L55jpld7gzA.

possible that Jackson took inspiration from Bowie's white gloves and that 'Let's Dance' may have stoked the cult of the white glove, as it manifested amongst some indigenous communities and subcultures.[55] Apart from the complex cultural signification of the white gloves, they are ludicrously impractical attire for a guitar player, rendering guitar playing impossible. By wearing the gloves while playing the guitar in the bar, Bowie mocks the fakery of pretending to play an instrument for the sake of a music video shoot (Figure 6.4). This visual device aimed at mocking his own fakery within the video production process is a 'tongue-in-cheek' Bowie-ism, much like the emphasis he placed on his treatment of the guitar as a prop in 'Be My Wife'.

Apart from white gloves and red shoes, the video includes a number of other visual references that exemplify Bowie's recontextualization of foraged materials in order to generate irony. For example, a parody of a well-known American

Figure 6.4 White gloves signify colonialism. 'Let's Dance' (David Mallet, 1983).

---

[55] For more on this, see Perrott, 'Moonwalking Backwards'. See also, 'Bowie's Waiata', *RNZ*, 22 November 2008, https://tinyurl.com/23dna4x2.

Express commercial underlines the reality that credit cards were not available to the Aboriginal population. Irony is also produced by the image of Joelene and Terry drawing Aboriginal designs on the wall of a Sydney art gallery, since (in the early 1980s) indigenous art was not considered worthy of exhibiting within many Australian galleries.

Bowie approved a Bollywood-style reworking of the original song and video for 'Let's Dance'. Released in South East Asian territories and beyond, this remix project produced the songs "China Girl (Club Mix)" and "Let's Dance (Club Bolly Remix)", for which an accompanying video was released in 2003 on MTV Asia.[56] The original sonic elements of "Let's Dance" are remixed in a Bollywood style, transforming it into a trance-like celebration. The video recontextualizes the visual narrative by embedding a few sequences from the original video within a 'kaleidoscopic montage of images'.[57] The montage comprises mostly still images of Asian faces and dancers overlaid with a moving graphic sequence comprised of text and patterns made up of the *boteh* (Persian) or *buta* symbol, an ancient symbolic predecessor to the paisley pattern, which is associated with Persian and Indian artforms, *Kashmiri* shawls, and other printed textiles.[58] These symbols form a pattern that dances on the surface of the video, providing an appropriate accompaniment to the *tabla* drums, sitars and Hindi backing vocals that were added to the re-mix. As with the original video, red shoes are a salient signifier in the remixed video, although having lost their sinister connotations within this Bollywood context. Responding to this project in 2003, Bowie said, 'Asian culture has had a fairly high profile within my work from the 1970s . . . it was not a difficult decision to give a green light to these remixes. I think they're pretty cool'.[59] This prominence of Asian culture in Bowie's work was to trigger another type of fan-engagement with the release of his next video, 'China Girl'.

"China Girl" – the song

Originally produced by Bowie and Iggy Pop, "China Girl" was released in 1977 as a single on Pop's album *The Idiot*. The song was initially arranged one night when

---

[56] placebooracle, 'David Bowie – Let's Dance (Club Bolly Remix)', *MTV Asia* (2003), YouTube video, 00:03:52, 14 October 2006, https://youtu.be/b8L24LuN9rU.
[57] Pegg, *The Complete David Bowie*, 160.
[58] '"Boteh" – The Journey from Persia to Paisley', *Rang Riwaaz*, 6 June 2021, https://tinyurl.com/32k48r9a.
[59] Pegg, *The Complete David Bowie*, 160.

the pair were playing around on toy instruments after a night out drinking. Playing a toy piano belonging to an eight-year-old child, Bowie devised a 'chirping riff' which features prominently in the final mix.[60] Days later, Pop wrote the lyrics, which were inspired by his affair with Kuelan Nguyen. This original song generated semantic ambiguity well before Bowie's video appeared. As O'Leary describes it, Pop sings:

> 'I'll ruin everything you are', yet he can't avoid doing so – his passion's too addicting and consuming – and it's not clear what he's ruining. He's more in love with his own depiction of her than whatever reality she offers; he's the man who fears he's poisoning his dreams, and spends his days raking through half-memories of them for impurities.[61]

Here, the lyrics are initially interpreted through the lens of a man realizing his capacity to invade and destroy his self-image of purity. However, O'Leary is quick to broaden his interpretation of these lyrics, adding, 'a widening of the lens finds Pop playing on the West's views of China itself [or 'the East']: a mirror reflecting its own flaws, a canvas on which it can project its own fantasies'.[62] This is an important contextual point, and one that should be considered by those who interpret the video for 'China Girl' as an isolated text, rather than what it actually is – a meta-commentary intended to build upon its collaborative origins. While the 1977 song already functioned as a commentary on Western stereotypical constructions of the East, Bowie intended his video to build upon this commentary, through a parody of 'Asian female stereotypes'.[63] Acknowledging Bowie's best intentions for the re-recorded song, Pegg perceives that 'Iggy's angrily growling vocal makes better sense of the lyric's forebodings about cultural imperialism and despoliation'.[64] By replacing Iggy's growling vocals with Bowie's harmonious crooning, 'cute' backing vocals and an oversimplified 'stereotypical' Asian guitar motif, Bowie transformed a sinister avant-punk song into a pastiche of a romantic pop song. That it works as pastiche is not fully realized by many audience members, since the frivolous elements of the re-recording complicated the song with a further layer of ambiguity.

---

[60] O'Leary, 'China Girl', *Pushing Ahead of the Dame*, 26 January 2011, https://tinyurl.com/3rkue95m.
[61] Ibid.
[62] Ibid.
[63] David Bowie, quoted in 'Bowie's China Girl, Geeling Ng, Remembers "Warm and Engaging" Star', *Stuff*, 12 January 2016, https://tinyurl.com/yzseexu8.
[64] Pegg, *The Complete David Bowie*, 61.

The song's 'Asian-sounding' guitar riff composed by Nile Rodgers sets the ironic tone, but only for those who perceive the irony intended in the simplification and exaggeration of a stereotypical sonic motif. The sonic elements of this opening riff are described by Ellie Hisama as 'superficial notions of what constitutes "oriental" music – parallel fourths played by the guitar'.[65] A similar response is expressed by Jonathan Kim, who said, 'the little plunky Asian-style riff … is the musical equivalent of someone saying "Ching chong ching", or the gong sound that went off in *Sixteen Candles* every time Long Duck Dong appeared on screen'.[66] A cutting but insightful point, showing how the strategic exaggeration or simplification of a stereotype might be perceived as ironic for some, but potentially as racist for those who have experienced racial stereotypes as identity markers constantly imposed by the West. In view of Kim's point, one has to wonder what led Rodgers and Bowie to believe this was a good choice of music. Rodgers told David Buckley that playing this opening riff to Bowie was 'the most nervous moment in my entire career', adding, 'I thought I was putting some bubble-gum over some artistic heavy record. I was terrified. I thought he was going to tell me that I'd blasphemed, that I didn't get the record and that I didn't get him, and that I'd be fired. But it was exactly the opposite. He said it was great.'[67] Perhaps Bowie considered the frivolity of this stereotypical sonic motif as a strategy to emphasize the very problem with racial stereotypes. Despite Bowie's best intentions to ironize racial stereotypes, Kim points out that he may have failed to communicate his message as broadly and successfully as he had intended:

> Bowie might very well have been trying to make a statement against anti-Asian racism with the song and video for 'China Girl'. But perhaps the more pertinent question is: Did Bowie succeed in communicating this message? Or was he unsuccessful or too clever to the point that 'China Girl' actually seems to *encourage* the kind of stereotyping and sexualization of Asian women he may have decried?[68]

Since these questions were raised in terms of the sonic aspects of the re-recorded song, it is important to pose these questions in the context of the video. Given

---

[65] Ellie Hisama, 'Postcolonialism on the Make: The Music of John Mellencamp, David Bowie and John Zorn', *Popular Music* 12, no. 2 (1993): 94.
[66] Jonathan Kim, 'An Asian's take on David Bowie's "China Girl"', *Rethink Reviews*, 30 March 2021, https://tinyurl.com/3pz8y5hk.
[67] Buckley, *Strange Fascination*, 338.
[68] Kim, 'An Asian's take on David Bowie's "China Girl"'.

the complexity of signification involved in the construction of the video, one must consider the relationship between linguistic, sonic and visual elements, along with the historical and geographic context in which the video was produced and released. However, we should consider Bowie's intentions for the video.

Bowie has expressed his abhorrence of racism in many ways and on numerous occasions. Having said that 'China Girl' is about 'invasion and exploitation',[69] Bowie has described the video as a 'vignette of my continuing fascination with all things Asian',[70] and as 'a very simple, very direct' statement against racism, through a parody of 'Asian female stereotypes'.[71] In an interview for Australian television, he elaborated, 'what I wanted to present was the imperialist Westerner coming to a foreign society and sort of dazzling the indigenous peoples with the idea of their own Western life, and that it's not necessarily a good thing to be jumping for'.[72] As discussed earlier, Bowie had already used symbolism, irony and metaphor to critique colonialist racism in 'Let's Dance'. With 'China Girl,' he wanted to use similar strategies to critique the racism inherent in Orientalism.

Orientalism

Orientalism is a way of seeing from a Western perspective that imagines, exaggerates, accentuates, and distorts the perceived characteristics of Asian, Middle Eastern and North African cultures and peoples, who are often represented as exotic, hyper-feminized and sexualized. In some texts, 'Orientals' are depicted as childlike, backward, uncivilized and dangerous. Particularly evident in nineteenth century art, literature, and histories produced by the West, this combination of 'traits' is similar to the 'noble savage' discourse, which nineteenth century artists and historians used to portray indigenous peoples as a duality of exoticism and desirability, yet savage and uncivilized; all of which was used as a means to justify colonization by the West.[73] Drawing on Michel Foucault's writing on the discursive conditions of knowledge, Edward Said redefined the term 'Orientalism' as a critical concept, arguing that the Orient is constructed by

---

[69] O'Leary, 'China Girl'.
[70] Pegg, *The Complete David Bowie*, 61.
[71] Bowie, quoted in 'Bowie's China Girl'.
[72] Bowie, 'Countdown with Molly Meldrum'.
[73] Andrew Bank, 'The Return of the Noble Savage: The Changing Image of Africans in Cape Colonial Art, 1800–1850', *South African Historical Journal* 39, no. 1 (2009): 17–43.

Western systems of knowledge, and that knowledge is intimately linked with institutions of power.[74] For Said, Orientalism is a self-perpetuating discursive system that provides the 'necessary knowledge for actual colonial conquest'.[75] Since Western representations of the East are inextricably connected to the Imperialist societies that produced them, they are inherently servile to an imperialist power.[76] Said argued that the texts of Orientalism (written histories, paintings, photographs, and films) 'can create not only knowledge but also the very reality they appear to describe'.[77] In other words, the Orient was constructed by the West, taking the form of a complex array of representations, which not only determined a Western understanding of the Orient, but 'provided the basis for its subsequent self-appointed rule'.[78] In this sense, the Orient can be understood as an abstract system of representations constructed by the West, which was also then performatively adopted or 'played out' by those who identify as 'Orientals'. This concept is sometimes discussed in relation to the discursive construction of the 'exotic Other', which is used as a means of establishing European identity as distinct from 'Others'.[79] These 'Others' have been feminized, infantilized and exoticized via literary texts, cultural forms and performative practices, to the extent that such markers of identification become played out by those constructed as 'Other'. As such, a Western representation of 'exotic Other' is not only stamped onto an ethnic people, but it can be internalized, forming an identity marker in a performative sense.[80] These ideas about Orientalism and representation provide an important context for the following discussion of the video for 'China Girl'.

'China Girl' – the video

Described by Mallet as a favourite of the videos he directed for Bowie,[81] 'China Girl' was shot in various Australian locations, including the Chinatown district of Sydney, Sydney Harbour and parts of the Australian outback. The video features

---

[74] Edward W. Said, *Orientalism* (New York: Vintage Books, 1979).
[75] Robert Young, *White Mythologies: Writing History and the West* (London: Routledge, 1990), 129.
[76] Said, *Orientalism*.
[77] Said, quoted in Young, *White Mythologies*, 129.
[78] Young, *White Mythologies*, 126.
[79] Suren Lalvani, 'Consuming the Exotic Other', *Critical Studies in Mass Communication* 12, no. 3 (1995): 263–86.
[80] For more on this, see Yiman Wang, 'Screening Asia: Passing, Performative Translation, and Reconfiguration', *Positions* 15, no. 2 (2007): 319–43; Kimberly Middleton, 'You Gotta Chink it Up: Asian American Performativity in the New Orientalism' (PhD diss., University of Notre Dame, 2003).
[81] Mallet, interview by Lisa Perrott.

Chinese actress Geeling Ng, who is now known as Geeling Ching (to avoid confusion I refer to her as 'Geeling'). Released in May 1983, the video was enthusiastically received by audiences across the globe, contributing to the success of the song – as indicated by charts and album sales.[82] 'China Girl' won Best Male Video at the 1984 MTV Video Music Awards, despite the controversy caused by the nude beach scene at the end of the video, which intertextually references the intimate beach scene in the film *From Here to Eternity* (1953). Bowie and Geeling were filmed lying in a naked embrace on the beach as the waves rolled over them. Perceiving the scene to be too *risqué* for a television audience, *Top of the Pops* initially banned the video. Much to the bemusement of Pegg, the show 'subsequently played an expurgated version that kept everything in wide shot and clumsily inserted slow-motion edits to spare us the sight of David's enviably well-toned bottom'.[83] When interviewed in 2009, Geeling clarified that 'contrary to popular belief, David and I did not have sex on the beach!'[84] Noting that she and Bowie were in view of the film crew and passers-by, she recalled how the scene was shot at 5 am, when the water was freezing, so it 'wasn't a great lubricant . . . not very romantic'.[85] Revealing another example of dampened intimacy, Geeling added, 'there's a scene where I sit up suddenly, as if woken from a dream, and David leaps on top of me. . . . I sat up and gave him a full Liverpool kiss in the face'.[86] She thought, 'Oh my God, I've just killed David Bowie, but he laughed and said "thank God I've got a hard head"'.[87] Mentioning the brief romantic relationship she had had with Bowie, Geeling recalled, 'I knew it was a passing phase. I was twenty-three. We lived in different worlds. But he gave me an experience I'll never forget.'[88] When interviewed after Bowie's death in 2016, Geeling said her 'China Girl' experience 'was completely surreal. . . . It's had the biggest influence on my life that I could have ever imagined.'[89] Although there has been much debate about the video's representation of Chinese women, Geeling said, 'I'm immensely

---

[82] Bowie's song 'China Girl' reached number 10 on the Billboard Hot 100. The song lasted on the chart for eighteen weeks. 'China Girl's' parent album, *Let's Dance*, was a huge commercial success, peaking at number 4 on the Billboard 200 and staying on the chart for sixty-nine weeks; Matthew Trzcinski, 'David Bowie's Hit Song "China Girl" Allowed Iggy Pop to get Married', *Cheatsheet*, 17 November 2021, https://tinyurl.com/bdhjmdm3.
[83] Pegg, *The Complete David Bowie*, 61.
[84] Pat Gilbert, *Bowie: The Illustrated Story* (Minneapolis: Voyageur Press, 2017), 177.
[85] Ibid.
[86] Dave Simpson, 'David Bowie and Me', *The Guardian*, 23 February 2013, https://tinyurl.com/2ubvj856.
[87] Ibid.
[88] Ibid.
[89] Nick Perry, 'David Bowie's "China Girl" Says Music Video Changed Her Life', *AP NEWS*, 13 January 2016, https://tinyurl.com/58mxakj8.

proud, utterly proud to be China Girl. I'll go to my grave with that. I'm blessed to have been part of that incredible talent.... It was so special, the time I spent with David, I would never trade for anything.'[90] Given her position in the video as representing Chinese women, these comments should be considered in relation to arguments that either Bowie, or the video, are racist. To investigate such perspectives, it is first necessary to examine the video in detail.

The opening sonic riff is accompanied by visual motifs that are reiterated at the end of the video. In the centre of the frame, an image of Geeling's torso appears from the distance. As though emerging from the sea, her cut-out image becomes progressively larger until she dominates the frame. This allusion to the divine birth of an exotic figure recalls images of Pierrot immersed in the sea in 'Ashes to Ashes' (Figure 5.4). Lowering her head and casting her eyes downward, Geeling appears submissive; her indirect address to camera signalling her status as an object to be looked at rather than possessing the agency to address the audience directly. She is wearing a veil or *chador*, a complex cultural signifier associated variously with the attire of Muslim women, adherence to Islamic beliefs, protection (and/or control) of women, mourning, modesty or dignity.[91] When this image of the *chador* is overlaid with motifs of entrapment, new meaning is generated (Figure 6.5). It becomes clear that Bowie is layering these signifiers to make a strong statement about Orientalism. Raising her arms as though to spread her wings, the sense of liberation implied by this gesture is counteracted by two decorative elements that appear to be marked on the surface of the video, both of which allude to entrapment. The first is a framing device in the form of a repeated pattern, much like the decorative frame around a Persian rug or tapestry. In this context, the patterned frame may connote entrapment within the Western 'frame' of Orientalism. The second is a criss-cross impression of barbed wire marks, signifying a brutal form of entrapment by a colonial power or militia. These 'drawn-on-the-surface' markings are in keeping with Mallet's intent to innovate non-conventional visual techniques to communicate specific messages. As was the case with 'Ashes to Ashes,' Mallet's signature transitions are distinctive: the residue of the earlier shot lingers while the new shot begins to dominate the frame. This visual layering is a method of spatial montage which generates new

---

[90] Corazon Miller, 'When an Ordinary Kiwi Became David Bowie's China Girl', *The New Zealand Herald*, 12 January 2016, https://tinyurl.com/3z6yubfb.

[91] Claire Alexander, 'The Motivations Behind Westerners' Obsession with the Islamic Veil', *The Cupola* (Spring 2016), https://tinyurl.com/394v9jsv.

Figure 6.5 Geeling wearing a *chador*. 'China Girl' (David Mallet, 1983).

meaning through the merging of different visual signs.[92] While the veiled woman fades to become the background image, a double bass player occupies the mid-ground and Bowie's face dominates the foreground, filling half the frame (Figure 6.6). As with the earlier shot, Bowie is encompassed by the patterned framing device; it is not only the Chinese woman who is trapped – Bowie and his bass player are also trapped within the Western frame of Orientalism.

The preliminary sequence of shots feature subtle alternations of focal length and colour, where figures move forward and backward across the 'Depth of Field,'[93] gaining or losing salience in comparison to others. For instance, an early shot in the sequence depicts Bowie's coral-tan face in sharp focus in the foreground. Filling half the frame, his face stands out against the blurry midground shot of the double bass player, who is lit with a purple gradient. This method of using focus and colour to differentiate the foreground and background continues into the next shot, where Geeling's face is projected onto a background screen.

---

[92] For more on this, see Bordwell, 'The Idea of Montage in Soviet Art and Film', 9–17.
[93] For an explanation of 'Depth of Field,' see David Bordwell and Kristin Thompson, 'Do Filmmakers Deserve the Last Word?' *Observations On Film Art*, 10 October 2007, https://tinyurl.com/5dsxsu5z.

Figure 6.6 Layered imagery in 'China Girl' (David Mallet, 1983).

Sharing this screen with the shadow cast by Bowie's head, Geeling's sharply focused face fills the right side of the frame, making her the dominant feature within the image. Bowie occupies the mid-ground as the less sharply focused part of the image, despite singing and dancing in his moderate 1980s style. A hand enters from the front of screen and strokes Geeling's face, introducing another foreground layer to this multi-layered image. While operating as a subtle means of allusion, these coordinated alternations of Depth of Field, colour, and layered zones of information exemplify Mallet's idiosyncratic approach to cinematography and editing (Figure 6.7).

'China Girl' also exhibits a number of motifs reiterated across the Mallet/Bowie videos. For instance, in a scene shot in the Australian outback, Bowie performs a colonialist execution. Accompanied by a military figure and dressed in the attire of colonial gentry, Bowie gestures with his hand to configure a gun held to Geeling's head. This scene was carefully planned so that the act of execution appears in reverse motion and is therefore experienced as strange rather than shocking. Mallet used this reverse motion editing technique very sparingly in 'Let's Dance' and 'Fashion'. Other elements reappear across the

Figure 6.7 Layered imagery in 'China Girl' (David Mallet, 1983).

Mallet/Bowie videos. For instance, the colonial attire worn by Bowie in the execution scene in 'China Girl' reappears in 'Loving the Alien', where he is shot alongside a woman dressed in an exotic 'Eastern' costume. As with 'China Girl', a double bass player features prominently in 'Wild is the Wind', 'The Drowned Girl', 'Let's Dance' and 'Loving the Alien'. While these examples show continuity across the Mallet/Bowie videos, they also show how collaborative assemblage is crucial to the seriality of Bowie's videos.

Critiques of 'China Girl'

Among the published critiques of 'China Girl' is the argument that the song and video are racist. Others take issue with the ambiguity of the imagery and the lyrics. Shelton Waldrep believes the meaning of the song is destabilized because the initial intention of the lyrics has been altered. He argues that, 'by shifting the song's intention from personal romance to something like politics or ideological critique, Bowie opened the text to multiple interpretations, but also destabilized meaning in the song, creating possibilities that he was perhaps not able fully to anticipate or control'.[94] If 'China Girl' had been intended to function as a form of ideological critique, Mallet may have used the editing technique of Soviet montage as a means to communicate a strong message through the merging of different visual ideas. While semantic juxtaposition is evident in both 'China Girl' and 'Let's Dance', my own audience research indicates that, although most viewers were familiar with montage and collage-like editing in music videos, many were disturbed by the juxtaposition of romantic imagery with scenes alluding to colonial execution and stereotypically racist images and gestures (such as the eye pulling gesture associated with racist, anti-Asian playground chants). The juxtaposition of visual imagery also clashes with the frivolous, pop music backing vocals, producing an audio-visual concoction that triggers incongruous affective responses, ranging from happiness and desire, to discomfort and confusion. A group of Chinese students expressed this feeling of discomfort and confusion after viewing the video for the first time, and their responses are summarized in Leonard Sanders' PhD thesis:[95]

> Some students cannot identify the gold-haired man (Bowie), wonder what is in the bowl ..., feel uncomfortable when the Chinese girl pushes up her nose, or Bowie pulls his eyes to make them slanted; but many students note the Chinese girl is the focus of the video, and comment on her transformation into ethnic dress, her makeup and her strange fingernails.[96]

Without knowing anything about Bowie and his artistic strategies, Sanders' students were not in a position to understand the use of exaggerated racial stereotypes. According to Sanders, his students were confused by the video's collage of imagery alluding to disparate time periods and geographical locations. While Bowie said he 'wanted to utilize the strange beauty of Australia ... to put it in a context where it hadn't been seen before',[97] the ambiguity of this collage-like flow of images appears to have opened up a space for confusion about the links between Australian locations and stereotypes associated with China. Intrigued by the comments made by Sanders' students, I decided to undertake my own audience research. I interviewed audience members of various ethnicities,

---

[94] Shelton Waldrep, 'The "China Girl" Problem: Reconsidering David Bowie in the 1980s', in Devereux, Dillane and Power (eds), *David Bowie: Critical Perspectives*, 147–59.
[95] Leonard Sanders, 'Postmodern Orientalism' (PhD diss., Postmodern Orientalism: Massey University, 2008).
[96] Ibid., 174.
[97] Bowie, 'Countdown with Molly Meldrum'.

genders and ages, and documented a range of their responses to the video. Most interviewees said they were confused about the presentation of Chinese stereotypes alongside distinctive Australian locations, such as the desert, the Chinatown district, and Sydney Harbour. A Chinese student of media studies said that she found it confusing to see an image of a Chinese woman running across the Australian desert holding a red flag, and questioned, 'maybe Bowie wanted to say she comes from a communist country? There is no communism in Chinese traditional culture'. She added that since all the actors in the video 'come from Western culture it's strange'.[98] This response highlights one of the potential pitfalls of editing a music video according to a non-continuity, montage or collage-like approach, particularly when a variety of signifiers are re-contextualized or placed alongside disturbing imagery such as an execution scene. This problem is exemplified by the following sequence in the video, which also provoked a strong response from the student I interviewed.

In a modern Chinese restaurant, Bowie sips from a Chinese tea cup and clumsily uses chopsticks to eat rice. Later, a monochromatic sequence accompanies the lyrics, 'I stumble into town, just like a sacred cow. Visions of swastikas in my head, plans for everyone.' We see Bowie running down a street (presumably located in Sydney's Chinatown). Happening upon a Chinese woman wearing a peasant costume and holding a steaming bowl of rice, Bowie grabs the bowl from her hands and throws the rice into the air; an act that triggers her transformation into a Westerner's idea of exotic beauty; she wears an elaborate ethnic costume and her face is painted with *oshiroi*, the white foundation worn by *geisha*. Bowie forcibly pulls her to him and their kiss is filmed in a 360-degree arc shot,[99] which gradually transforms from grayscale into colour. The romance of this whirlwind kiss is undermined by the lyrics, 'My little China girl, you shouldn't mess with me. I'll ruin everything you are', and this audio-visual incongruity generates an uncomfortable feeling of threat and uneven power dynamics. This sequence exemplifies the way in which Bowie stitched together linguistic, sonic, and visual elements as a means of alluding to problematic Western attitudes toward 'the Orient'. Despite his best intentions, Bowie's strategic use of collage and allusion has not always been understood in the way he intended. In response to this sequence, my interviewee pointed out that 'Bowie doesn't know how to use chopsticks'. By including this detail, the

---

[98] Research participant. Interview by Lisa Perrott, 17 January 2022.
[99] For an explanation of 'arc shot', see chapter 3.

director 'shows no understanding of Chinese culture.... It's bizarre for Chinese, why a Peking Opera costume suddenly appears, and why Bowie took the bowl of rice and threw it up. What did that mean? Chinese people couldn't understand what these things are supposed to mean.'[100] Since the video uses stereotypes that are exclusively understood by Westerners, this Chinese woman wondered if the video was made for a Western audience. Perhaps in 1983, it didn't occur to Bowie and Mallet that a woman raised in China might experience their use of Orientalist stereotypes as confusing. This question is considered by Ellie Hisama, who compares 'China Girl' with Mellencamp's song of the same title. Describing 'China Girl' as a 'complex piece ... in the context of Orientalist politics', Hisama breaks down the video, demonstrating her understanding of the strategies used by Bowie as a critique of Orientalism:

> ... its narrative of Western Man meets Asian woman seems so overdone, and thus done tongue in cheek. The act of stroking her hair while she is on her knees, as if she were an obedient dog; the photo of a debonair Bowie prominently displayed upon her bedside table; and the moment in which he lunges upon her passive body on the bed while he sings 'I'll give you a man who wants to rule the world' all contribute to an exaggerated, self-mocking portrait of white male-Asian female relationships.[101]

Although Hisama has identified the video's strategic use of exaggeration, irony and self-parody, she cannot accept that these strategies work, at least not through her own interpretive lens as an Asian woman. Acknowledging the tension she experiences when undertaking a critical interpretation of the video, Hisama says that:

> Although reading his 'China Girl' as a brilliant piece of irony would leave my admiration for Bowie's work intact ... I am still unable to convince myself to accept this interpretation. For while the song seems sensitive to the domination and corruption by white men of Asian women, it nevertheless homogenizes Asian female identity in a manner which I do not perceive as being critical. When the Western man laments to his little chinagirl that he will 'ruin everything you are', he takes one admirable step towards realizing that he is appropriating her. Yet she remains nameless, reduced to a sex and a race. And despite the narrator's claim that she has the power to get him to shut up, the chinagirl is never permitted to speak in her own voice – the first and only time she gets the opportunity to say anything, she mouths her line while Bowie delivers it in a

---

[100] Research participant. Interview by Lisa Perrott.
[101] Hisama, 'Postcolonialism on the Make'.

monotone. Thus, although their conversation seems to be interactive, it is actually monological: Bowie appears to allow an Other to speak, but the 'dialogue' only underscores his authority to represent, and at the same time confers upon himself the role of hero in a Kevin Costner-style rescue fantasy, thereby enacting a new form of colonialism.[102]

Hisama's analysis provides some insight into the tension between acknowledging the critical intentions behind the song and video, perceiving the strategic use of exaggeration and irony, and ultimately interpreting both the song and video as not only a failure to be critical, but as 'enacting a new form of colonialism'.[103] Hisama's comments echo those of my Chinese interviewee, who said her main issue with the video was that the story is told through the perspective of the Western man, while 'the Chinese woman has no voice'.[104] While this raises crucial issues about who is allowed the agency to speak, I wonder if this is the very point Bowie was intending to make – that Western representations of 'the Orient' render 'Others' as exotic and voiceless. If one accepts that Bowie's actions in the video underscore his authority to represent, then one would have to perceive Bowie as playing himself in the video. However, if he was playing the role of a racist colonizer to critique this figure (as he did in 'Let's Dance'), then it is the Costner-style hero figure – not Bowie – who is rendering the woman as exotic and voiceless. The trouble is that for the most part, Bowie comes across as 'himself' – the smiling, handsome, apparently 'mask-less' Bowie in 1983 interviews. Apart from the execution scene, it's not entirely clear that he is playing a role that might represent the West's control over the representation of the East. With so many layers of representation, it's not surprising that there is confusion about who is doing the representing, and what the message is. Cat Zhang provides yet another perspective about the video's layers of irony:

> One of the reasons 'China Girl' was – and remains – so confusing to me is because of its many layers of irony. At first listen, it can sound really racist. And then, after several listens, it actually feels as if Bowie is, with incredible insightfulness, dismantling all of the layers of objectification and Orientalism and sexism that are wrapped up in this stereotype of the 'China girl'. You can listen to the song and feel like either he's perpetuating that stereotype or he's actually understanding it

[102] Ibid, 95.
[103] Ibid.
[104] Research participant. Interview by Lisa Perrott.

better than anyone else ever did. He always seemed like somebody who, if you sat down and talked to him, he would have listened and understood.[105]

I have presented a variety of different interpretations here to show that audience members make sense of music videos by drawing upon their access to an array of cultural resources, previous experiences, discourses, and knowledge of artistic strategies. To make sense of 'China Girl', it also helps to consider this video within the context of the artistic strategies employed by Bowie across his *oeuvre*. In particular, the strategic use of pastiche and gesture in this video are evident in Bowie's earlier work, often appearing as moments of subversion and critique. I have not yet read a critique of 'China Girl' that mentions the meaning of Geeling's lipstick smear at the end of the video (Figure 6.8). As noted in chapter four, this was a gesture performed by Bowie four years earlier in 'Boys Keep Swinging'. In the context of that video, the gesture appeared as an act of defiance against

Figure 6.8 Geeling performing the lipstick smear. 'China Girl' (David Mallet, 1983).

[105] Cat Zhang, 'What Novelist Susan Choi is Listening to Right Now', *Pitchfork*, 3 January 2020, https://tinyurl.com/3dkfpdm9.

normative gender codes. When Geeling performs this gesture in 'China Girl', it appears as an act of defiance against the codes of Orientalism. Understanding such strategic use of gesture requires critical analysis informed by a knowledge of Bowie's artistic approach and his stated intent to make a critical statement about racism.

When considering all of these debates about 'China Girl', it is instructive to listen to the voice of Geeling, who is a successful actress and businesswoman living in New Zealand. When interviewed in 2022 by Carly Flynn, Geeling expressed pride in being publicly recognized as 'China Girl'. When Flynn asked her, 'The point of you being in that video was to expose Asian stereotypes. . . . Did it do its job?' Geeling responded:

> I think the message might have been too subtle . . . and that's David. He travels in a different plane. And so I feel like, if you didn't perhaps read about it, you wouldn't have understood what he was trying to say. Particularly, you know with shooting me in the head, where I'm wearing the Mao outfit and all of that sort of thing . . . and he's got the English suit on, with the top hat etc., and it's all about colonialism. I think if you didn't know, you'd kind of be going, I don't really know what this is [about]. But you know, we did win best video of the year, so . . .[106]

When I talked with Geeling in 2021, she reiterated similar thoughts and emphasized her ongoing admiration of Bowie and Mallet. When considering Flynn's question of whether the video did 'its job', it is also important to consider a diverse range of audience interpretations. If a Chinese viewer feels that the video has rendered her voiceless, then it must have failed to deliver a clear message to a diverse audience. Interestingly, the interviewee who made this statement sent me a message later that day, saying that after watching several live performances of the song, she was convinced that 'Bowie was just playing and parodying a white man in that video. The expressions in the video look very frivolous, and I now think Bowie performs it in that way on purpose.'[107] She concluded, 'Banksy said art should comfort the disturbed and disturb the comfortable. I think David Bowie achieved both these ways. I felt a little bit disturbed this afternoon and now I feel comfortable when I knew it is his (or the director's) trick.'[108]

---

[106] Geeling Ching, interviewed by Carly Flynn, Tom Thexton, 'What You Don't Know About podcast: China Girl – "The phone call from Bowie that changed my life"', *Today FM*, 2 August 2022, https://tinyurl.com/3nt3a9v8.

[107] Email comment written by an interviewee of Chinese descent, 17 January 17 2022, following an interview conducted by the author on that date.

[108] Ibid.

Imago[109]

This chapter explores the personal, cultural and political context in which Bowie emerged with a new persona in 1983, with a new drive to use the art of music video as a means for critiquing issues such as racism, colonialism and Orientalism. Not only was he vocal about his intentions during media interviews, Bowie was also not afraid to confront his audience with discomforting signifiers of racism and Orientalism. In 'Let's Dance', the *verité* footage of the local inhabitants, along with the arrangement of the imagery, confronts viewers with the realities of racism and colonial oppression. Despite the discomfort generated by the video, it was successful in bolstering album sales, along with Bowie's emerging status as a mega rock star. Although 'China Girl' also played a significant role in increasing Bowie's popularity at the time, the song and video have since been the source of much criticism, including audience responses of discomfort at signifiers that have been perceived as racially ambiguous. After examining a variety of published critiques as well as comments by interviewees, I conclude that, despite Bowie's intentions to use layers of irony as a critique of racism and Orientalism, the collage-like assemblage of the video has led to a partial failure in communicating this message clearly to a diverse audience. It is problematic that some viewers feel the video renders Chinese women as voiceless, and that some experience elements of the video as confusing or discomforting. However, my research shows that the video also opens room for further thought, and that for some, discomfort is a passage toward deeper levels of interpretation. In fact, this notion of discomfort, as creatively productive and potentially enlightening, is at the heart of Bowie's approach to music video – and a key finding of this book, as we shall see in the epilogue.

---

[109] Imago is the final stage of metamorphosis.

Epilogue

The final chapter concluded with my observation that discomfort is at the heart of Bowie's creative process. From 'Love You till Tuesday' to 'China Girl', we have seen how discomfort threads its way through Bowie's music videos, leaps out of screens and seeps into our bodies. If there are two vital messages that we can take away from the videos examined in this book, it is to embrace discomfort, and to respect the collaborative process. Through his videos, Bowie demonstrates the value of these tenets – not only for the creative process and the audience experience, but as principles for living and growing.

Contributions, insights and dangling threads

I hope this book will be a source of inspiration for fans, scholars, and practitioners, and that it will contribute new insights to the existing body of literature on the music videos, audio-visual media, and art of David Bowie. By undertaking an in-depth study of Bowie's contribution to establishing music video as an artform, this book builds upon valuable research across disciplinary areas. For instance, it supports Emily Caston's argument that music video developed as a collaborative artform, years before the launch of MTV. It also reinforces Mathias Korsgaard and Tomáš Jirsa's definition of music video as a 'hybrid audio-visual configuration', an 'intertextual space of perpetual remediations where one medium transforms the other'.[1] By probing this space, pulling apart the layers and examining how this remediation process works in practice, this book champions the study of audio-visual relations, while illustrating the usefulness of multimodal analysis as a flexible method. Since the method does not restrict its focus solely to one mode, it demands an excavational approach to analysis, whereby each layer is examined before holistic connections are explored. Although time-consuming and intellectually demanding, the strength of this method lies in its capacity to detect the production of new meaning, as it emerges from the volatile relations between sonic, visual and literary modes.

---

[1] Jirsa and Korsgaard, 'The Music Video in Transformation', 117.

While I am confident that this book will make a useful contribution to knowledge, it has taken a different shape from what I had planned. As mentioned, my initial aim to interview each director was thwarted by circumstance. Sadly, several of Bowe's collaborators from this early period are no longer alive. Although this situation required rethinking my methodological process, it led to a tenacious approach to contextual research and in-depth analysis. I needed to deviate from my initial plan in other ways too. When I began this project in 2017, I had intended to analyse a comprehensive selection of Bowie videos from 1969 to 2016. However, it became clear that to do so within the word limitations of one book would not do justice to Bowie's videos, which are extremely complex audio-visual forms that should be considered within a broad context. While Bowie underwent much change in his creative output, music video as an artform has undergone major changes over the past five decades. For these reasons, I decided to limit the timeframe of this book to 1969–83, on the basis that I would examine the latter timeframe in a second book.

Collaboration

In hindsight, I began to realize that valuable insights could still be gained without having conducted interviews with each director. It is testament to the communication skills of Bowie's collaborators that their voices are so eloquently articulated though their art. This is perfectly exemplified by Mick Rock's photographs and videos. My analysis of his videos demonstrates his special ability to draw out the essence of a performer, thereby 'bottling' their 'aura'. In retrospect, what becomes clear is that it is not only Bowie's aura that is captured in Rock's still and moving images, but that of Rock himself. This is one of the many surprises that emerged from my research. With each chapter, further insights surfaced. Just as it has been fascinating to learn of Dorfman's affinity for visual music and his art practice across several mediums, it is also extremely satisfying when detailed analysis reveals his artisanal 'fingerprints' to be imprinted in 'Be My Wife' and 'Heroes'. It was also intriguing to see Mallet's innovation manifested in the use of techniques and aesthetics that brought to life Bowie's avant-garde visions – a collaborative outcome that is particularly striking in 'Ashes to Ashes'.

The analyses in this book reveal the specific ways in which these directors each played an important part in establishing music video as an artform. By taking time to explore their contributions, we learn how these directors each taught Bowie something unique about how to use the medium, and about the collaborative process. For instance, it was through working closely with Rock that Bowie experienced the value of a non-hierarchical, symbiotic approach to collaboration. The trust upon which this relationship was founded enabled Bowie to relax and master the art of performing directly to the camera. Similarly, working with Dorfman involved a mutual appreciation for painting, visual music, and creating across mediums – a basis from which Bowie further developed the art of posing, and using his body as a sculpture upon which to paint with light. Having developed these tools for performing in music video, Bowie was assisted by Mallet to further develop his use of gesture, signification and intertextuality. While Mallet taught him much about how to communicate his ideas visually and technically, he also stepped back and gave Bowie the opportunity to learn about directing music videos. Mallet supported him to experiment with storyworld development, and with communicating ideas through analogy, signification, and gesture.

Creative process

While this book casts a spotlight on the significant contributions of Bowie's collaborators, it also highlights that collaboration was central to Bowie's creative process, which is underpinned by the notion of alchemy. The idea of new meaning being created through the synthesis of volatile 'elements' is reiterated in many of the reflective comments made by those who worked with Bowie. While visual ideas for 'Ashes to Ashes' were generated by bouncing thoughts backwards and forwards with Mallet, video shoots with Rock and Dorfman portray a different type of alchemy – one in which performance and light are captured by the eye of the director and the shutter of the camera. Even before the videos were created, there were many instances of alchemy in the recording studio, as Bowie undertook aleatory composition practices with Visconti and Eno. As mentioned, there have already been insightful explorations of how this process transpired with regard to Bowie's musical composition. This book builds upon such studies, to explore the specific ways in which experimentation and chance occurrence are manifested in his music videos.

While Bowie has been described as a 'magpie' in order to denote his rampant foraging when writing songs, such foraging was also at play in the creation of his music videos. As we have seen, Bowie appropriated many poses, gestures and stylistic features, which he synthesized and reiterated through his performances and videos. When we examine his videos, we see Anthony Newley's light entertainer antics, the self-touching gestures gleaned from Hollywood starlets and the lipstick smear borrowed from drag performances that Bowie had seen in Berlin. All these examples demonstrate the power of foraging and synthesis as artistic strategies, and the suitability of music video as a forager's canvas.

Artistic strategy

One of my aims for this book was to demonstrate that Bowie's videos are artforms and should be studied as such. Approaching each video as an artwork in its own right, I have undertaken a layered analysis of the different modes that comprise each video, taking into account formal properties, aesthetics and techniques. However, to gain meaning from an artwork, it is important to consider the social, cultural and historical context in which it is situated. By devoting time to researching this context, I hope that the analyses in this book are further enriched, and that readers find them insightful. By exploring these contextual aspects, we learn that Bowie was a master of many artforms and that he had a hunger for experimenting with artistic strategies. While he drew on the tenets of visual music across various mediums, he used music video as a means to explore new configurations of sound, image and word. Through examining Bowie's videos, we learn that he drew on the tenets of surrealism – not only to entice his audience into a deeper understanding of art and culture but also to subvert normative structures of thought, and to provoke a rethinking (or reimagining) of taken-for-granted perceptions of the world. He used strategies such as defamiliarization, *détournement*, parody and irony, thus subverting normative gender codes, racial stereotypes, and dominant notions of rock music. While Bowie used strategies that were practiced by the proponents of artistic traditions such as visual music and surrealism, he also developed his own methods, such as mimicry, self-quotation, gestural migration and performativity. He experimented with the signification of material objects such as the guitar, the Droog costume, black bomber-jacket, white gloves and red shoes.

By tracing Bowie's artistic approach across fourteen years, we can chart the development of his use of artistic strategies. Chapters two and three show how, during the late 1960s and early 1970s, Bowie was playfully mimicking and synthesizing the signifiers and gestures that he had foraged. Chapter four demonstrates the way that, in the mid-1970s Bowie started using these signifiers in a more sophisticated manner, making use of strategies such as parody, irony and *détournement*. Chapter five shows that by 1979, Bowie had mastered the art of allusion, and was combining persona and masking with intertextuality and worldbuilding. He was articulating these strategies with such complexity that my analysis of 'Space Oddity' and 'Ashes to Ashes' required excavating through numerous layers of references and allusions. In chapter six, we see that in 1983, Bowie began using artistic strategies for the purpose of drawing attention to the oppression brought about by racism, colonialism and Orientalism. This involved layering his videos with further strategies, such as the symbolism of white gloves and red shoes, references to the atrocities committed by colonialism, and his strategic (though troublingly subtle) use of stereotype as a means of drawing attention to the representation of the 'Other'.

While each chapter has shed light on Bowie's use of artistic strategies within his music videos, when we reflect upon all the videos in this book, they appear as vehicles for the transit of particular characters, themes, and tropes, all of which form threads of loose continuity across his *oeuvre*. This supports my argument that Bowie was a transmedia navigator, one that paved the way for other artists to stitch together worlds – not through narrative convention – but through analogy, dialogism and intertextuality. Not only are Bowie's videos built through collaborative process and dialogue, they are also thickened with layers of intertextual references to ancient mythology, literature, cinema, art traditions and popular music. However, these references are not painted on the surface in an explicit or obvious manner. Using the strategy of allusion, Bowie strategically buried these references deep within a stratified, drillable text.

Reflecting on the videos discussed in this book, it is apparent that while Bowie uses music video as a canvas, he treats time as a malleable medium that is threaded through the weave of his videos. His videos operate as time-travelling vessels that transport characters and storyworld components through time and space. This point is demonstrated in chapters two and four, where I chart the travels of 'Space Oddity' through multiple videos. The notion of Bowie's videos as mobile palimpsests is further elaborated by examining re-edited videos made by fans, therefore providing support for my metaphor of the music video as a TARDIS. By travelling through time and referring us to the past and future, Bowie's videos play a pivotal role in remediating traditional artforms, thus demonstrating music video's affordance for remediation and intermedial transit.

Scaffolding from this study of music video as a collaborative, time-travelling artform, my forthcoming book examines Bowie's music videos from 1984 to 2016, and beyond. While exploring the ways in which music video has transformed within this time frame, the second book demonstrates Bowie's contribution to this process, leading the way for fans to play an active part as collaborators in the creation of music videos.

The preface for this book opened with a story about the motivating presence of Bowie in a dream. While this served as a metaphor for the extent to which Bowie has accompanied me during this writing adventure, the dream felt real, and I did feel a sense of being visited as I stood in front of those screens at the *David Bowie Is* exhibit. Now that the book is complete, the spare room can now be vacated for other guests. It's been five years, and my brain hurts a lot!

Bibliography

Abdulmajid, Iman. 'Watch That Man: Interview by Iman'. *Bust Magazine* (October 2000). https://tinyurl.com/mvzjv6pr.

Adamson, Glenn. 'Did David Bowie Invent the Music Video?\ *Frieze* (5 April 2018). https://tinyurl.com/4c5km77r.

Alexander, Claire. 'The Motivations Behind Westerners' Obsession with the Islamic Veil'. *The Cupola* (Spring 2016). https://tinyurl.com/394v9jsv.

Allen, Graham. *Intertextuality: The New Critical Idiom* (London: Routledge, 2000).

Andersen, Hans Christian. 'The Red Shoes'. *New Fairytales* 1, no. 3 (Copenhagen: C.A Reitzel, 1845).

Ardrey, Caroline. 'Dialogism and Song: Intertextuality, Heteroglossia and Collaboration in Augusta Holmes's Setting of Catulle Mendes's "Chanson"'. *Australian Journal of French Studies* 54, no. 2–3 (2017): 235–52.

Auslander, Philip. 'Framing Personae in Music Videos'. In *The Bloomsbury Handbook of Popular Music Video Analysis,* edited by Lori Burns and Stan Hawkins, 91–109 (New York: Bloomsbury, 2019).

Austerlitz, Saul. *Money For Nothing: A History of the Music Video from the Beatles to the White Stripes* (New York: Continuum, 2007).

Baker, Logan. 'A Complete Guide to Continuity Editing in Film and Short Videos'. *The Beat* (9 September 2022). https://tinyurl.com/3m2vfxsf.

Bakhtin, Mikhail. *Dialogic Imagination: Four Essays* (Austin: University of Texas Press, 1981).

Bank, Andrew. 'The Return of the Noble Savage: The Changing Image of Africans in Cape Colonial Art, 1800–1850'. *South African Historical Journal* 39, no. 1 (2009): 17–43.

Barthes, Roland. *Image-Music-Text* (London: Fontana, 1977).

Baylis, Nicola. 'Making Visible the Invisible: Corporeal Mime in the Twenty-first Century'. *Theatre Quarterly: NTQ, Cambridge* 25, no. 3 (August 2009): 274–88.

Benson-Allott, Caetlin. 'Going Gaga for Glitch: Digital Failure @nd Feminist Spectacle in Twenty-FIrst Century Music Video'. In *The Oxford Handbook of Sound and Image in Digital Media*, edited by Carol Vernallis, Amy Herzog and John Richardson, 127–37 (Oxford: Oxford University Pres, 2014).

Blair, Alison. '"Oh man, I need TV when I got T. Rex": Bowie and Bolan's Otherwordly Carnivalesque Intermediality'. *Celebrity Studies* 10, no.1 (2019): 75–88.

Bolter, Jay, and Richard Grusin. *Remediation: Understanding New Media* (London: MIT Press, 2000).

Bonasera, Carmen. 'Estrangement, Performativity, and Empathy in Bo Burnham's Inside (2021)'. *Between*, 12, no. 23 (2022): 93–116.

Bonner, Michael. 'Lindsay Kemp on David Bowie: "I taught him how to make an entrance and how to make an exit"'. *Uncut* (25 August 2018). https://tinyurl.com/4d5r9j6d.

Bordwell, David. 'The Idea of Montage in Soviet Art and Film'. *Cinema Journal* 11, no. 2 (1972): 9–17.

Bordwell, David. 'Observations in Film Art: Now Leaving Platform 1' (2009). https://tinyurl.com/u38t62vd.

Bordwell, David, and Kristin Thompson. 'Do Filmmakers Deserve the Last Word?' *Observations On Film Art* (10 October 2007). https://tinyurl.com/5dsxsu5z.

Bordwell, David, Janet Steiger and Kristin Thompson. 'The Classical Hollywood Cinema – Cap 5'. *Leyendocine* (1 May 2007). https://tinyurl.com/2nm6krzd.

Bowie, David. Interview by Tim Rice. *Friday Night, Saturday Morning*, BBC. YouTube video, 00:17:47 (10 October 1980). https://tinyurl.com/2wbvpre2.

Bowie, David. *Moonage Daydream: The Life and Times of Ziggy Stardust* (London: Palazzo, 2002).

Bowie, David. Teenage Wildlife, 'David Bowie – Scary Monsters Interview, PART 1 (12" Promo 1980)'. YouTube video, 00:07:51 (26 March 2009). https://tinyurl.com/yseam5yb.

Bowie, David. 'Life On Mars? Yesterday and Tomorrow'. *DavidBowie.com* (22 June 2014). https://tinyurl.com/5n8astap.

Bowie, David. Quoted in 'Bowie's China Girl, Geeling Ng, Remembers "Warm and Engaging" Star'. *Stuff* (12 January 2016). https://tinyurl.com/yzseexu8.

Bowie, David. 'David Bowie '83 the "Let's Dance" Interview on Countdown w/ Molly Meldrum'. Interview by Molly Meldrum, 6 November 1983, YouTube video, 00:06:39 (27 January 2016). https://tinyurl.com/uv8dmmu8.

Bowie, David. 'David Bowie on Making Let's Dance & Black Artists | MTV Full 1983 Interview'. *MTV NEWS*, YouTube video, 00:17:07 (11 January 2017). https://youtu.be/L3i53rjh-PA.

Bowie, David. Interview by Andy Peebles, 7 December 1980, quoted in Nacho Video, 'David Bowie in New York 1980. The Elephant Man, Scary Monsters & Other Strange People', YouTube video, 00:37:48 (5 December 2020). https://youtu.be/F1fTtwGqdQw.

Boyd, William. 'William Boyd: How David Bowie and I Hoaxed the Artworld'. *The Guardian* (12 January 2016). https://tinyurl.com/jxbt4vmu.

Brecht, Bertolt. 'On Chinese Acting'. *Tulane Drama Review* 6, no.1 (1961): 130–6.

Broackes, Victoria, and Geoffrey Marsh, eds., *David Bowie Is* (New York: V&A Publishing, 2013).

Brooker, Will. *Forever Stardust: David Bowie Across the Universe* (London: I.B. Taurus, 2017).

Brougher, Kerry, Olivia Mattis and Jeremy Strick, eds., *Visual Music: Synaesthesia in Art and Music Since 1900* (New York: Thames and Hudson, 2005).

Brown, Mick. 'Lindsay Kemp: The Man Who Taught Bowie His Moves'. *Bowie Wonderworld* (September 1974). https://tinyurl.com/59behzcb.

Brown, Timothy. 'Subcultures, Pop Music and Politics: Skinheads and "Nazi Rock" in England and Germany'. *Journal of Social History* 38, no. 1 (2004): 157–78.

Buckley, David. *Strange Fascination* (London: Virgin, 2005).

Buckley, David. *David Bowie: The Music and the Changes* (New York: Omnibus Press, 2015).

Buckley, David. 'Revisiting Bowie's Berlin'. In *David Bowie: Critical Perspectives*, edited by Eoin Devereux, Eileen Dillane and Martin Power, 215–29 (London: Routledge, 2015).

Burns, Lori. 'Interpreting Transmedia and Multimodal Narratives: Steven Wilson's "The Raven That Refused to Sing"'. In *The Routledge Companion to Popular Music Analysis: Expanding Approaches*, edited by Ciro Scotto, Kenneth Smith and John Brackett, 95–113 (New York: Routledge, 2018).

Burns, Lori. 'Dynamic Multimodality in Extreme Metal Performance Video: Dark Tranquillity's "Uniformity", Directed by Patric Ullaeus'. In *The Bloomsbury Handbook of Music Video Analysis*, edited by Lori Burns and Stan Hawkins, 183–200 (New York, Bloomsbury, 2019).

Burrows, Marc. *The London Boys: David Bowie, Marc Bolan, and the 60s Teenage Dream* (Barnsley: Pen & Sword History, 2022).

Carpenter, Alexander. '"Give a Man a Mask and He'll Tell the Truth": Arnold Schoenberg, David Bowie, and the Mask of Pierrot'. *Intersections* 30, no. 2 (2010): 5–24.

Caston, Emily. *British Music Videos, 1966–2016: Genre, Authenticity and Art* (Edinburgh: Edinburgh University Press, 2020).

Caswell, Estelle. 'Why Cartoon Characters Wear Gloves'. *Vox* (2 February 2017). https://tinyurl.com/2k5622rw.

Chapman, Ian. *David Bowie: FAQ* (Connecticut: Backbeat Books, 2020).

Ching, Geeling. 'What You Don't Know About podcast: China Girl – "The phone call from Bowie that changed my life"'. Interview by Carly Flynn, Tom Thexton, *Today FM* Audio, 00:46:00 (2 August 2022). https://tinyurl.com/3nt3a9v8.

Chion, Michel. *Audio-Vision: Sound on Screen* (New York: Columbia University Press, 1994).

Cinque, Toija, and Sean Redmond. *The Fandom of David Bowie.* Cham: Palgrave Macmillan, 2020.

Cinque, Toija, Angela Ndalianis and Sean Redmond. 'David Bowie On-Screen'. *Cinema Journal* 57, no. 3 (2018): 126–30.

Cinque, Toija, Christopher Moore and Sean Redmond, eds., *Enchanting David Bowie: Space|Time|Body|Memory* (New York: Bloomsbury, 2015).

Clerc, Benoît. *David Bowie All the Songs: The Story Behind Every Track* (New York: Black Dog & Leventhal Publishers, 2022).

Constantineau, Wayne. 'Mime and Media: The Parallel Worlds of Étienne Decroux and Marshall McLuhan'. *Dalhousie French Studies* 71 (2005): 115–34.

Copetas, Craig. 'Beat Godfather Meets Glitter Mainman'. *Rolling Stone* (28 February 1974). https://tinyurl.com/b8hf7c7f.

Cromelin, Richard. 'David Bowie: The Darling of the Avant Garde'. *Phonograph Record* (January 1972). https://tinyurl.com/3axx4kv4.

Ćurčić, Slobodan. 'Divine Light: Constructing the Immaterial in Byzantine Art and Architecture'. In *Architecture of the Sacred: Space, Ritual and Experience from Classical Greece to Byzantium*, edited by Bonna D. Westcoat and Robert G. Ousterhout, 307–37 (Cambridge: Cambridge University Press, 2012).

Cutchins, Dennis. 'Bakhtin, Intertextuality and Adaptation'. In *The Oxford Handbook of Adaptation Studies*, edited by Thomas Leitch, 71–86 (Oxford: Oxford University Press, 2017).

Daisy. 'Mick Rock – Beyond the Velvet Rope RIP'. *My Punk Rock London Life* (18 November 18 2021). https://tinyurl.com/ycxvvs92.

Dant, Tim, and Graeme Gilloch. 'Pictures of the Past: Benjamin and Barthes on Photography and History'. *European Journal of Cultural Studies* 5, no.1 (2002): 5–23.

Debord, Guy, and Gill J. Wolman. 'Methods of *Détournement*'. *Les Lèvres Nues* no. 8 (1956), Nothingness.org, https://tinyurl.com/yttkn8sm.

Deevoy, Adrian. 'David Bowie: Boys Keep Swinging'. *Q Magazine* (June 1989).

Deguzman, Kyle. 'The Arc Shot – Examples and Camera Movements Explained'. *Studio Binder* (23 May 2021). https://tinyurl.com/5a4rfs4n.

DeMain, Bill. 'The Sound and Vision of David Bowie'. *Performing Songwriter Magazine* (September 2003). https://tinyurl.com/44xs8dkv.

DeMain, Bill. 'The Story Behind the Song: Heroes by David Bowie'. Loudersound.com (4 February 2019). https://tinyurl.com/u4ukrbxa.

Derfoufi, Mehdi. 'Embodying Stardom, Representing Otherness: David Bowie in "Merry Christmas Mr. Lawrence"'. In *David Bowie: Critical Perspectives*, edited by Eoin Devereux, Aileen Dillane and Martin Power, 160–77 (London: Routledge, 2015).

Derrida, Jacques. *Specters of Marx: The State of the Debt, the Work of Mourning and The New International* (New York: Routledge, 1994).

Devereux, Eoin, Aileen Dillane and Martin J. Power, eds. *David Bowie: Critical Perspectives* (London: Routledge, 2015).

Devereux, Eoin, Aileen Dillane and Martin J. Power. 'Saying Hello to the Lunatic Men: A Critical Reading of "Love is Lost"'. *Contemporary Music Review* 37, no. 3 (2018): 257–71.

Di Pirajno, Alberto Denti. *A Grave for a Dolphin* (London: Andre Deutsch, 1956).

Dixon, Ian, and Brendan Black, eds. *I'm Not a Film Star* (New York: Bloomsbury, 2022).

Donnelly, Kevin. 'Experimental Music Video and Television'. In *Experimental British Television*, edited by Laura Mulvery and Jamie Sexton, 166–79 (Manchester: Manchester University Press, 2015).

Du Noyer, Paul. 'An Interview with David Bowie for the April 1990 issue of Q Magazine'. *Q Magazine* (6 February 1990). https://tinyurl.com/3cxbm6fw.

Duttlinger, Carolin. 'Imaginary Encounters: Walter Benjamin and the Aura of Photography'. *Poetics Today* 29, no. 1 (2008): 79–101.

Fisher, Mark. 'What is Hauntology?' *Film Quarterly* 66, no. 1 (2012): 16–24.

Fisher, Mark. *Capitalist Realism: Is There No Alternative?* (New Alresford: John Hunt Publishing, 2013).

Fisher, Mark. *Ghosts of My Life: Writings on Depression, Hauntology and Lost Futures* (Alresford: Zero Books, 2014).

Fishkind, Scott. 'The History of Rock: An Interview with the Iconic Mick Rock'. *As If* (22 July 2020). https://www.asifmag.com/story/interview-with-mick-rock.

Fiske, John. 'MTV: Post-Structural Post-Modern'. *Journal of Communication Inquiry* 10, no. 1 (1986): 74–9.

Fitch, Richard. 'In This Age of Grand Allusion: Bowie, Nihilism and Meaning'. In *David Bowie: Critical Perspectives*, edited by Eoin Devereux, Eileen Dillane and Martin Power, 19–34 (London: Routledge, 2015).

Fukuyama, Francis. 'The End of History?' *The National Interest* no. 16 (1989): 3–18.

Gilbert, Pat. *Bowie: The Illustrated Story* (Minneapolis: Voyageur Press, 2017).

Gillespie, Michelle, and Catherine Clinton, eds. *Taking off the White Gloves: Southern Women and Women Histories* (Missouri: University of Missouri Press, 1998).

Glynn, Stephen. *A Hard Day's Night: Turner Classic Movies British Film Guide* (London: Bloomsbury, 2005).

Goddard, Michael. 'Audiovision and *Gesamtkunstwerk*: The Aesthetics of First – and Second – Generation Industrial Music Video'. In *Music/Video: Histories, Aesthetics, Media*, edited by Gina Arnold, Daniel Cookney, Kirsty Fairclough, and Michael Goddard, 163–80 (London: Bloomsbury, 2017).

Haben, Amy. 'Stanley Dorfman: Top of the Pops and Beyond'. *Please Kill Me: This is What's Cool* (15 April 2019). https://tinyurl.com/mfr7vbbe.

Hann, Michael. 'Watch the Reworked Video for David Bowie's Life on Mars'. *The Guardian* (4 November 2016). https://tinyurl.com/zhjusdyp.

Hawkins, Stan. *The British Pop Dandy* (Abingdon: Routledge, 2009).

Hawkins, Stan. 'David Bowie: 1947–2016'. *Contemporary Music Review* 37, no. 3 (2018): 189–92.

Hebdige, Dick. 'The Meaning of Mod'. In *Resistance Through Rituals: Youth Cultures in Post-war Britain*, edited by Stuart Hall and Tony Jefferson, 87–98 (London: Routledge, 1993).

Heller, Jason. 'How Ashes to Ashes Put the First Act of David Bowie's Career to Rest'. *NPR* (6 October 2017). https://tinyurl.com/2whjrj5n.

Heller, Jason. 'Anthems for the Moon: David Bowie's Sci-fi Explorations'. *Pitchfork* (13 January 2016). https://tinyurl.com/y3h78sea.

Heller, Jason. 'David Bowie Gave the Punk Movement Both Fuel and Fire'. *AV Club* (27 January 2016). https://tinyurl.com/4cbvek5j.

Helman, Peter. 'Hear David Bowie's Previously Unreleased 1982 "Let's Dance" Demo Featuring Nile Rodgers'. *Billboard* (1 August 2018). https://tinyurl.com/df3h478z.

Herman, David. *Basic Elements of Narrative* (Hoboken, NJ: Wiley, 2009).

Hisama, Ellie. 'Postcolonialism on the Make: The Music of John Mellencamp, David Bowie and John Zorn'. *Popular Music* 12, no. 2 (1993): 91–104.

Hughes, Rob, and Stephen Dalton. 'David Bowie Remembers Berlin: I Can't Express the Feeling of Freedom I Felt There'. *Uncut* (April 2001). https://tinyurl.com/yrr3n5z4.

Jackson, Mark, ed. *Stress in Post-War Britain: 1945–85* (New York: Routledge, 2015).

Janov, Arthur. *The Primal Scream: Primal Therapy, The Cure for Neurosis*. New York: Dell Publishing, 1970.

Jenkins, Henry. *Convergence Culture: Where Old and New Media Collide* (New York: New York University Press, 2006).

Jenkins, Henry. 'The Aesthetics of Transmedia: In Response to David Bordwell (Part 3)' (2009). https://tinyurl.com/mrw6z8a6.

Jenkins, Henry. 'Transmedia Education: The 7 Principles Revisited', *Confessions of an Aca-fan*, 21 June 2010. https://tinyurl.com/4pxh6ej4.

Jenkins, Henry. 'Confessions of an Aca-fan'. *Henry Jenkins* (22 October 2011). https://tinyurl.com/a5pew2tm.

Jirsa, Tomáš, and Mathias Korsgaard. 'The Music Video in Transformation: Notes on a Hybrid Audiovisual Configuration'. *MSMI* 13, no. 2 (2019): 111–22.

Johnson, David. 'Wormholes, the Time Vortex, and TARDIS: Time Travel and "Dr Who"', *Wondrium Daily* (8 April 2021). https://tinyurl.com/yc3r2hv9.

Johnson, Katherine. 'David Bowie Is'. In *David Bowie: Critical Perspectives*, edited by Victoria Broackes and Geoffrey Marsh, 1–19 (New York: V&A Publishing, 2013).

Jones, Allan. 'Goodbye To Ziggy And All That'. *Melody Maker* (29 October 1977), Bowiegoldenyears.com. https://tinyurl.com/4nprfxd4.

Jones, Josh. 'David Bowie and Klaus Nomi's Hypnotic Performance on SNL (1979)' (5 September 2014), *Open Culture*. https://tinyurl.com/56e97cae.

Jung, Carl. *The Archetypes and the Collective Unconscious* (Princeton: Princeton University Press, 1969).

Kardos, Leah. 'I Don't Want to Leave, or Drift Away: The Transition from David Bowie's Lodger to Scary Monsters'. *Academia.Edu*. https://tinyurl.com/2p8stf3a.

Kardos, Leah. *Blackstar Theory: The Last Works of David Bowie* (New York: Bloomsbury, 2022).

Keazor, Henry, and Thorsten Wübbena. *Rewind, Play, Fast Forward: The Past, Present and Future of Music Video* (Bielefeld: Transaction Publishers, 2010).

Kim, Jonathan. 'An Asian's take on David Bowie's "China Girl"'. *Rethink Reviews* (30 March 2021). https://tinyurl.com/3pz8y5hk.

Korsgaard, Mathias. *Music Video After MTV: Audiovisual Studies, New Media, and Popular Music* (Abingdon: Routledge, 2017).

Kristeva, Julia. *The Bounded Text. Desire in Language* (New York: Columbia University Press, 1980).

Kurth, Richard. 'Pierrot Lunaire: Persona, Voice, and the Fabric of Allusion'. In *The Cambridge Companion to Schoenberg*, edited by Jennifer Shaw and Joseph Auner, 120–34 (Cambridge: Cambridge University Press, 2010).

Ladd, Mike. 'The Lesser Known History of the Maralinga Nuclear Tests – And What it's Like to Stand at Ground Zero'. *ABC News* (24 March 2020). https://tinyurl.com/499j49js.

Laing, Dave. 'Listening to Punk'. In *The Subcultures Reader*, edited by Ken Gelder, 448–59 (London: Routledge, 2005).

Lajosi, Krisztina. 'Wagner and the (Re)mediation of Art: *Gesamtkunstwerk* and Nineteenth Century Theories of Media'. *Frame* 23, no. 2 (2010): 42–60.

Lalvani, Suren. 'Consuming the Exotic Other'. *Critical Studies in Mass Communication* 12, no. 3 (1995): 263–86.

Leigh, Wendy. *Bowie: The Biography* (New York: Gallery Books, 2014).

Lidbury, Olivia. 'Sandy Powell's David Bowie Homage Was One the Best Looks at the Baftas'. *The Telegraph* (15 February 2016). https://tinyurl.com/yp7eb9j4.

Lobalzo Wright, Julie. 'The Boy Kept Swinging: David Bowie, Music Video, and the Star Image'. In *Music/Video: Histories, Aesthetics, Media*, edited by Gina Arnold, Daniel Cookney, Kirsty Fairclough and Michael Goddard, 67–78 (New York: Bloomsbury, 2017).

Loder, Kurt. 'David Bowie: Straight Time'. *Rolling Stone* (12 May 1983). https://tinyurl.com/39y97b67.

McKenzie, Mairi. 'Football, Fashion and Unpopular Culture: David Bowie's Influence on Liverpool Football Club Casuals 1976-79'. *Celebrity Studies* 10, no. 1 (2019): 25–43.

McLuhan, Marshall. *Understanding Media: The Extensions of Man* (Cambridge: MIT Press, 1964).

Mcquade, Christopher. '"I loathed it." What David Bowie Learnt from His Brief Spell in Adland'. *The Drum* (11 January 2016). https://tinyurl.com/2p8u767s.

MacKinnon, Angus. 'The Future Isn't What It Used to Be'. *New Musical Express* (13 September 1980). https://tinyurl.com/3a79uwhc.

Mallet, David. Interview by Lisa Perrott (17 February 2021).

Mallet, David. Interview by Eoin Devereux (16 April 2014).

Marks, Craig, and Rob Tanenbaum. *I Want My MTV: The Uncensored Story of the Music Video Revolution* (London: Penguin Group, 2011).

Marks, Laura. 'Video Haptics and Erotics'. *Screen* 39, no. 4 (1998): 331–48.

Marsh, Geoffrey. 'Astronaut of Inner Spaces'. In *David Bowie Is*, edited by Victoria Broackes and Geoffrey Marsh, 27–68 (New York: V&A Publishing, 2013).

Marshall, Colin. 'Jump Start Your Creative Process with Brian Eno's "Oblique Strategies" Deck of Cards (1975)'. *Open Culture* (2 July 2013). https://tinyurl.com/mrje8chb.

Mecklenburg, Karen. 'David Bowie, interviewed by Television Week', *The New York Times*, 13 December 1981, YouTube video by Richard's David Bowie Channel, 15 February 2020, https://youtu.be/d7aJWFAu0Fo.

Mendelssohn, John. 'David Bowie: Pantomime Rock?' *Rolling Stone* (1 April 1971). https://tinyurl.com/mushsbkp.

Mendes, Ana Cristina, and Lisa Perrott, eds. *David Bowie and Transmedia Stardom* (Abingdon: Routledge, 2020).

Middleton, Kimberly. 'You Gotta Chink it Up: Asian American Performativity in the New Orientalism'. PhD diss. (University of Notre Dame, 2003).

Miller, Corazon. 'When an Ordinary Kiwi Became David Bowie's China Girl'. *The New Zealand Herald* (12 January 2016). https://tinyurl.com/3z6yubfb.

Miller, Mark. 'It's a Wurlitzer'. *Smithsonian Magazine* (April 2002). https://tinyurl.com/4vxmnzv7.

Miyao, Daisuke. 'Cinema and the Haptic in Modern Japan'. *Screen Bodies* 3, no. 1 (2018): 23–36.

Morley, Paul. 'Dali, Duchamp and Dr Caligari: The Surrealism that Inspired David Bowie'. *The Guardian* (22 July 2016). https://tinyurl.com/26ts6vdc.

Murray, Charles Shaar. 'David Bowie: Who Was That (Un)masked Man?' *New Musical Express* (12 November 1977). https://tinyurl.com/mrheyrye.

Naiman, Tiffany. '"More Solemn Than a Fading Star": David Bowie's Modernist Aesthetics of Ending'. In *The Bloomsbury Handbook of Popular Music Video Analysis*, edited by Lori Burns and Stan Hawkins, 297–313 (New York: Bloomsbury, 2019).

Naremore, James. *Acting in the Cinema* (Berkeley: University of California Press, 1988).

Ndalianis, Angela. 'Bowie and Science Fiction / Bowie as Science Fiction'. *Cinema Journal* 57, no. 3 (2018): 139–49.

Neville, Miles, and Perry Neville. *Bowie In His Own Words* (London: Omnibus Press, 1980).

Nichols, Bill. *Introduction to Documentary* (Bloomington: Indiana University Press, 2010).

Nick. 'David Bowie – Life on Mars? (Original Unedited Version, Remastered by Nacho)'. *David Bowie News* (17 December 2021). https://tinyurl.com/2p89ka5s.

Nick. 'David Bowie – Life on Mars? 2016 Mix Re-edit Mick Rock'. *David Bowie News* (4 November 2016). https://tinyurl.com/5fdbxkmj.

October, Dene. 'Transition Transmission: Media, Seriality, and the Bowie-Newton Matrix'. *Celebrity Studies* 10, no.1 (2019): 104–18.

O'Leary, Chris. *Pushing Ahead of the Dame*. https://tinyurl.com/nfxd4xhu.
O'Leary, Chris. *Rebel Rebel: All the Songs of David Bowie: From '64 to '76* (Alresford: Zero Books, 2015).
O'Neil, Richard. 'The Gypsy Exception'. *The Guardian* (14 November 2007). https://tinyurl.com/bdhzejhn.
Onlylovecanleavesuchamark. 'Space Oddity [1979 Re-record]'. *Don't Forget the Songs 365* (12 August 2012). https://tinyurl.com/mr3as54p.
Paget, Derek, and Jane Roscoe. 'Giving Voice: Performance and Authenticity in the Documentary Musical'. *Jump Cut: A Review of Contemporary Media* 48 (2006). https://tinyurl.com/nhfycu5b.
Paglia, Camille. 'Theatre of Gender: David Bowie at the Climax of the Sexual Revolution'. In *David Bowie Is*, edited by Victoria Broackes and Geoffrey Marsh, 69–98 (London: V&A Publishing, 2013).
Pareles, Jon. 'David Bowie, 21st Century Entrepreneur'. *The New York Times* (9 June 2002). https://tinyurl.com/sxydrhx5.
Pegg, Nicholas. *The Complete David Bowie* (London: Titan Books, 2016).
Perone, James. *Music of the Counterculture Era* (London: Greenwood Publishing Group, 2004).
Perrott, Lisa. 'Bowie the Cultural Alchemist: Performing Gender, Synthesizing Gesture and Liberating Identity'. *Continuum* 31, no. 4 (2017): 528–41.
Perrott, Lisa. '"Accented" Music Video: Animating Memories of Migration in "Rocket Man"'. *Music, Sound and the Moving Image* 13, no. 2 (2019): 123–46.
Perrott, Lisa. 'The Alchemical Union of David Bowie and Floria Sigismondi, "Transmedia Surrealism" and "Loose Continuity"'. In *Transmedia Directors: Artistry, Industry and New Audiovisual Aesthetics,* edited by Carol Vernallis, Holly Rogers and Lisa Perrott, 194–220 (New York: Bloomsbury, 2019).
Perrott, Lisa. 'The Animated Music Videos of Radiohead, Chris Hopewell, and Gastón Viñas: Fan Participation, Collaborative Authorship, and Dialogic Worldbuilding'. In *The Bloomsbury Handbook of Popular Music Video Analysis,* edited by Lori Burns and Stan Hawkins, 47–68 (New York: Bloomsbury, 2019).
Perrott, Lisa. 'Experimental Animation and the Neosurrealist Remediation of Popular Music Video'. *Animation Practice, Process & Production* 8 (2019): 85–106.
Perrott, Lisa. 'Time is Out of Joint: The Transmedial Hauntology of David Bowie'. *Celebrity Studies* 10, no.1 (2019): 119–39.
Perrott, Lisa. 'Moonage Daydream: Brilliant Bowie Film Takes Big Risks to Create Something Truly New'. *The Conversation* (14 September 2022). https://tinyurl.com/3aecydm7.
Perrott, Lisa. 'Ziggy Stardust, Direct Cinema and the Multimodal Performance of Gesamtkunstwerk'. In *I'm Not a Film Star*, edited by Ian Dixon and Brendan Black, 25–51 (New York: Bloomsbury, 2022).

Perrott, Lisa. 'Moonwalking "Backwards into the Future": "Poi E," Music Video, and Documentary'. In *Travelling Music Video*, edited by Mathias Bonde Korsgaard and Tomáš Jirsa (New York: Bloomsbury, 2023).

Perrot, Lisa. *David Bowie and the Transformation of Music Video (1984–2016 and Beyond)*. London: Bloomsbury Academic (forthcoming).

Perrott, Lisa, Holly Rogers and Carol Vernallis. 'Beyonce's Lemonade: She Dreams in Both Worlds'. *FilmInt* (2 June 2016). https://tinyurl.com/rw6w5jrj.

Perry, Nick. 'David Bowie's "China Girl" Says Music Video Changed Her Life'. *AP NEWS* (13 January 2016). https://tinyurl.com/58mxakj8.

Peters, Michael. 'On the Edge of Theory: Dadaism, (Ca-Caism), Gagaism'. *Review of Education, Pedagogy, and Cultural Studies* 34, no. 5 (2012): 216–26.

Potter, Jordan. 'How John Lennon Gave Primal Scream Their Name'. *Far Out* (11 January 2022). https://tinyurl.com/5n8ke7ux.

Railton, Diane, and Paul Watson. *Music Video and the Politics of Representation* (Edinburgh: Edinburgh University Press, 2011).

Reed, Katherine. *David Bowie and the Moving Image: A Standing Cinema* (New York: Bloomsbury, 2023).

Reilly, Nick. 'Is Jodie Whittaker Channelling David Bowie in her "Dr Who" Reveal?' *NME* (17 July 2017). https://tinyurl.com/3pku5jx9.

Richards, Sam. 'Watch Tony Visconti Discuss His New Mix of David Bowie's "Space Oddity"'. *Uncut* (15 November 2019). https://tinyurl.com/cp6atwsx.

Richardson, John, Claudia Gorbman and Carol Vernallis, eds. *The Oxford Handbook of New Audiovisual Aesthetics* (New York: Oxford University Press, 2013).

Richardson, John. *An Eye for Music: Popular Music and the Audiovisual Surreal* (New York: Oxford University Press, 2012).

Riefe, Jordan. 'Music Video Pioneer Stanley Dorfman Recalls Bowie, Sinatra and Lennon'. *The Hollywood Reporter* (2 November 2016). https://tinyurl.com/mr4372vf.

Riwaaz, Rang. '"Boteh" – The Journey from Persia to Paisley' (6 June 2021). https://tinyurl.com/32k48r9a.

Rock, Mick. 'Mick Rock Talks Bowie, Iconic Photographs'. Interview by King 5 News Desk (29 June 2017). YouTube video, 00:06:21. https://youtu.be/cf89gEmzSuk.

Rock, Mick. *Moonage Daydream: The Life and Times of Ziggy Stardust* (UK: Doppelganger, 2002).

Rogers, Holly. 'Twisted Synaesthesia: Music Video and the Visual Arts'. In *Art or Sound*, edited by Germano Celant, 383–8 (Venice: Fondazione Prada, 2014).

Rogers, Holly. *Visualising Music: Audiovisual Relationships in Avant-Garde Film and Video Art* (London: Lambert Academic Publishing, 2010).

Rook, Jean. 'Waiting for Bowie and Finding a Genius Who Insists He's Really a Clown'. *Daily Express* (5 May 1976). https://tinyurl.com/bdddnhys.

Roscoe, Jane. 'Real Entertainment: Real factual Hybrid Television'. *Media International Australia*, 100 (2001): 9–20.

Rüther, Tobias. *Heroes: David Bowie and Berlin* (London: Reaktion Books, 2014).
Ryan, Marie-Laure. 'Story/Worlds/Media: Tuning the Instruments of a Media-Conscious Narratology'. In *Storyworlds Across Media: Toward a Media-Conscious Narratology*, edited by Marie-Laure Ryan and Jan-Noël Thon, 25–49 (Lincoln: University of Nebraska Press, 2014).
Said, Edward. *Orientalism* (New York: Vintage Books, 1979).
Sammond, Nicholas. *Birth of an Industry: Blackface Minstrelsy and the Rise of American Animation* (Durham: Duke University Press, 2015).
Sanders, Leonard. 'Postmodern Orientalism'. PhD diss. (Palmerston North: Massey University, 2008).
Scoates, Christopher. *Brian Eno: Visual Music* (San Francisco: Chronicle Books, 2013).
Seabrook, Thomas Jerome. *Bowie in Berlin: A New Career in a New Town* (London: Outline Press, 2008).
Sharma, Tr.fowpe. 'Rosa Luxemburg in the Works of Brecht," *Revolutionary Democracy* 15, no. 1–2 (April-September 2009). https://tinyurl.com/5n7vkmbx.
Sheppard, Jordan. 'Penderecki and the Sound of Horror'. *The Artifice* (14June 2019). https://tinyurl.com/kpv3mmxs.
Simpson, Dave. 'David Bowie and Me'. *The Guardian* (23 February 2013). https://tinyurl.com/2ubvj856.
Smith, Justin. 'Absence and Presence: *Top of the Pops* and the Demand for Music Videos in the 1960s'. *Journal of British Cinema and Television* 16, no. 4 (2019): 492–544.
Stark, Tanja. 'Crashing Out with Sylvian: David Bowie, Carl Jung and the Unconscious'. In *David Bowie: Critical Perspectives*, edited by Devereux, Eoin, Aileen Dillane and Martin Power, 82–110 (London: Routledge, 2015).
Storey, Robert. *Pierrot: A Critical History of a Mask* (Princeton: Princeton University Press, 1978).
Straw, Will. 'Music Video in its Contexts: Popular Music and Post-modernism in the 1980s'. *Popular Music*. 7, no. 3 (1988): 247–66.
Straw, Will. 'Music Video in its Contexts: 30 Years Later'. *Volume!* 14, no. 2 (2018): 187–92.
Stubbs, Jeremy. 'Surrealism's Book of Revelation: Isadore Ducasse's *Poésies*, *Détournement* and Automatic Writing'. Romantic Review 87, no. 4 (1996): 493–510.
Sukhanova, Svetlana. '"Don't Ask Me How David's Mind Worked": George Underwood and Steve Schapiro about David Bowie'. Birdinflight.com (25 January 2019). https://tinyurl.com/3m4z3t7y.
Taylor, Tom. 'Watch Rare Never Broadcast Footage of David Bowie Performing on the *Old Grey Whistle Test* in 1972'. *Far Out* (12 April 2021. https://tinyurl.com/yw3c3jtf.
Thain, Laura. 'Walter Benjamin on Photography and Film'. *Viz* (n.d.). https://tinyurl.com/3cedm9u9.
Thompson, Kristin, and David Bordwell. *Observations on Film Art* (25 May 2011). https://tinyurl.com/yc3swj92.
Trammel, Matthew. 'David Bowie and the Return of the Music Video'. *The New Yorker* (12 January 2016). https://tinyurl.com/msc548u5.

Trynka, Paul. *Starman David Bowie: The Definitive Biography* (London: Sphere, 2011).
Trzcinski, Matthew. 'David Bowie's Hit Song "China Girl" Allowed Iggy Pop to get Married'. *Cheatsheet* (17 November 2021). https://tinyurl.com/bdhjmdm3.
Turner, Dave. 'David Bowie Let's Dance Festival Carinda'. YouTube video, 00:02:41 (7 October 7, 2018). https://youtu.be/aapW2DyIlLw.
Van Gogh, Johanna. 'Shibui'. *The Painters Keys* (20 May 2008. https://painterskeys.com/shibui/.
Vernallis, Carol. *Experiencing Music Video* (New York: Columbia University Press, 2004).
Vernallis, Carol. *Unruly Media: YouTube, Music Video, and the New Digital Cinema* (New York: Oxford University Press, 2013).
Visconti, Tony. *A New Career in a New Town (1977–1982)* (USA: Rhino/Parlophone, 2017).
Visconti, Tony. 'David Bowie's Heroes Producer Gets to the Heart of the Song'. *BBC Arts* (10 January 2020). https://tinyurl.com/483kmh4v.
Waldrep, Shelton. *Future Nostalgia: Performing David Bowie* (New York: Bloomsbury, 2015).
Waldrep, Shelton. 'The "China Girl" Problem: Reconsidering David Bowie in the 1980s'. In *David Bowie: Critical Perspectives*, edited by Devereux, Eoin, Aileen Dillane and Martin Power, 147–59 (London: Routledge, 2015).
Wang, Yiman. 'Screening Asia: Passing, Performative Translation, and Reconfiguration'. *Positions* 15, no. 2 (2007): 319–43
Watts, Michael. 'Confession of an Elitist'. *Melody Maker* (18 February 1978). https://tinyurl.com/2drrp988.
Watts, Michael. 'Oh! You Pretty Thing'. *Melody Maker* (22 January 1972), quoted in 'Bowie: "I'm gay and always have been"'. *The Bowie Bible* (27 August 2018). https://tinyurl.com/bd4jh8h5.
Wolf, Mark. 'Transmedia World Building: History, Conception, and Construction'. In *The Routledge Companion to Transmedia Studies*, edited by Matthew Freeman and Renira Rampazzo Gambarato, 141–7 (New York: Routledge, 2019).
Wells, H.G. *The Time Machine* (London: William Heinemann, 1895).
Wells, H.G. *The Chronic Argonauts* (London: Royal College of Science, 1888).
Wiegand, Chris. 'Lindsay Kemp: I Tried to Get David Bowie to do Puss in Boots'. *The Guardian* (12 January 2016). https://tinyurl.com/47ahtak8.
Wilcken, Hugo. *David Bowie's Low (33 1/3)* (New York: Bloomsbury, 2005).
Wilde, Oscar. *The Picture of Dorian Gray* (London: Ward, Lock and Company, 1891).
Xcel, Bauer. 'David Bowie and Kenny Everett's Space Oddity'. *Mojo* (23 July 2013). https://tinyurl.com/38ecshee.
Young, Robert. *White Mythologies: Writing History and the West* (London: Routledge, 1990).
Zhang, Cat. 'What Novelist Susan Choi is Listening to Right Now'. *Pitchfork* (3 January 2020). https://tinyurl.com/3dkfpdm9.

Index

absurd 8, 54, 80, 92, 109, 138, 142
acting 38, 42, 77, 83–4, 86, 89–90, 116, 144, 159, 160, 198, 228
actor 37, 41, 59, 86, 89, 130, 175–6, 180, 193, 226
aesthetic xx, 6, 9–11, 13, 17, 20–2, 26, 33–4, 40, 54, 73, 78–9, 94–5, 102, 106–7, 110, 118–19, 136, 143, 152, 157, 178, 186, 190, 198–9, 234, 236
affordance xix, 9–10, 13–15, 24, 27, 38, 40, 105, 185, 188, 237
album cover art 25, 34, 66, 110, 175–6, 180
aleatory 8, 91, 106, 107, 109, 122, 133, 154, 235
alien 22, 52, 58, 66, 88, 94, 103, 125–7, 134, 168, 178–9, 206, 209, 224
alienation 52, 86, 147, 153–4, 161, 180–1, 183, 186
allusion 22, 51, 54, 127, 133–4, 163, 172, 182, 186, 188, 211, 221, 223, 226, 237
Alomar, Carlos 122, 133, 171
alterity 22, 134, 181
ambiguity 38, 72, 75, 78, 84, 92, 134, 216, 224–5
America (USA) 15, 19, 20, 32–3, 59, 68, 72, 76, 79, 80–1, 84–5, 92, 107, 109, 113, 140–2, 186, 190, 202, 207, 212, 214
analogical 8, 92, 150, 172, 188
analogue 5, 57, 68, 79, 105–6, 113
analogy 188, 235, 237
androgynous 91, 95, 98, 211
anthropomorphize 115–17
archetype 8, 13, 22, 27, 38, 163, 180–1, 186, 188, 210
art history 3–8, 25, 91, 106, 110, 127, 154–5, 167
artform xv, xvi, xviii, xix, xx, 1–5, 9–10, 12–13, 15–16, 18–19, 27–8, 36, 38, 63, 66, 95, 105–6, 172, 183, 198, 215, 233, 233–4, 236–8

artifice 29–30, 38–9, 43, 47, 61–3, 72, 86, 102, 103, 181
artisanal xvi, 103, 169, 234
artistic xv–xx, 1, 4–8, 10, 16, 18, 20–2, 24, 26, 30–2, 34–5, 39, 49, 64–8, 89–91, 95, 100, 103–6, 111, 123, 127, 131–2, 136, 142–4, 153–4, 158–9, 164–7, 180–3, 188, 191, 198–203, 207, 217–18, 225, 229, 230, 236–7
  strategy xx, 34, 158, 181, 183, 202, 236–7
artwork 5, 34, 69, 155, 176, 236
'Ashes to Ashes' xx, 7, 14, 20, 25, 145, 154, 157, 158, 161–91, 221, 234–5, 237
"Ashes to Ashes" 161–3, 182
assemblage 12, 15, 26–7, 57, 165, 171–2, 182, 185, 188, 224, 231
associations 59, 106, 127, 162, 167, 179, 186, 188, 210–11, 213
astronaut 51, 54, 86, 150, 153, 162, 164, 178–9
audience xvi, xx, 3, 10, 16–17, 20, 26, 36, 38, 40, 42, 47, 50, 53–4, 74, 77, 78, 81, 84–5, 88–9, 95, 97–100, 111, 116, 118, 137–8, 142, 144, 146, 150, 180, 192, 202–3, 207, 209, 216, 220–1, 225, 227, 229–31, 233, 236
audio-visual xii, 4, 6, 9, 11–12, 14, 28, 32, 34, 58, 76–8, 93, 105, 111, 114, 132, 153, 165, 171–2, 182, 185, 192, 196, 198, 225–6, 233–4
aura 67, 69, 70, 71, 86, 103, 234
Austerlitz, Saul 4
Australia 201, 205–8, 215, 218–19, 223, 225–6
authenticity 29, 30, 43, 60–3, 72, 80, 86, 88, 89, 95, 102–3, 116–17, 124, 182, 190
authorship 16, 24, 26–8, 33
  collaborative 78
  dispersed 27, 49, 55

avant-garde 6–8, 11, 34, 36–37, 74, 107, 109, 110, 121, 139, 142, 178, 180, 182–183, 198, 216, 234

Baal (the character) 195
Baal (EP) 194, 195
Baal (play) 194, 195
Baal (BBC TV movie) 195
Bakhtin, Mikhail 27
Barthes, Roland 27, 86
BBC 17, 19, 42, 45, 50, 56, 58, 61, 77, 84, 93, 111, 165, 194, 195
Beatles, The 17, 18, 29, 205
Belew, Adrian 137–8
'Be My Wife' 34, 107, 110–19, 126, 127, 129, 154, 214, 234
"Be My Wife" 112, 113
Benjamin, Walter 69, 70, 86
Berlin xix, 105–10, 120–1, 123–4, 128, 130, 137, 139, 143, 155, 159, 190, 236
'Blackstar' 133
Blondie 11, 132
bohemian 34, 35, 43
Bolder, Trevor 61, 73, 76
Bordwell, David 21, 45, 89, 137, 175, 222
'Boys Keep Swinging' 7, 19, 107, 132–40, 142, 144, 191, 229
 Saturday Night Live (SNL) version 140–3
"Boys Keep Swinging" 132–4
Brecht, Bertolt 52, 86, 194–5
Brel, Jacques 41, 59
Broackes, Victoria 164
Brooker, Will 24
Buckley, David xvi, 108, 124, 217
Buñuel, Luis 22, 167, 176–7
Burns, Lori 11–12, 26
Burretti, Freddie 94
Burroughs, William 25, 110
Buxton, Adam 122, 157–8
Byzantine 127, 129

Cabinet of Dr Caligary, The 151–2
camera xix, 12, 40, 42, 45–7, 53, 55, 57, 65–78, 81–90, 96–100, 103, 116, 118, 125–30, 148–54, 169–70, 175, 184–5, 187, 193, 199, 221, 235
 360-degree arc shot 90, 226

address to 29, 47, 71, 88–9, 114, 118, 173, 221
angle 42, 46, 89, 118, 129, 151, 153, 165
close-up (CU) 6, 74, 76–7, 82–3, 88, 95–6, 98, 118, 127, 129, 148–50, 167, 173, 174, 175, 193, 197
frontality for 89, 90, 130
lens 29, 46–7, 53, 65, 82, 84, 85, 88, 90, 98, 100, 116, 118, 129, 148, 150, 168, 192
movement 72, 83, 90, 103, 118, 125, 127–30, 149–50, 193
tracking shot 98, 128, 150
wide shot 74, 77, 118, 150, 197, 220
zoom 46, 90, 116, 167
canvas xix, 1, 10, 24, 94, 105, 114, 120, 145, 155, 165, 181, 216, 236–7
capitalism 186, 207, 209–10
Carpenter, Alexander 38, 39, 49, 180–3
Caston, Emily 2, 15–19, 32–3, 47, 233
chance composition 8, 121–3, 132, 160, 164–5, 170–2, 235
character 22, 24–6, 38–9, 47, 51, 54–5, 59, 66–7, 76, 80, 116, 135, 137, 143, 148, 150, 154, 160–1, 164, 168–9, 172–3, 178–84, 186–7, 189, 204, 212, 237
'China Girl' xx, 139, 207, 209, 215–31, 233
"China Girl" 215–17
Ching, Geeling (Ng, Geeling) xii, 220–3, 229–30
chord, musical 45, 60–1, 90–3, 122, 133, 171, 205
chorus 73, 92, 113, 134, 162, 195, 203, 204
cinematic 26, 55, 63, 71, 89, 93–4, 96, 100, 111, 118, 129, 144, 196–8
cinematography 18–19, 33, 47, 136, 173, 194, 199, 223
Cinéma vérité 17, 83, 101, 206, 231
Cinque, Toija xv, 22
clown 28–9, 38–9, 92, 107, 114, 157–8, 163–4, 166, 168, 180, 185
collaborative process xii, xv, 1, 12, 15–16, 172, 233, 235, 237
collage 66, 111, 171–2, 225–6, 231
collective unconscious 163, 188, 210
colonialism 202, 207, 209, 213–14, 228, 230–1, 237

Index

colour 5, 8, 12, 20, 61–2, 68, 70, 76, 85, 92, 94, 96, 101–2, 105, 118–20, 127, 165, 168–71, 173, 180, 185, 222–3, 226
Commedia dell'arte xx, 4, 20, 38–40, 95, 180–1
composition 7–8, 33, 55–6, 60, 91, 93, 105–7, 109, 113, 118–19, 122, 132, 154, 161, 165, 172, 174, 182, 194, 205, 235
convergence 4, 9, 15–16, 25, 76
costume 10, 36, 47, 50, 62, 70, 84, 95, 113, 135, 142–3, 145, 167, 176, 224, 226–7, 236
creative process xiv–xvi, xix, 7, 12, 15, 24, 67, 78, 109, 121–2, 131–2, 233, 235
Crowley, Aleister 205
cultural xv–xvi, xix, 1–3, 7, 9, 12, 14, 17, 25–7, 30–3, 35, 43, 52, 63, 73, 77–9, 84, 92, 132, 134, 139, 146, 171, 179, 183–4, 198, 206–7, 210–12, 214, 216, 219, 221, 229, 231, 236
culture xvii, 2–3, 6, 24, 27, 34–5, 55, 58–9, 73, 86, 92, 95, 108–11, 121, 142, 155, 198, 215, 218, 226–7, 236
   counterculture 33, 76, 78
   popular 81, 92, 111, 132, 178
   subculture 25, 32–5, 72–3, 78, 164, 168, 176, 178, 186, 214
cut-up technique 110
cyborg 172, 178–9
"Cygnet Committee" 51, 58–9

Dada 6, 8, 142
Dalí, Salvador 22, 176, 177
dance 5, 10, 20, 31, 36, 41, 46, 73–4, 77–8, 83, 193, 203, 205–6, 210, 215
dancing xiv, 33, 72, 82, 100, 111, 134, 141, 204, 206, 210, 211, 223
dandy 34, 35, 39, 42, 47, 127, 181, 186
David Bowie (1967) 33, 36, 40
Davis, Dennis 133, 171
death xvii, 22, 36, 49, 101, 112, 140, 145, 153–4, 186, 188–9, 195, 198–9, 220
Decroux, Étienne 37–8
defamiliarize 8, 59, 86, 136, 168, 185, 188, 336
Defries, Tony 65, 70, 81

Depth of Field 22, 193, 197, 222–3
Derrida, Jacques 14, 185
détournement 8, 212, 236–7
Devereux, Eoin xvii, 163, 165, 172, 180–1, 183–5, 187
dialogic 24, 27, 28, 237
Diamond Dogs 110, 151
diegetic 47, 48, 116, 172
Dietrich, Marlene 75, 135, 137, 140, 167
director xv, xviii, xx, 6, 8, 15–20, 33, 37, 49, 55, 66, 71, 86, 103, 106, 110–11, 125, 130–2, 154, 159, 164–7, 196, 227, 230, 234–5
discomfort 63, 88, 138, 161, 163, 195, 204, 206, 209, 225, 230–1, 233
dispersed authorship 27, 49, 55
dissonance 8, 14, 22, 77, 172
Divine Mercy, The 127–8
Doctor Who 13, 17, 25, 54
documentary 16, 33, 66–7, 72, 132, 165
Dorfman, Stanley xv, xix, 6, 19, 68, 106, 110–11, 114–15, 117–20, 125, 127, 129–31, 154, 234–5
drag 109, 135–9, 142–3, 155, 236
dramatic 38, 76, 97, 118, 143, 147, 151, 163, 182, 190–1
drawing 120, 151, 175, 215
drillability 26–7 134, 211, 237
drumbeat 59–61, 149
drums 60–1, 113, 133, 147, 193, 215
Dudgeon, Gus 50–1
dyschronia 14, 184
dystopia 51, 58–9, 163, 168, 175, 185–6

editing xii, 8, 12, 16, 18–19, 33, 45–6, 56, 72, 74, 76–9, 81, 83, 90, 93, 97, 100–2, 111, 129, 135–7, 141, 144, 150, 164, 172–3, 194, 196, 199, 220, 223, 225–6
   180-degree rule 45, 77, 120, 129
   continuity editing 8, 46, 77, 120, 226
   cross-cut 77, 135–7, 175
   cut-away 78, 100, 130
   dissolve 119–20, 129–30, 150–1, 172–3, 175, 193, 196–7
   jump-cut 46, 47, 77
   re-edited videos 16, 56, 78–9, 93, 101–2, 237

transition 118–20, 129, 136, 150, 155, 165, 172, 175, 193, 197, 221
Elephant Man, The xviii, xx, 160, 189
emotion 59–60, 62, 86, 91–2, 112, 121–2, 124, 129, 131, 147, 159–63, 188–90, 192–3, 196, 199
enigma 21, 57, 76–8, 84, 91, 93, 97, 100, 112–13, 121, 126, 129, 131, 133–5, 154, 168, 186–7, 205
Eno, Brian xix, 6, 68, 106–7, 109–10, 122, 127, 143, 146, 154, 235
estrangement 7, 59, 135, 142, 150, 165, 168–9, 171
Everett, Kenny 56, 132, 136, 140, 146, 150
exotic 218–19, 221, 224, 226, 228
experimentation 1, 6–10, 12, 18–20, 22, 30–2, 40, 60, 63, 68, 91, 105–7, 109–10, 114, 122, 133, 146, 163, 235–6
expressionist 151–3, 164–5, 180, 182–3, 193–4

fan xiv, xv, 3, 16, 21–2, 27, 40, 54–7, 62, 78, 86, 95, 100–2, 133–4, 157, 202, 211, 213, 215, 233, 237–8
  fan-made videos 16, 56–7, 157
fashion 25, 42, 84, 95, 160, 211
'Fashion' 189, 223
feminine 75, 77, 135, 137
feminized 22, 74, 98, 100, 145, 218–19
Ferguson, Nick xix, 106, 125, 130–1
film xviii–xx, 2–6, 9–11, 15–22, 24–5, 29–34, 37, 39–40, 42, 47, 50, 53, 55, 58, 60, 63, 65–7, 69, 74, 76–7, 86–9, 94–7, 105, 110–11, 118, 120, 125, 128, 144, 150–3, 155, 158–9, 162, 167, 169–70, 173–4, 178–9, 185, 190–1, 198, 206, 210, 212–13, 219–20
  promotional (promo) 37, 40, 63, 105, 110, 111, 158
film noir 150, 152, 190–1
fine art 2, 111, 118, 127
Fisher, Mark 14, 58, 184–6
Fiske, John 2
'Five Years' 57, 61–3
"Five Years" 57–62
flickers of authenticity 86, 102, 190

foraging xviii, 22, 28, 34, 123, 135, 205, 213–14, 235–7
fourth wall, breaking 47, 53, 98, 149
framing 12, 26, 46, 74, 82, 90, 96, 98, 118, 125, 127, 129–30, 221–2
French New Wave 33, 47
Fripp, Robert 127
future nostalgia xx, 15, 52, 58–9, 163, 183–5, 188, 191, 199

gaze 6, 71, 74, 76, 78, 83, 88–90, 95, 98, 100, 118, 120, 128, 130, 143, 148
geisha 94, 95, 100, 226
gender 6, 44, 59, 75, 134, 139, 212, 226
  codes 8, 84, 100, 137, 230, 236
  roles 32, 133
Genet, Jean 36–7, 80
genre 31, 33, 63, 66
German expressionist 151–3, 173
Gesamtkunstwerk (total work of art) 4–6, 8, 23
gesture xx, 9, 12, 22, 38, 42–3, 48, 53, 63, 72, 74–7, 82, 87, 95, 97–100, 110, 114, 116, 129, 133, 135, 137–40, 142, 153, 176, 213, 221, 223, 225, 229–30, 235–7
  gestural migration xix, 110, 142, 236
glam 66, 71, 77, 95
gloves, white 118, 209–14, 236–7
Ground Control 50–3, 147–50, 161, 168, 172
guitar 44–5, 73, 76, 112–19, 125, 129, 137–8, 146–9, 171, 193, 214, 216–17, 236
  acoustic 44, 61–2, 90, 146–9, 204
  bass 61, 73, 113, 122, 133, 147, 171

hairstyle 33, 95, 113, 137, 186
haptic 74, 94–6, 197
hauntology 14, 21, 58, 184–6
Hawkins, Stan 34–5
Heckel, Eric 110
'Heroes' xviii, 90, 94, 107, 111, 120–1, 125–31, 154, 234
"Heroes" 106, 120–4
Heroes 106, 110, 120–1
Hingston, Tom 25, 153, 191
Hisama, Ellie 217, 227, 228

Hollywood 4, 6, 21, 74–5, 81, 100, 135, 191, 236
Hunky Dory 74–5, 93, 130
Hutchinson, John 'Hutch' 40, 50–2

identity xvii, 3, 8, 12, 24, 32, 39, 59, 66, 181, 202, 209, 217, 219, 227
illusion 77, 94, 102, 103, 116, 119, 145
Image, The 144
Iman 123–4, 134
improvisation 38, 121–2, 124, 165, 186, 195
indigenous 206, 207, 211, 214, 215, 218
intermedial xviii, 2, 4, 37–8, 95, 110, 159, 160, 237
intertextuality 2, 12–13, 20, 25–8, 53, 56, 73, 110, 117, 126, 135, 150–1, 153, 174, 178–9, 183, 220, 235, 237
irony 98, 112, 116, 134, 144, 182, 206, 209, 211, 214–15, 217–18, 227–8, 231, 236–7
"It's No Game (Part 1)" 60

Jackson, Michael 20, 213–14
Jagger, Mick 45–6, 134
jazz 190–1, 193
Jenkins, Henry 21–2, 25–6
Jirsa, Tomáš 12, 28, 233
'John, I'm Only Dancing' 66, 73–9, 82, 84, 117
"John, I'm Only Dancing" 72
Jones, David 33, 35, 63, 67
'Jump They Say' 139
Jung, Carl 160, 163, 182–3, 210
juxtaposition 7, 118, 169, 172, 206, 209, 225

kabuki 4, 36–7, 95, 167
Kardos, Leah xvi, 56, 133, 184
Keaton, Buster 113–15
Kemp, Lindsay xix, 31, 35–8, 71, 74, 80
King, Joelene 206, 208, 211–13, 215
Klimt, Gustav 127
Kristeva, Julia 27
Korniloff, Natasha 167
Korsgaard, Mathias 4–5, 9–12, 19, 28, 233
Kubrick, Stanley 25, 50

Lady Gaga 6–7, 140
Laroche, Pierre 94–5

"Laughing Gnome, The" 80, 134, 164
'Lazarus' 25, 133
Leigh, Wendy 41
Lennon, John 53, 60, 72, 92, 111, 147, 189–90, 199–202
'Let Me Sleep Beside You' 40, 45–6, 117
"Let Me Sleep Beside You" 44
'Let's Dance' xx, 118, 205–15, 218, 223–5, 228, 231
"Let's Dance" 203–5, 215
'Life on Mars?' 66, 74, 84, 90, 93–102, 110, 118, 126
"Life on Mars?" 90–2
light xii, xix, 5, 8, 12, 19, 40, 45–7, 57, 61–2, 76–7, 82–3, 85, 87, 90, 94, 105, 111, 114, 118–20, 125–32, 136–7, 145, 149–55, 165, 168, 173, 180, 190–4, 197–9, 235
  back-light 127, 129–30, 46, 57, 76, 125, 127, 129–30
  chiaroscuro 190–1, 199
  Divine Light 127, 129, 131
  exposure 94, 96, 120
  high-key 82–3, 94, 119, 126, 129
  low-key 76, 82–3, 87, 94, 128, 151
  noir 150, 152
  theatrical 47, 190
lipstick smear 137–41, 213, 229, 236
Lodger 106, 121, 133, 144–5
London 28, 31–3, 35, 38, 42–3, 48, 52, 61, 67, 69, 74, 78–9, 84, 94, 109, 144, 147, 159, 168, 176
'Look Back in Anger' 107, 143–5
loose continuity 2, 20, 22, 47, 49, 237
Lorde 140–1
'Love is Lost' 183, 185
'Love You till Tuesday' 29–30, 40, 42–3, 233
"Love You till Tuesday" 41–2
Love You till Tuesday 29–31, 34, 39–42, 47, 49–52, 63, 71
'Loving the Alien' 209, 224
Low 25, 106–7, 112–14, 122
Lye, Len 6, 169
lyrics 7, 12–13, 22, 41–4, 49, 51–2, 58–9, 72–3, 80, 91–3, 97–8, 100, 105, 108, 112–14, 116, 121–4, 130–4, 142, 161–4, 168, 171, 183, 185–6, 192, 195, 199, 203–5, 210–11, 216, 224, 226

McLuhan, Marshall 37, 39
Major Tom 22, 25–6, 50–4, 86, 90, 147–8, 150, 154, 161–2, 165, 168, 172–4, 178–80, 183–4, 186, 198
makeup 36, 76, 94–5, 100, 102, 113, 139, 225
Mallet, David xii, xv, xix–xx, 19, 55, 106, 131–2, 136, 138–9, 143–4, 146, 148–54, 157–9, 164–78, 188, 190–4, 196–8, 206, 208, 210–14, 219, 221–5, 227, 229–30, 234–5
Man Who Fell to Earth, The 24–5, 150, 153–4, 179
Man Who Sold the World, The 85, 133
marionette 114, 129, 141
masculinity 75, 77, 84, 134, 137, 142, 145, 211
mask xix, 4, 22, 29, 31, 37–9, 47–9, 57, 63, 82–3, 86, 95, 114, 120, 180–1, 186, 190, 193, 198, 201, 209–211, 228, 237
'Mask (A Mime), The' 39–40, 47–9, 95, 144
medium xiii, xviii, xix, 1, 3–5, 9–10, 13–14, 16, 18, 21–5, 28–30, 33, 39–40, 49, 63, 65, 71, 76, 89, 95, 105, 110–11, 140, 154, 160, 163–4, 180–1, 185–6, 190, 233–7
melody 91, 122, 147, 205
metaphor xx, 13, 27, 49, 52, 86–7, 90, 174, 179, 186, 190, 198, 209, 211, 218, 237–8
mime xix, 4, 10, 12, 23, 30–1, 36–2, 47–9, 54, 63, 75, 82, 95, 97, 116, 181, 186, 193
minimalist 28, 40, 47, 76, 82, 85, 94, 100, 113, 118–19, 126, 130, 145, 147
mod 33–4, 42, 137
Mondrian, Piet 119
montage 74, 215, 221, 225–6
  Soviet 137, 175, 225
'Moonage Daydream' (1972) 66
Moonage Daydream (2022), film 16, 65–6, 96
Moonage Daydream (2002), book 66
Morgen, Brett 16, 66, 96
motif 113, 153, 216–17, 221, 223
MTV (Music Television) xx, 2–3, 15–16, 19–20, 77, 159, 164, 180, 186, 201–3, 211, 215, 220, 233

Mueller, Otto 123
multimodal xix, 11, 12, 26, 233
Murray, George 122, 171
music video
  definition of 12–17, 28
  fan-made 16, 56, 57
  official 17, 55, 57, 62, 66, 72, 93, 100–2, 110–11, 132, 140–2
  phases of production 17–20
  prehistory of 3–10, 91
  promotional film (promo) xviii, xix, 4, 9–10, 16–18, 29, 30–3, 35, 37, 40, 42–3, 45, 47, 50–5, 61–3, 66, 73–6, 83–8, 90, 93, 103, 105, 110–11, 158
  TARDIS 13, 28, 237
musical arrangement xiv, 12, 44, 52, 59, 61, 73, 92–3, 112–13, 121, 133, 147, 163, 171, 182, 204
myth 8, 13, 27, 35, 157–8, 162–3, 188, 237

Nacho xii, 56, 61, 78–9, 100–2
narrative 8, 21–3, 26, 51–2, 126, 172–4, 206, 215, 227, 237
Ndalianis, Angela 25
New Romantic 166, 168, 176–8, 186, 198
New York 79, 86, 100, 159–61, 189
Newley, Anthony 29, 41–2, 113, 236
Newton, Thomas Jerome 22, 24–6, 179, 181
'No Plan' 25, 153
Nomi, Klaus 142–3
nursery rhyme 162–3, 178, 182, 185

object 7, 22, 25, 27, 34, 74, 76, 83, 88–90, 94, 100, 103, 114–16, 118–19, 130, 148, 181, 185, 187–8, 221, 236
  objectification 34, 228
  salience 89–90
Oblique Strategies 107, 122, 132
October, Dene 24–5
'Oh, You Pretty Things' 57
O'Leary, Chris xvi, 41, 44–5, 49–52, 59–60, 73, 80, 92, 113–14, 123, 133–4, 143, 145, 147, 163, 171–2, 176, 191–2, 195, 203–5, 211, 216
Old Grey Whistle Test, The xix, 31, 57, 61–3

Orientalism 100, 218–19, 221–2, 227–8, 230–1, 237
Orwell, George 25, 185
Otherness 181, 211, 219, 228, 237

Paglia, Camile 135–7
painter 5, 22, 24, 37, 106, 110, 144
painterly 114, 119–20, 130, 185, 198
painting xii, xix, 5, 9–10, 23, 69, 93–5, 97, 100, 102–3, 105–6, 110–11, 118–19, 122–4, 127, 129, 144, 155, 169, 190, 195–8, 219, 235
palimpsest 14, 93, 237
pantomime 30, 38–9, 42, 47, 181, 186
paratexts, musical 34, 66, 180
Paris 108, 111, 114, 127
parody 29, 39, 45, 116–18, 133–6, 142–3, 154, 182, 214, 216, 218, 227, 230, 236–7
pastiche 117, 139, 216, 229
Pegg, Nicholas xvi, 52, 59, 72–3, 93, 124, 132, 205, 210, 216, 220
Penderecki, Krzysztof 60
performativity 3, 34, 39, 86, 132, 134, 139, 219, 236
persona xx, 3, 22, 38–9, 47, 49, 65–7, 70, 77, 80, 95, 144–5, 157–8, 161, 176, 180–3, 189, 210–11, 230–1, 237
photograph xii, xix, 5, 9–10, 65–72, 74–5, 86, 103, 129, 187, 219, 227, 234
photographer 5, 66–7, 70–1, 103, 174, 187
piano 60–1, 91–3, 97, 113–14, 147, 171, 185, 216
Pierrot xix, 22, 29, 31, 38–9, 47, 49, 95, 114, 120, 158, 165–9, 172–89, 198, 211, 221
Pierrot Lunaire 180–3
pitch, shifting 163–4, 182, 185, 196
Pitt, Kenneth 40–2
Pop, Iggy 59, 80, 215–16
pop art 85, 94–5, 102, 143
pose 12, 22, 33, 42–3, 45, 71, 76, 82–4, 110, 125, 129, 145, 235–6
Presley, Elvis 41, 45–6, 134
prop 39–40, 76, 117, 119, 129, 165, 214
punk 6, 33, 73, 76–9, 84, 117, 127, 133, 216
puppet 22, 114, 125, 141–3, 155, 181
purging 106, 108, 159, 161–2, 183, 189, 198–9

Quatermass xviii, 25, 58, 165–6, 178
'Queen Bitch' 57, 73
queer 59, 72–3

racism xx, 199, 202, 206–7, 209, 212, 217–18, 221, 224–5, 228, 230–1, 237
RCA 72, 79, 85–6, 113, 144, 179
'Rebel Rebel' 117
rebellion 78, 83–4, 90, 113
recording 16, 19, 41, 50–2, 55–6, 61, 72–3, 85–7, 90, 93, 101, 120–2, 124, 145–7, 150, 159, 161, 191–2, 216
studio 45, 51, 72, 79, 85–7, 90, 101, 120–4, 133, 147, 155, 159, 190, 192, 201, 235
red shoes 209–15, 236–7
Reed, Lou 59
remediation xvi, xix–xx, 4, 7–13, 18, 20–1, 28, 30–1, 47, 57, 63, 119, 155, 158, 183, 233, 237
representation xvi, 2–3, 9, 13, 20, 22, 26, 39, 52, 55, 65, 67, 71, 77, 100, 103, 163, 178, 180–2, 184, 187, 199, 202, 207, 209, 218–21, 228, 237
rhythm 5, 11, 60, 73, 76, 80, 105, 113, 132, 147, 171, 193
Richardson, John 6–7
Roberts, Terry 206, 208, 211–12, 215
Rock, Mick xv, xix, 18, 55, 65–2, 74–9, 81–90, 93–4, 96–103, 118, 234–5
rock music 2, 23–4, 30, 33, 41, 43, 57, 59, 66, 69, 71, 77, 79–80, 95, 109, 113, 116–17, 144, 179–80, 203, 210–11, 231, 236
Rodgers, Nile 204–5, 217
Roeg, Nicholas 24, 150
Rogers, Holly xii, 6, 11
Rolling Stones, The 17–18, 44, 81
Romanek, Mark 8, 139
Ronson, Mick 60–1, 73, 76, 93, 101
'Rubber Band' 40

Said, Edward 218–19
saxophone 73, 193
Scary Monsters xx, 145, 159–64, 180, 184, 199
Schiele, Egon 110
Schoenberg, Arnold 5, 163, 180–3

Schwab, Coco 193
science fiction 13–14, 25, 50–1, 53–4, 125, 165, 185–6
scream 60, 114, 124, 163–4
"Scream Like a Baby" 164
sculpture xix, 5, 6, 10, 119, 127, 129, 204, 235
self-quotation 60, 133, 236
'Sense of Doubt' 110
seriality 21, 24, 26, 58, 80, 224
set design 12, 46, 53, 151, 153, 155
sexuality 8, 73, 76–7
Shibui 94, 101
Sigismondi, Floria 8
signification 22, 127, 205, 211, 214, 218, 235–6
   signify xx, 8, 22, 26, 39, 60, 84, 95, 97, 110, 117–18, 130, 137, 153, 175, 185–8, 210–15, 221, 226, 231, 237
silhouette 57, 125, 127, 192, 197
Simone, Nina 191
Sinatra, Frank 91, 195
singing 36, 41–3, 50, 52, 59, 61, 77, 97–8, 113–14, 116, 124, 129, 134, 137, 141, 146, 148–50, 163, 168, 172, 192, 206, 216, 223, 227
Smith, Justin 16, 18
sound 120, 124, 127, 132–3, 150, 159, 167, 171, 185, 191, 204, 217, 236
space xv, 11–14, 25, 55–6, 74, 80, 83, 87, 88, 118–19, 122, 126, 145–7, 150, 153–4, 161–2, 166, 168, 172, 178–9, 186, 193, 225, 237
   intertextual 13, 27–8, 233
   outer xv, 51, 53–4, 56, 88, 100, 127, 145–7, 153, 161–2, 179, 186
   psychological 153, 186
   sonic 51, 87, 107, 147, 150
   space capsule 80, 85–7, 90, 125, 145, 166, 175, 178–9
   travel 32, 50
'Space Oddity' 14, 49, 52–6, 198, 237
   (1969) 40, 52–6, 87, 153
   (1972) 55, 66, 85–90, 102, 117, 153
   (1979) 25, 55–6, 90, 107, 117, 145–6, 148–54, 173, 179, 187, 198
"Space Oddity" 49–51, 55–57, 85, 90, 146–7, 161, 171, 186

Space Oddity 65, 85, 175–6
sprechstimme 163, 182
stagecraft 31, 36–7, 40
stardom xiv, xvii, 20, 23, 48–9, 67, 113, 118
Stark, Tanja 183
'Stars (Are Out Tonight), The' 133, 138, 183
stereotype 216–18, 225–8, 230, 236–7
storyboard 159, 164–6, 173
storyworld xiii, xv, 13, 17, 20–1, 25–6, 49–50, 55, 59, 90–1, 154, 157, 159, 161–2, 173, 179–80, 184, 186, 198, 235, 237
Strange, Steve 176, 186
strategy xx, 5–8, 20, 30, 34–5, 37, 63, 77, 81, 83–6, 89–90, 96, 105, 109, 113–14, 132, 142, 153, 158, 173–4, 181–3, 198, 202–3, 207, 209–11, 217–18, 225–30, 236–7
string instruments 44, 60–1, 92–3, 97, 116, 122, 146–7
Stylophone 50–1, 56
subconscious 8, 37, 80, 119, 123, 184, 204
subversion 6–8, 13, 22, 35, 76–8, 92, 109, 116–17, 132–4, 137, 142–3, 202, 229, 236
surrealist xx, 6–8, 20, 22–3, 80, 92, 154, 164–5, 167, 170, 172–4, 182, 220, 236
symbolism 8, 27, 38, 68, 113, 163, 187–8, 207, 209–11, 213, 215, 218, 237
synthesizer 127, 146, 147, 171, 185, 204

television 2, 10, 17–19, 21, 31–2, 40, 57, 61, 85, 132, 137, 138, 141, 150, 153, 158, 186, 191, 207, 218, 220
   series xviii, 13, 25, 58, 75, 154
   show xix, 16, 31, 38, 42, 50, 56, 57, 132, 136–7, 140–3, 145–6, 149
temporal dissonance 8, 14, 22, 172, 184–5
texture 24, 94, 98, 105, 119–20, 147, 182, 196–7
theatre 4–5, 20, 35, 37–8, 40, 74, 76, 158, 160, 181, 183, 185–6, 190, 195, 206
theatrical xviii, 4, 9–10, 21, 31, 36–44, 47, 63, 76, 95, 113, 180–1, 190
'The Drowned Girl' xx, 150, 158, 190, 194, 196–9, 224

"The Drowned Girl" 195
'The Jean Genie' 37, 66, 81–5
"The Jean Genie" 79–80
The Rise and Fall of Ziggy Stardust and the Spiders from Mars 59, 61, 66
Thin White Duke, The 22, 181
timbre 5, 22, 105
time xiii, xv–xvi, 3, 12–14, 22, 24–7, 34, 40, 43, 45, 49, 52, 56–62, 69, 73, 76–9, 83, 92–5, 105–13, 121, 154, 157, 172, 178, 181, 184, 190, 203, 207, 211, 225, 237–8
    time is out of joint 14, 185
    time-travel xvi, 13–14, 16, 26, 28, 49, 55, 154, 178–80, 185–6, 237–8
Thomson, Malcolm J. xix, 30, 40, 43, 45–8, 50, 52–5, 71, 87
Top of the Pops (TOTP) 17, 44, 56, 77, 84, 111, 220
total work of art (*Gesamtkunstwerk*) 4, 74
transition 31–2, 34, 57, 63, 120, 143
    editing techique 118–20, 129, 136, 150, 155, 165, 172, 175, 193, 197, 221
transmedia xvii, 2, 20–8, 153, 237

Un Chien Andalou 22, 167, 174–8
Underwood, George 171, 176
United Kingdom (UK) 31–3, 58, 72, 76, 78, 81, 84, 111, 132, 146

'Valentine's Day' 82, 90, 118
verisimilitude 46, 77, 116
Vernallis, Carol 6, 11
Visage 176, 178, 186–7

Visconti, Tony xix, 50, 56, 106–7, 120–4, 133, 146–7, 150, 154, 164, 171, 185, 192–3, 235
visual art 1, 4–6, 35, 63, 67–8, 105, 111, 155, 180
visual music 3–6, 8, 11, 34, 105–6, 234–6
vocal 22, 41–2, 50–2, 57–8, 60–1, 77, 87, 90, 107, 113, 121, 124, 129, 131, 133, 147, 150, 153, 157, 163–4, 171–2, 182, 185, 191–6, 198–9, 204–5, 215–16, 225, 227–8, 230–1, 234
volatile audiovisuality 10–12, 233, 235

Wagner, Richard 4
Wakeman, Rick 93, 97
Waldrep, Shelton 34, 184, 224–5
"Warszawa" 106, 122
'When I Live My Dream' 40
'When I'm Five' 40, 134
Who, The 18, 76
'Wild is the Wind' xx, 90, 150, 158, 190–4, 196–9, 224
"Wild is the Wind" 192
Woodmansey, Woody 59, 61, 93
worldbuilding 2–3, 21, 23, 25–6, 154, 237
Wurlitzer 167, 185

YouTube xviii, 1–2, 16, 55–7, 78, 110, 123
    comment 45, 55, 135, 137–8, 187, 192

Ziggy Stardust 45, 49, 57, 65–7, 70, 76–8, 81–5, 90, 113, 144–5, 181, 211
Ziggy Stardust and the Spiders from Mars 31, 62, 74, 79, 81

www.ingramcontent.com/pod-product-compliance
Lightning Source LLC
Chambersburg PA
CBHW051632230426
43669CB00013B/2265